*Border Witness*

Recovered continuity script from *The Pilgrim* (1923)

514. MS: The US-Mexico borderline. Reverend Pym, in a state of extreme indecision, considers the choice between confronting a pursuing lawman in Texas or crossing over into a lawless Mexico.

515. MLS: Pym walks off, undecided, with one foot on either side of the international boundary line.

*The screen goes black.*

---

*Producciones DMQ*

# Border Witness

## REIMAGINING THE US-MEXICO BORDERLANDS THROUGH FILM

## Michael Dear

UNIVERSITY OF CALIFORNIA PRESS

*The publisher and the University of California Press Foundation
gratefully acknowledge the generous support of the Kenneth Turan
and Patricia Williams Endowment Fund in American Film.*

University of California Press
Oakland, California

All photographs, diagrams, and screenshots are by Michael Dear.

Library of Congress Cataloging-in-Publication Data

Names: Dear, M. J. (Michael J.), author.
Title: Border witness : reimagining the US-Mexico borderlands through film /
    Michael Dear.
Description: Oakland, California : University of California Press, [2023] |
    Includes bibliographical references and index.
Identifiers: LCCN 2022025053 (print) | LCCN 2022025054 (ebook) |
    ISBN 9780520391932 (cloth) | ISBN 9780520391949 (paperback) |
    ISBN 9780520391956 (epub)
Subjects: LCSH: Borderlands in motion pictures. | Mexican-American Border
    Region—In motion pictures.
Classification: LCC PN1995.9.M48 D43 2023 (print) | LCC PN1995.9.M48 (ebook)
    | DDC 791.43/658721—dc23/eng/20221003
LC record available at https://lccn.loc.gov/2022025053
LC ebook record available at https://lccn.loc.gov/2022025054

Manufactured in the United States of America

32  31  30  29  28  27  26  25  24  23
10  9  8  7  6  5  4  3  2  1

This book is dedicated
to all borderland peoples,
and to Norma Iglesias Prieto,
who began this whole enterprise.

Este libro está dedicado
a todos los pueblos fronterizos,
y a Norma Iglesias Prieto,
quien inició toda esta empresa.

# Contents

# Introduction

I grew up in Wales acquiring an inexplicable childhood attachment to Mexico. It was nurtured by watching "cowboy flicks" starring the likes of Tom Mix and the Cisco Kid but—more consequentially—it featured those majestic landscapes from the American West. It's how I became habituated to seeing Mexico through film. I arrived in the US in the early 1970s and lived along the Canada-US boundary line for more than a decade, but later became a US citizen. Always I returned to Mexico, north, south, east, and west. By the early 2000s, I felt ready to travel along both sides of the entire US-Mexico border, a voyage that took four years to complete. So in some ways this book is the culmination of a lifetime's learning about Mexico and the US through direct experience and representations in film.

My purpose in this book is to explore how the images in border-focused films of the past century reflected cross-border attitudes in each country, from the early silent films through present-day global blockbusters. Whose stories were being told in border films, and whose ignored or distorted? What kind of plots, narratives, and themes did filmmakers favor, and how did these choices alter over time? Do onscreen images accurately portray real lives? And what does a century of border filmmaking reveal about our nations' future?

International relations between Mexico and the US have always been tinged by mistrust and prejudice. Today cross-border attitudes are worse than at any time since the era of post–World War II optimism. The US federal government in Washington, D.C., consistently regards Mexico as a junior partner in all things including trade, politics, and filmmaking (one clear exception that comes to mind is *futbol*). Conventional wisdom is that the southern border is the source of all evils, meaning undocumented immigration; threats to national security; and the trafficking of drugs, guns, and human beings. Public opinion in the US is dominated by a shrill anti-immigrant rhetoric, punitive policing and lawmaking, racism that too often bleeds into violence, and an irrational belief that building walls will solve the nation's problems.

Meanwhile in Mexico City, a highly centralized federal government rarely bothers to look northward unless and until cross-border commerce with its premier trading partner is threatened. Despite the prosperity and political clout of its northern border states, Mexico's population else-where continues to regard the north as a remote, inconsequential back-water, where (I've heard it said) people eat catfood, and the towns they live in are not really Mexican. Mexicans who live along the borderline confront the insult and indignities of the US-built border wall every day. By now a generation of young people have lived their entire lives in the shadow of walls.

Successive US presidents (George W. Bush, Barack Obama, and Donald Trump) have elected to fight the nation's largest domestic wars—drugs, national security, and immigration—by using border communities as battlegrounds. At the same time, twenty-first-century Mexican presidents (Vicente Fox, Felipe Calderón, Enrique Peña Nieto, and Andrés Manuel López Obrador) have wrestled to maintain economic growth and stability in the face of threats posed by ascendant drug cartels. Borderlanders resent interference from their respective national capitals because there lurk powers to confiscate land, impose unwanted regulations, authorize military-style occupations, and curtail civil liberties. The police and mili-tary forces occupying the US are eerily reminiscent of the foot soldiers of drug cartels occupying parts of Mexico. While both federal governments strive to assert their authority, their endemic corruption confounds the practices of democracy in both countries.

My interest lies in the "in-between" spaces where two nations converge. For me, the border zone is like a piñata: one small tap, and out pours a cascade of wonders, confections, and sometimes things. Over ten million people live in border-adjacent communities, most of them dwelling in a series of "twin towns" that straddle the borderline. (The best-known twins are Tijuana and San Diego, and Ciudad Juárez and El Paso.) Well over a billion dollars' worth of trade crosses the international boundary every day, and taken together, the ten border states reputedly would comprise the third largest economy in the world. Hundreds of thousands of border residents cross daily to the other side for purposes relating to work, family, shopping, play, schooling, and affairs of the heart. Many border families have lived in this border ecology for several generations, some even before the US-Mexico boundary was created in 1848. They are fond of reminding visitors that it was the border that moved, not they or their forebears.

The border is also a state of mind. People on both sides insist that they have more in common with each other than with residents of either home nation. For them, the borderline unites rather than divides. They speak with uninhibited affection and pride about their "in-between" status and connections. Though bodies and minds may be divided by the line, border-landers thrive on the fusions that proximity and adjacency permit. Cross-border lives are so pervasive that people have often said to me: "I forget which side of the line I'm on." One time I was sitting with a binational group of longtime border friends on the Avenida Revolución in Tijuana, at the restaurant where the Caesar salad reputedly was invented. All of us are super-aware of our cross-border connections and comfortable with various expressions of an "in-between" identity, referring to one another as "transborder" citizens and calling San Diego and Tijuana twin cities, *ciudades hermanas* (sister cities), or *ciudades amistosas* (friendly cities). I sometimes think of this closely connected border space and the people who live in it as a "third nation." (I don't mean this literally; the San Diego-Tijuana twins won't be sending delegates to the United Nations any time soon.) The term offers a different perspective on the US-Mexico border:

not as an edge where hostile nations grind together but as a shared space where two peoples connect.

Not everyone likes this idea. Some of my salad-sharing companions are hostile to the idea of a third nation, regarding it as an infringement on Mexican identity and sovereignty. I understand their caution, but I find the view of border spaces as a kind of quasi-independent ministate opens the door to refreshing insights into divided worlds. One of my objectives in this book is to explore this new way of seeing.

Exploring the mental maps of real people is a messy business, involving assessment of personal feelings, identities, and complicated histories. There have been a few opinion polls measuring cross-border attitudes and sentiments regarding people on the other side, but I needed something more. I began searching for an independent source that could cast light onto borderlanders' feelings about cross-border connections. My hope was to find a source that covered the entire geography of a two-thousand-mile border zone on both sides, as well as incorporating a history that reached back centuries to the 1848 treaty that caused the original borderline to exist. At first, this seemed an all but impossible ambition.

But then it came to me that this is exactly what border film was offering.

I have been going to the movies since before I can remember. Watching films in theaters has been a lifelong devotion and pleasure. The earliest films I recall are those Saturday morning Westerns involving gunfights between Mexican bandits and gringo heroes who too often interrupted the action in order to serenade a horse. They were joined by extravagantly dressed Western women who manifestly preferred horses over any man. The border landscapes favored in these films were always exotic and bewitching even if the plots were more than a tad repetitious.

Time passed, and cowboys were replaced by cops; the bad guys still had guns and wisecracks, and the women still veered between saints and sinners (the latter with hearts of gold, naturally). Western landscapes soon gave way to the thrall of dark, gritty urban locations, but border films remained blood soaked and melodramatic. Only much later did border films acquire a distinct identity and diversify into tales of revolution, social concern, romance, migration, sex, drugs, cartels, and *la migra* (Spanish slang for US immigration police). The men in these films seemed more than ever damaged and violent, but women became more adventurous and stronger.

Most recently the attention of border-oriented filmmakers was riveted by the devastations caused by drug cartels and the corrupt establishments in politics and law enforcement. Coincidentally, this occurred just as the tectonic plates of US and Mexican film cultures collided. The consequent trauma unfolded over decades but was spectacularly capped in 2019 when Hollywood awoke to find that five out of the previous six Best Director Academy Awards had been awarded to Mexicans: Alfonso Cuarón (twice), Alejandro González Iñárritu (twice), and Guillermo del Toro.

This would not have come as a surprise to many observers beyond Hollywood. In the mid-twentieth century, Mexico was a hemispheric presence in film, and after the 1990s the country reemerged as a global force in film and television. The Hollywood studio system supporting twentieth-century filmmaking had begun showing overt signs of stress and imminent collapse. So the emergence of three Grandmaster filmmakers from Mexico, the revitalization of Mexican film and television, and the apparent fragility of Hollywood's dominance simply confirmed that a new world order of film was imminent. Amid this maelstrom, in the year 2000, a distinctive genre of border film was born. Another of my principal objectives in this book is to explain why this happened and to reveal what the border film genre consists of.

I have had the extraordinarily good fortune to work with first-class film scholars during my professional life. Over many years at the University of Southern California I absorbed a belated education at one of the nation's premier film schools. There were movie stars in cafés, in markets, and on sidewalks. I participated on a number of film projects, the most fun being screen time in *City of Gold*, a documentary film on Jonathan Gold (the first Pulitzer prize-winning restaurant critic) directed by Laura Gabbert for Sundance Selects. In Los Angeles—truly a border city—I fell in with a circle of people active in film and crossed the border to meet artists, filmmakers, and critics in Baja California and Mexico City. Then in the 1990s I was approached by a group of Mexican and Chicano artists wanting to learn more about Los Angeles, the city where they worked. Thanks to them I acquired a second belated education, this time in Latinx and

Chicanx art history and practice. I began paying serious attention to Mexico. After 2009 my film education continued through UC Berkeley's Film and Media department, where I taught a class in film and was introduced to the Pacific Film Archive.

After sojourning in these different galaxies, I began scribbling notes about border film. My attention was piqued by the gap between what I knew about the borderlands and what border filmmakers chose to portray onscreen. The gap seemed large, and my essay continued to grow. There was much more to say than I expected.

My foremost challenge lay in choosing a selection of border films from a vast archive of border-related films accumulated in the century-long catalogs of two nations. (It was vitally important that I should be conversant in the films of both countries.) A few "classics" of the burgeoning genre emerged quickly, but my curiosity bent toward more quirky films that illuminated something beyond the iconic. I began by defining a *border film* simply as taking place in a borderland setting, with a thematic focus on the lives of border people and their cross-border connections. To be considered a contender, the chosen film would do more than treat the border as mere scenery or backdrop; instead it would demonstrate the border's transformative impact on person and plot. The highest echelon in the hierarchy would be reserved for films that rendered the border as the topical focus or subject of the film (in which case, the film is said to be *about* the border).

The catalogs of two nations' films are too much to consider in a single book, so I have confined my interest to fictional feature films originating from Mexican and US sources. Occasional reference is made to documentary films, television programs, and films originating beyond the US and Mexico whenever their perspectives provide special insight. Throughout, I endeavor to maintain a balanced presentation of Mexican- and US-origin films, even though long-established practices of international coproduction make it increasingly difficult (and unhelpful) to attribute a single country of origin to such films.

My wide-ranging inquiry is broken down into three parts. Part 1 describes the origins of border films in the silent film era, setting standard themes and stereotypes even in these early offerings. I explain some ground rules for using films as "evidence," and provide short histories of film and border film in both countries. The remainder of part 1 presents the first crop of border film "classics" that appeared in the first half of the twentieth century. Thematically they dealt with revolutionary war and modernization, the first great migrations of rural Mexicans to the city and the US, and the reputation of border cities as distasteful places of crime and vice.

Part 2 tracks the growth and diversification of border films during the second half of the twentieth and the early decades of the twenty-first centuries. During this period, filmmakers began devoting more attention to a wider range of border-related topics. As the geopolitical boundary increased in political prominence toward the end of the twentieth century, the number and quality of border films increased. The principal themes of these later decades revealed a maturation of filmmakers' palette, encompassing the aftermath of the Spanish conquest; the increasing prominence and diversity in portraits of borderland women; the rise of drug cartels; the trials endured by migrants in search of their "American Dream"; the use of borderland settings to convey acute moral tales (e.g., pertaining to race and miscegenation); and some surprising and welcome diversions into comedy, fantasy, science fiction, and spirituality.

Part 3 gathers the book's accumulated evidence to define an overarching border film "genre," based on identifying the principal elements of a distinctive *cinematic imagination* expressed in the contents of my film choices. These imaginary worlds are compared with the actual world of real borderland people, leading to a provocative reconsideration of the realities confronting borderland residents as well as the future of border film.

Following the introductory materials, each chapter is generally arranged thematically by category or subgenre (e.g., drama, comedy), chronology (according to the historic period covered in the film, not the year of its release), and topic (migration, war, etc.). Throughout the book, brief historical digressions assist in understanding the events featured on-screen.

My book blends film and media studies with the geography, history, and politics of the US and Mexico. I use film not as an object of conventional criticism, theory, or philosophy but as *evidence* of the ways borders were represented over a hundred years of film releases originating in both countries. Images from the films are complemented by photographs of real borderland landscapes in order to encourage an independent level of reader interpretation of the evidence.

I favor James Baldwin as a guide for film analysis. His notion of *witness* involved judging film representations by comparing them with what he had experienced in real life. Ultimately the book rests on my selection of over 120 border films (though many more were considered). I do not pretend to offer a comprehensive account or catalog of over a century of border filmmaking. What I offer instead is an unabashedly idiosyncratic and opinionated report based in four decades of experience, research, writing, and activism along the southern border. Taken together, these films make a persuasive case for a border film genre as well as a credible cartography (or road map) for the past, present, and even future of our two nations. Along the way, the book also demonstrates that both nations have much to learn from the ways borderlanders conduct their daily interconnected lives.

PART 1 Origins

"How far away is the Mexican border?"

"No-one knows exactly. It's never been decided."

—the outlaw Ben Wade questioning the barmaid Emmy
in *3:10 to Yuma* (1957)

# 1 Border Witness

FROM THE PACIFIC OCEAN
TO THE GULF OF MEXICO

I began traveling the entire length of the US-Mexico border on December 17, 2002. I visited both sides of the line, starting from Tijuana–San Diego on the Pacific Ocean and ending at Matamoros–Brownsville on the Gulf of Mexico, a total of just under four thousand miles there and back. I started before the US undertook to fortify its southern boundary and so became an unintentional witness to the border's closure. My binational exploration was completed on February 5, 2006, but I have continued visiting up to the present, adding thousands more miles to my borderland travel log.

On the very first night of our borderline trip, the incredible beauty of the Algodones Dunes lured Héctor and me from the paved highway to where our car promptly sank up to its belly in the sand. Within minutes two Border Patrol vehicles confronted us, having spotted our plight via their surveillance cameras. We were a hundred yards from the border and approximately the same distance from Interstate Highway 8. The agents stayed with us for the three hours it took to extricate ourselves in order to protect us from being hit by speeding smugglers who used this desert road to drop off their human or narcotics cargos, which were then picked up by prearrangement with vehicles on I-8 for distribution nationwide.

*Figure 1.1.* Outward bound, in the company of the US Border Patrol.

From the beginning, I anticipated devoting most of my time to examining drug, national security, and immigration issues. Instead, I quickly became absorbed in the lives of people who pursued cross-border lives: Mexicans who lived in Tijuana, where the cost of living was lower, while working in San Diego, where wages were higher; and Americans on fixed incomes, who settled in Mexico in order to stretch their retirement savings. Outside the cities there were few fences, and people constantly crossed the line without documentation to shop or visit family, graze their farm animals, or join weekend softball games.

In those first months of travel, I shared some of this freedom. "Unofficial" crossings were easy—there was even a guide book![1] At San Luis Río Colorado, in the Mexican state of Sonora just south of Yuma, Arizona, I walked around a freestanding boundary monument, taking photographs. Every time I crossed the imaginary line into Mexico, two old guys watching me would yell: "You're illegal!" and then fall around laughing. After a while, I walked across the line and chatted with them.

On February 2, 1848, the Treaty of Guadalupe Hidalgo was signed, ending the Mexican-American War. The treaty required designation of a

*Figure 1.2.* Morning departure, Mexicali, Baja California Norte.

*Figure 1.3.* Morelos Dam, Baja California Norte. Built in 1950 to access waters from the Colorado River for use by agricultural *ejidos* in the Mexicali Valley.

"boundary line with due precision, upon authoritative maps, and to establish upon the ground landmarks which shall show the limits of both
republics."[2] The consequent surveys were undertaken by a joint US–
Mexico commission charged with surveying the two-thousand-mile border line and marking it with monuments. Just over one-third that distance
ran along the land boundary from the Pacific Ocean to the junction with
the Rio Grande/Río Bravo at a town called Paso del Norte, and from
thence to the Gulf of Mexico. The water boundary was defined as the
deepest point in the river channel.[3]

The first survey took eight years to complete. The terrain and climate
were often difficult and life-threatening in mountain and desert; the survey crews were not always welcomed by indigenous people; and the surveyors had to contend with a handful of maps from different sources, none
of which were entirely accurate (the map marking the location of Paso del
Norte, for example, was one hundred miles off true).[4] Uncertainties were
exacerbated as the two nations continued squabbling about the boundary's exact location. The most consequential dispute led to the 1853 Gads-
den Purchase (known as the Treaty of Mesilla in Mexico), whereby the US
delivered $10 million to Mexico and in return acquired a coveted corridor
connecting Paso del Norte to Baja California, thus enabling access for a
rail link to the Pacific coast. The first survey placed only fifty-two monuments along the entire length of the line, almost all on the land boundary.
After the war, military bases and "twin towns" were established on each
side of the line to consolidate the territorial holdings of each nation.

A second boundary survey was undertaken between 1892 and 1894 on
the land boundary alone, primarily because the precise location of the line
had been masked by population growth in the borderlands. Also, many
boundary markers had been stolen, moved, or damaged beyond repair.
By century's end, the number of monuments was increased to 258, but in
many places the precise location of the line remained vague.[5] In one dispute in 1893, a Texas Ranger inadvertently strayed into Mexican territory
in pursuit of an alleged criminal. After Mexico protested the incursion,
the US Department of State responded that the lawman had entered an
ill-defined boundary zone and that "the boundary line between the United
States and Mexico has never been so settled as to be known except by citizens of long residence on the border."[6] The lawman claimed that he had

encountered no markers indicating the line and that the boundary line lay in a river channel that was known to have migrated to a different location.

On the Pacific Ocean lies Tijuana, the largest border city in Mexico. It began as a scattering of indigenous tribes that later fell under the thrall of Spanish missionizing. By the time that the Mexican-American War ended in 1848, the Rancho de la Tía Juana was the largest cattle-ranching settlement in the Tijuana River valley. Indeed, it was the *only* settlement marked on maps created by boundary surveyors after the war. A small customs house was built in 1874, attracting a few modest residences. The region's ranching economy was tied to California, supplying food and other products required by the booming gold and silver mines to the north. After the mid-1880s, Baja was caught up in the speculative land and property boom in Southern California. Sales did not match expectations, but optimism was such that a formal urban plan for Tijuana was published in 1889 with the intention of guiding city growth and promoting development.

By 1900, Tijuana had a population of about two hundred people. Then the world accelerated around it. San Diego rose as a commercial and military port, and Tijuana began to attract tourists from California. In 1916 a horse-racing track called Agua Caliente was built in Tijuana a quarter mile from the international boundary. The town emerged as a popular playground for visitors, including Hollywood film stars. Innovations in irrigation technology, improved rail connections, and US and Canadian investments began the transformation of harsh deserts into major agricultural interests in the region, including eastward into the Imperial and Mexicali Valleys. Tijuana entered a golden age for tourism when the 1919 Volstead Act brought Prohibition to the US. Thirsty Americans flocked south across the border in search of liquor and entertainment to slake a thirst that could not be legally quenched at home. The Agua Caliente racetrack became a casino and tourist complex, and by 1930, Tijuana's population had risen to eighty-four hundred. (Around the same time, Ciudad Juárez added two new international bridges over the river boundary to cope with increased tourist traffic.) The booze- and gambling-fueled boom couldn't last, of course. The Volstead Act (the National Prohibition Act) was terminated in 1933, and Mexican president Lázaro Cárdenas shuttered all gambling establishments in the country.

In the eastern half of the continent on the Gulf of Mexico lay Browns-ville, Texas, across the Rio Grande/Río Bravo from its border twin, Mat-amoros, in the state of Tamaulipas. Matamoros was the only border town that had built fortifications for self-protection, and the border twins re-membered many conflicts: the Texas Revolution; the Mexican-American War; and the Battle of Palmito Ranch, which was the final land battle of the US Civil War. By the end of the nineteenth century, Brownsville had around seven thousand inhabitants, over half of whom were Mexicans accustomed to the ways of their American neighbors. An 1893 almanac recorded that the twin towns were so integrated that it was hard to believe they were parts of separate republics:

> It is interesting to watch the tide of travel between the republics. [. . .] The Mexican women, with their almost uniform dress of black and white, with heads bare and graceful "rebozos" draped about their shoulders; the "ran-chero," with jingling spurs on his high-heeled boots, a gaudy sash, white shirt, and heavy, broad-brimmed "sombrero"; merchant and clerks, intent upon the business to be transacted at the Customhouse, the banks, or the market of the sister city; Spanish ladies tastefully and richly dressed, spar-kling with jewels and shielding their bright eyes from the glare of the sun on the water with their proverbial weapon, the fan, which is also the only sun-shade they ever carry; Englishmen, Frenchmen, American, Irishmen, and Africans; and they nearly all use the Spanish language or its Mexican "patois," in the affairs of daily life.[7]

By the end of the twentieth century, Brownsville had grown into a sprawling settlement of around 180,000 inhabitants. Prosperous Mat-amoros had half a million. Every year a ceremony is held celebrating the Brownsville-Matamoros concord. The six border states in Mexico (from west to east: Baja California Norte, Sonora, Chihuahua, Coahuila, Nuevo León, and Tamaulipas) contained 18.2 million people, or 16 percent of Mexico's total population. The four US border states (California, Arizona, New Mexico, and Texas) were home to 66.9 million people, or 21 percent of the US population. Taken together, the ten border states would have comprised one of the largest economies in the world.

In 1945 the US government constructed the first fences designed to curtail the flow of unauthorized migrants from Mexico, along both sides of the All-American Canal near Calexico, California, and Mexicali, Baja California. The barrier was over five miles long and consisted of posts connected by chain-link fencing recycled from camps where Japanese Americans had been interned during World War II. Later, on a much grander scale, the 237-mile Western Land Boundary Fence Project was mostly constructed between 1948 and 1951, extending from Tijuana to El Paso.

In the mid-1990s, undocumented immigration into the US had reached chaotic proportions. Crowds of unauthorized crossers would sometimes assemble at the border crossing and literally rush the barriers. The US responded by building more elaborate fences to deter unlawful crossings in major towns and cities, including San Diego, California; Nogales, Arizona; and El Paso, Texas. This time the fencing was constructed from steel mats that had been used to provide temporary landing strips for US aircraft during the war in Vietnam. Still, beyond the major cities, most of the borderline remained open territory.

After the attacks of September 11, 2001, President George W. Bush created the Department of Homeland Security (DHS), charged with ensuring operational control over the nation's borders. The general consensus among borderlanders is that life got nastier along the line after 9/11.

The centerpiece of DHS operations was the Secure Border Initiative (SBI), which included constructing seven hundred miles of fencing along the land boundary with Mexico, at a cost of over $2 billion. "The Wall" took various forms, including steel ramparts, wire-mesh fences, closely spaced concrete pillars and bollards, vehicle barriers, and razor wire. In some places, no fewer than three layers of fencing divided the two countries, and the intervening tracks were groomed to permit high-speed chases. Paradoxically, the US was also investing heavily—in cooperation with Mexico—to increase the number of ports of entry connecting the two sides. Yet determined migrants managed to find ways over, under, through, and around the Wall.

Anti-immigrant sentiments quickly resurfaced in the US. The Minutemen Project was a high-profile vigilante group whose members volunteered to patrol the border. In 2008 I visited the Mountain Minutemen encampment on a prominent hilltop called Patriot Point, near Campo, California, just east of Tecate, Baja California. In the clear desert morning, flashes of sunlight sparkled on small aluminum plates fixed to a short informal fence that Minutemen volunteers had constructed to protest government delays in defending the borderline. Each plate was engraved

*Figure 1.4.* Fence reconstruction at Playas de Tijuana, on the Pacific Ocean. The rusted fences were originally installed during the mid-1990s Operation Gatekeeper era.

with hostile messages directed toward migrants, such as "Drop dead" and "You are not welcome in the USA. Stay out or die."

Captain Robert "Lil' Dog" Brooks was a former military man and retired offshore fisherman who'd been on self-appointed guard duty at Patriot Point for three years. Armed with a gun and wearing a black baseball hat with the motto "Mountain Minutemen, Patriot Point Posse," Brooks gazed in disgust at the fencing, saying: "What a place! If you were going to give America an enema, this is where you'd insert the tube." One year later, Brooks was gone from Patriot Point. I heard from someone that he'd gone back to ocean fishing in Alaska, but a US Border Patrol officer told me that Brooks was now in prison in Arizona, having been caught running illegal immigrants across the line.

Barack Obama took office as US president in 2009. Throughout his first term and much of his second, he continued the policies of his predecessor:

*Figure 1.5.* Patriot Point, along the California/Baja California border, extending eastward toward the Colorado River. Formerly a popular site for undocumented migrant crossings.

*Figure 1.6.* Holtville Cemetery for unidentified migrants, Imperial Valley, California. The sign warns against treading on the graves which are shallow and prone to collapse.

"Prevention through Deterrence" involving fortifications, policing, and surveillance to discourage unauthorized crossers; and "Enforcement with Consequences," aimed at deterring migrants by imposing tougher penalties. Only later in his second term did Obama introduce changes that improved the circumstances of migrants in the US, including curbing abuses of authority by Immigration and Customs Enforcement (ICE) personnel.

Bush's SBI regime was a free-spending, loosely targeted bonanza for the security, intelligence, and detention industries. The subsequent Obama era was described to me by a senior US diplomat as "calming." His administration closed programs that were ineffective or abusive and improved the situation of some migrants already in the US. It also oversaw record levels of deportation.

By January 2013, DHS contractors had installed a total of 651 miles of fencing, mostly along the land portion of the border—regarded as the practical upper limit on wall building, since some terrain was too precipitous to build on or was interrupted by bodies of water. The consensus of expert opinion is that the Wall had no effect on rates of undocumented migration across the US-Mexico boundary line. Any decline in the rate of border apprehensions was associated with the presence of more agents on the ground, increased raids in the workplace, the proliferation of interior checkpoints, and draconian prosecution and deportation policies. Also significant was the decline in job opportunities in the US due to economic recession, and improvements in the Mexican economy that gave Mexicans less reason to migrate.[8]

The land boundary portion of the US-Mexico line terminates at the Rio Grande—known in Mexico as the Río Bravo del Norte (Wild River of the North)—at the twin cities of Ciudad Juárez and El Paso. According to the Treaty of Guadalupe Hidalgo, the international boundary follows the deepest channel in the river, historically a problem because the course of the river has constantly shifted over time.

The massive growth of population and maquiladora employment in Ciudad Juárez spawned extensive suburban growth in the early 2000s. The Riberas del Bravo was a new town of over eleven thousand housing units built to provide workers with easier access to the principal maquiladora

*Figure 1.7.* The Official Center of the World, Felicity, California. I stood inside this architectual folly on March 15, 2009, at 3.10.55pm; it's one of the many unexpected places in the Southwestern deserts.

districts on the east side of Juárez. Sometime in the mid-2000s the neighborhood was taken over by drug cartels.

More than 430 women were murdered in the state of Chihuahua in the ten years following 1993, and hundreds more simply disappeared, mostly in and around Ciudad Juárez, Chihuahua's largest city. One-third of the victims had been sexually assaulted; others had been mutilated or showed signs of torture. Their bodies were dumped in desolate desert places. The femicides attracted international attention to Juárez, but news coverage dropped off as violence associated with drug cartels exploded in Chihuahua and other border states. In the five years after 2006, the Mexican national murder rate was 14 per 100,000 inhabitants; but in Juárez, the rate was 189 per 100,000. (The US rate in 2011 was 4.7 homicides per 100,000 persons, the lowest since 1963.)

*Figure 1.8.* Riberas del Bravo, on Highway 2 east of Ciudad Juárez, Chihuahua.

At first the corpses of femicide victims were discovered in remote locations beyond Juárez. Then, in 2001, eight bodies were discovered within
the city limits. When I visited the site three years later, eight tall pink
crosses had been erected, each bearing the first name of a murdered
woman. The memorial lay in a small depression formed by the intersection
of two major traffic arteries that were slightly elevated above ground level,
creating a curious feeling of intimacy even in the midst of traffic. While
I was photographing there, three vehicles approached me at speed, clearly
not looking for a parking spot in the shade. I knew that they were not local
police, who tend in border cities to travel around standing in the backs of
flatbed trucks carrying automatic weapons. Today's intruders were federal
police from the since-disbanded Agencia Federal de Investigación. They
were firm but not aggressive in questioning, explaining that I was tres-
passing on an "active" crime scene. After some long tense moments, the
matter was resolved amicably. I felt most threatened when they took away
my passport to verify my identity.

The mid-2000s were bleak years of drug wars along the border. In
2004 I was driven to a Juárez conference in a special bus along closed

*Figure 1.9.* Reynosa, Tamaulipas. Flyer protesting the murders of Mexican women, 2003. The poster added below it invites applications from young women seeking work as receptionists and hostesses for an "important business."

streets accompanied by a large police motorcycle escort, watched over by groups of police posted along the route. As the violence metastasized, the city's population fell by over a quarter of a million as residents fled. Many crossed the river to El Paso. Around this time, an artist friend told me that no one was safe now because the "bullets no longer have names on them."

*Figure 1.10.* PAQUIMÉ, Chihuahua. Southwest of Paso/Juárez, these restored structures mark the site of a major regional trading center that flourished during the period between 1250 and 1340.

I was always careful along the border, never deliberately courting danger (as many sensation-seeking border writers are prone to do). My travel etiquette was simple: keep alert and use your common sense; having some Spanish always helps, but traveling with people with local knowledge is the gold standard in personal safety. There's one other caution: be prepared for the unexpected.

One fine day in 2014, I was having difficulty finding a monument just outside Nogales on the Sonoran side of the line. I noticed a cluster of three teenage males hanging out near the border wall. On a nearby house there was a handwritten note: "SE RENTAN A SOLTEROS Y SOLTERAS," basically, "Rooms for rent to singles." It was targeted at migrants without papers who were intending to cross over into the US. The young men were cartel lookouts, employed to monitor all activities at this informal crossing site. I was ready to leave, but my local host approached the

*Figure 1.11.* Statue outside a casino at the Tigua Indian
Reservation, Ysleta, Texas. Ysleta del Sur Pueblo is just downriver
from El Paso, and is one of the oldest communities in Texas.

boys and began an animated conversation. He returned to tell me that
he knew the boys' mother, so we were "family." He also knew that lookouts always had binoculars at hand, so he asked them if I could borrow
a pair. One of the teenagers returned with a pair of binoculars powerful
enough to spot life on Mars, and I located my monument instantly. We

thanked them and waved goodbye. It felt as though we were leaving a family reunion.

Another time, on my own, I was literally ambushed along a California line by two heavily armed men in camouflage uniforms resembling combat soldiers from some desert war. (They really did jump out from behind bushes, brandishing guns in my direction!) It took me a long time to convince them that I was none of the following: (a) an undocumented migrant, (b) a drug runner, or (c) a threat to American national security.

During my early days along the river, I received a warm welcome at Marfa Border Patrol station in west Texas. As usual, the interview was mediated by a communications expert employed to protect line officers from people like me. As I was leaving, one veteran agent gestured for me to join him outside. He began talking about life on the line: the camaraderie between agents, the traditions, the challenges and thrills of "sign cutting" (tracking), the great beauty of deserts, and his worries that transportation upgrades on the Mexican side would increase the flow of undocumented people crossing along the Marfa sector. He seemed aware that a way of life was passing.

The Big Bend is a beautiful, impassable jumble of massive mountains and boulders. People say it's where gods dumped the leftovers once the task of creation was completed. The deeply incised canyons and treacherous floods presented impassable obstacles to the boundary survey teams after the 1846–48 war between the US and Mexico. Big Bend National Park is today part of a large collection of environmentally protected lands on both sides of the international boundary line.

Further downstream in the Lower Rio Grande Valley, a collaboration between the American IBWC and Mexico's CILA created a five-mile-long earth- and rock-filled dam across the Rio Grande/Río Bravo del Norte. It was dedicated in 1953 and intended for flood control, conservation purposes, and to produce hydroelectric power. It also inspired a bombastic display of aggressive eagles.

The advantage of small places is that you see things more clearly. After 9/11, the informal ferries that crossed the river between Mexico and the US were suspended. Small villages like Boquillas del Carmen, in Coahuila, were devastated by the loss of tourist income. So women across the border in Terlingua, Texas, collected fabric that they donated to Boquillas

*Figure 1.12.* Rio Grande/Río Bravo del Norte, at Big Bend, Texas.

*Figure 1.13.* Commemorative monument, Amistad Dam, near Ciudad Acuña on the Texas/Coahuila border.

*Figure 1.14.* US Border Patrol Bicycle Brigade, Laredo, Texas. The streets of Laredo, Texas, are full of US Border Patrol officers on foot, on bicycles, and in vehicles, rendering the city uncommonly safe for its residents, who are predominantly of Mexican origin.

women, who sewed it into quilts and returned the finished products for sale in Terlingua. The proceeds from the sales were then delivered back to the quilters in Boquillas.

Laredo, Texas has a population of nearly three hundred thousand people, 95 percent of whom are of Mexican origin. Many people told me: "You can move the borderline twenty miles north and not many people around here would notice." The masthead of the local newspaper is emblazoned with seven flags of various sovereignties that have presided over Laredo in the past: France, the Republic of the Rio Grande, Mexico, the United States, Texas, the Confederate South, and Spain. Things are always more complicated than they seem in Texas, and bitter memories never die.

Further downriver, McAllen, Texas, had the distinction of drawing a greater share of Mexican spending than any other US city, affecting everything from retail sales to home purchases and vacation destinations. Most of the money came from the major industrial metropolis of Monterrey (in the state of Nuevo León), only two hours away by fast toll road. Many McAllen malls ran special bus services to attract shoppers from Mexico. So common is the trip from Monterrey to McAllen that a new Spanish verb was coined: *macalenear*, literally "to do McAllen."

In 2016, Donald J. Trump was elected US president, after running an election campaign that demonized Mexican immigrants as rapists and criminals. He promptly launched a crusade to build more walls, even though his advisers stated publicly and plainly that walls did not work. His plans met intense opposition and moved very slowly until a mad rush late in his term. Ultimately, he claimed to have completed 402 miles of fortifications. However, only 25 of these miles covered locations where no barriers had previously existed. The rest of the new construction either replaced dilapidated sections of existing barriers or duplicated existing structures.

Trump ignored evidence that the main source of undocumented immigration into the US was now people who arrived legally and overstayed their visas. Instead, he adopted virulently anti-immigrant policies: increasing detention, prosecution, and deportation rates; deliberately separating parents and children of families detained while crossing the border without documentation; attacking "sanctuary" cities in the US—municipalities that limit their cooperation with the federal government on immigration enforcement—through the courts; and removing protections for hundreds of thousands of children, known as Dreamers, born in the US to undocumented parents. On the international scene, Trump prohibited entry into the US by nationals from predominantly Muslim countries deemed hostile to the US and curtailed programs assisting refugees and asylum seekers.

The new president of Mexico, a left-leaning populist named Andrés Manuel López Obrador (known as AMLO), treated Trump with courtesy and spent most of his time trying to avoid bruising confrontations. But Trump was no friend of Mexico. He unceremoniously retired the North American Free Trade Agreement (NAFTA), replacing it with the US–Mexico–Canada Agreement (USMCA), ratified in March 2020. Under pressure, AMLO adjusted Mexican practices for dealing with immigrants from Central America, preventing them from crossing over to pursue claims for asylum in the US. And as cartel-related violence began once more to rise, AMLO seemed unwilling to challenge narco authority. Many civic officials, political candidates, and journalists were murdered.

After his 2020 inauguration, President Joe Biden was confronted with the legacy of Trump's daunting catalog of anti-immigrant policies. He took immediate executive action to undo many of Trump's edicts, adjusting the enforcement practices of ICE, lifting travel bans on nationals from Muslim and African countries, and protecting certain at-risk immigrant groups from deportation. By 2020, the annual US border and immigration budget exceeded $25 billion, a sixteenfold increase since 1994, when it was $1.5 billion.[9]

In today's altered borderlands, life is tougher. The wall has created a mean place. Arizona residents refer to the occupied zones as a "police state." A Mexican teenager was shot ten times in the back in April 2014 by a US Border Patrol officer firing without any provocation across the line from Nogales, Arizona, into Nogales, Sonora. The teenager, José Antonio Elena Rodríguez, died as he was walking at night, just blocks from his home, along the border fence through which officer Lonnie Swartz fired. A civil prosecution of the assailant was pursued by the American Civil Liberties Union (ACLU) on behalf of the boy's mother, all the way to the US Supreme Court. A key point in the prosecution's case was that the protections of the US Constitution apply across the fence into Mexico because the twin Nogales towns are an integrated single community. (They are commonly referred to collectively as Ambos Nogales, or Both Nogales.) I helped prepare and signed an amici curiae, or "friends of the court," brief. It ended with this astonishing conclusion: "In considering this case, *amici* urge the Court to recognize that Ambos Nogales—though it extends into two countries—is a single community of families, workers, and businesses. When a person who lives here walks beside the border, he walks beside a fence that is a mundane and unremarkable fixture in his world. He walks past shops that cater to tourists; he walks where his neighbors come to work. He walks through the middle of his community."[10] However, the US Supreme Court voided the lower court decision that had given Rodríguez's family standing in American courts, having earlier ruled in a separate case involving a cross-border shooting that constitutional protections did not extend across the line. A US agent could fire a gun and kill someone through the fence into Mexico, but a victim's family could not seek justice in American courts.

And yet unexpected kindnesses decorate the border landscape. Not so long ago in Arizona, I struggled to photograph a boundary monument that had been concealed behind a new fence. A passing Border Patrol officer suggested I should climb the fence to get the photograph. (Was he messing with me? Tempting me to break the law? Was he a practitioner of Mexico's *ley de fuga*, or "law of flight," whereby police would free prisoners only to shoot them in the back as they fled?) I declined the invitation. Sensing my reluctance, the agent himself scaled the fence and took the photograph I sought.

Surveys of residents in cross-border twin cities confirm that the borderlands are increasingly regarded as an economically integrated and bicultural society, where two countries, two languages, and two cultures come together to become one. And people want their lives back. For them this adds up to ending the occupation by police, immigration, and national guard authorities; removing the border wall and replacing it with other more effective methods of border surveillance and control; repairing the damage caused by wall construction and security operations, to be paid for by the governments and contractors who created the mess; and diverting the billions of dollars earmarked for wall construction to expanding the number and capacity of cross-border ports of entry.

Brownsville in Texas is the southernmost city in the United States and lies a short distance upstream from where the Rio Grande/Río Bravo enters the Gulf of Mexico. Its twin city is Matamoros, in the Mexican state of Tamaulipas. Some of the latter's wartime fortifications are still evident in the townscape. Construction of Fuerte (Fort) Casamata was conceived in 1830 as part of a general fortification system for Matamoros. The fort served as a supply base in the 1846 hostilities against the US and saw action during the Mexican Revolution. It is now a regional history museum.

Not far from the fort lies the compact, well-proportioned central square (or *zócalo*) housing Matamoros's municipal buildings, a church, bandstand, banks, shops, and more. It is frequently used for commemorative occasions, musical offerings, or political meetings. The absence of a *zócalo* in western border settlements such as Tijuana and Mexicali is regarded as evidence that they are not "real" Mexican towns.

Playa Bagdad is on the Gulf of Mexico, just south of the principal mouth (*desembocadura*) of the Rio Grande/Río Bravo. This small port was

*Figure 1.15.* Museo Casamata in Matamoros, Tamaulipas.

*Figure 1.16.* Zócalo in Matamoros, Tamaulipas.

established in 1848 but lost its significance after the Civil War; today it is little more than a cluster of beachside buildings. I had reached the eastern limit of the Mexico-US boundary line and started walking north along the beach toward the river boundary terminus. After a half hour or so, a truck pulled up alongside me. The two men inside were in uniform, but I couldn't see if they were police. They warned that the *desembocadura* was more than five miles away, and they offered me a ride for the price of a couple of sodas. I gladly accepted and jumped into the open back of the truck. Truth be told, there's not much to see around the river mouth: just two small dunes separated by a narrow river channel. Some picnickers lounged near a lighthouse, though not in great numbers. There was no physical evidence of a boundary monument, even though years earlier I had seen one marked on the original nineteenth-century survey maps at the Mapoteca archive in Mexico City. I sat watching the ubiquitous Border Patrol vehicle on the opposite side of the river. The truck had arrived moments after me, followed as I ventured upstream, and lingered after I departed.

Twenty years after my borderland odyssey began, I retain two enduring impressions of border life. First, it is a miracle how borderland residents on both sides of the line manage to transcend the hideous intrusions of the walls and armies of occupation and still maintain the connections that have characterized cross-border lives for centuries. The second miracle is how much civility still lingers along the line.

# 2 Bisected Bodies

I begin with Charlie Chaplin's feet.[1]

At the climax of *The Pilgrim* (a 1923 silent film), Chaplin's ex-jailbird character confronts a desperate dilemma as he stands astride the well-marked US-Mexico borderline, a foot firmly placed on either side. In the US he faces prosecution by a looming, vindictive lawman, but in Mexico he confronts a perilous future in a land seemingly beset by lawlessness. Chaplin's character is unable to decide between the two options. The film ends as he stumbles comically toward the horizon with his left foot planted firmly in the US and his right in Mexico. His body is, in effect, bisected, cut in two by the border.

Chaplin had the knack of playing the same personality in virtually every character he inhabited.[2] In *Pilgrim*, he is an escaped convict disguised in parson's clothing to conceal his real identity. He takes a train, having selected a destination by poking a finger randomly at a railway timetable. Upon arrival, he is mistaken for a real priest the town is expecting. Much of the consequent action is a conventional comedy of errors. When, for example, he is handed a Bible to conduct a church service, Chaplin (now known as the Reverend Pim) places a hand on the Bible in the manner of a criminal preparing to swear an oath to tell the truth and nothing but the truth.

Complications multiply. Pim is recognized by a convict who once knew him in prison, and who tries enticing him back to a life of crime. Eventually, Pim manages to acquit himself honorably, and he even finds time to woo a beautiful woman. Retribution is, however, inevitable. Pim is recognized by a gruff lawman, who escorts him to the boundary marker between Mexico and the US. The sheriff orders Pim to pick flowers on the Mexican side. When Pim crosses back to present him with the bouquet, the ranger dismounts from his horse and forcibly boots Pim over the line into Mexico.

Realizing the lawman's intention to exile him on the other side of the border, Pim at first seems ready to embrace his future. An intertitle has him exclaim: "A new life! Peace at last!," but instantly he is surrounded by a handful of sombrero-wearing pistoleros who spring from the bushes, and whose ensuing gunplay shatters his reverie. Terrified, Pim retreats again to the boundary marker, but hesitates as he straddles the line, fearful of the law in the US and the lawlessness in revolutionary Mexico. Disconsolate and undecided, Pim trudges off with one side of his bisected body in the US, the other in Mexico.

Charles Chaplin was director, producer, writer, and star of *The Pilgrim*, so it is safe to assume that little was left to chance in the film. Yet it is difficult to escape the sense that this closing sequence was an afterthought. Up to that point the border did not feature in the plot. Had Chaplin simply seized an opportunity for an amusing twist to his otherwise fairly conventional tale? A deeper look suggests more.

*The Pilgrim*'s representation of the early twentieth-century US-Mexico border landscape looks authentic enough. It's a flat expanse of sparsely vegetated emptiness, interrupted by a solitary signpost identifying the international boundary, the hazy outlines of far-distant mountains on the horizon. While the border location functions as a convenient background for Chaplin's antics, it is also an apt, witty comment on Pim's outsider status. Even in this short scene, the boundary line has tangible meanings and consequences for Pim and the sheriff. The lawman is well aware that Mexico is a suitable place to exile lawbreakers from the US. For Pim, a single step into Mexico will change everything: from his being a citizen to a noncitizen, from native to alien, from comfortable custom to unfamiliar challenge, from white to brown, and from rule of law to the anarchy of revolution.

*Figure 2.1. The Bridge* (2013). A bisected corpse straddles the international boundary line in the middle of an El Paso–Ciudad Juárez bridge crossing.

One hundred years after *The Pilgrim*, a television miniseries provided a different perspective on bisected bodies, this time in a far more literal sense. *The Bridge* (2013) is a border detective drama that opens with the discovery of a corpse on a heavily trafficked bridge connecting Ciudad Juárez in the state of Chihuahua with El Paso, in Texas. The dead body precisely straddles the international boundary line in the middle of the bridge. Its upper portion is in El Paso, but the lower section is in Juárez; one corpse divided between two countries, or so it appears. But we know that there is only plotline in all fiction, that things are never as they seem.

Police on either side of the line bicker over who has jurisdiction in this case. The US officer (Diane Kruger) is insistent that the case belongs to her. The Mexican officer (Demián Bichir) is happy to concede ownership since he already has more corpses than he can cope with. But as forensic investigators prepare to move the corpse, they realize that it is in fact two bisected bodies. Each is severed at the waist then shoved together neatly with an almost cult-inspired devotion. Even closer inspection reveals that one half of the body has brown skin, but the other half is white. This case belongs in both countries.

A century of filmmaking separates *The Pilgrim* and *The Bridge*, yet both feature a body apparently sliced in two by the US-Mexico boundary line, in metaphorical and literal senses. Chaplin confronted an existential dilemma; *The Bridge's* macabre fusion of one brown and one white demi-corpse epitomizes the brutal collision of two nations engulfed in criminal violence. When I first placed these two images alongside each other, I recognized the plot of a border film narrative. From the silent comedy traditions of Charlie Chaplin to the present-day epidemics of violence instigated by Mexico's drug cartels, the two images bracketed the time and space between then and now. We've already been introduced to Chaplin's bisected body, but for now I can set aside the mix-'n'-match corpses on the El Paso-Juárez bridge. They are not going anywhere.

Released a decade before *Pilgrim*, *Shorty's Trip to Mexico* (1914; unfortunately later retitled *Licking the Greasers*) offers a kind of guidebook for navigating border film. It features an Anglo adventurer named Shorty (played by Shorty Hamilton) who smuggles guns across the US border in support of the rebel cause during the Mexican Revolution. Shorty is an honorable man endowed with a casual heroism, who is smitten by an undying love for Anita, his beautiful Mexican sweetheart (Ramona Radcliffe). Shorty's principal antagonist across the line is a cruel and corrupt military general who lacks empathy for the Mexican people but has an army at his disposal.

The action ricochets back and forth across the international boundary line, which features prominently in the film. In the film's concluding scenes, Shorty dons a sombrero and darkens his skin color in order to cross into Mexico and rescue Anita from the clutches of the despicable general. Together they recklessly drive a stolen car back to the US, arriving at a border crossing marked by a stone monument typical of those constructed after the 1848 Treaty of Guadalupe Hidalgo. (The monument featured in this scene looks authentic, even down to the commemorative plaque affixed to its side. As was typical of the times, no fencing or other materials mark the border's extension beyond the obelisk.) Two US border guards on horseback grant passage to the fugitive pair, who cross safety into the US. Moments later, the same officers easily dissuade a small army of Mexican troops from pursuing Shorty and Anita across the line. In the happy-ever-after finale, Shorty declares his intention to marry Anita, affectionately promising: "And your future name and address is to be Mrs. Shorty USA."

## WHAT MAKES A "BORDER FILM"?

I define a *border film* as taking place in a borderland setting, with a topical focus on the lives of border people and a special concern for their cross-border connections. I prefer the brevity and flexibility of this compared to more detailed alternatives.[3] I also need a way to distinguish between those films that make only brief reference to the border from those that are deeply centered at the border. For this, I adopted the categories of background, character, and subject that Thom Anderson used to demonstrate how Los Angeles in film evolved from being a simple setting or background to a central concern of film productions. I have adjusted Anderson's scheme for my purposes as follows:[4]

> *Border as background*: The border location is purely incidental to plot and character, existing solely to provide a setting or backdrop—and nothing more—for the film's narrative. (Anderson suggests that such films could be understood as occurring in "anyplace.") Border-as-background films are rarely relevant for my investigation, so I can set them aside without loss.

> *Border as character*: The border has an enabling or transformative impact on person and plot. It is an explicit, active presence in a film's narrative, often manifest as the borderline's physical proximity. It has a physical, material form and presence, but can also pertain to mental or cognitive awareness of borders, in such perceptions as the "American Dream." Through its influence on plot, protagonist, and action, the border may be said to have acquired "agency" in border-as-character films. (Anderson refers to the LA suburbs as "bit parts or players" in some films.)

> *Border as subject*: The border is explicitly adopted as a thematic focus; in essence, the film is *about* the border. This category represents the deepest level of engagement; the borderline is accorded pervasive, fundamental, and enduring consequences for plot, protagonist, and action. In border-as-subject films, the border cannot be overlooked or ignored; if the border content were deleted, no coherent film would remain. (Anderson suggests this happens when a film becomes "self-conscious" of a place and its obsessions.)

According to this scheme, *The Pilgrim* qualifies as a border film. But of what kind, exactly? The film's principal plotline has no border theme (it's about Chaplin's escape and transformation), and the border is introduced only in the final scene of the film. Nevertheless, the conundrum posed by Pim's potential exile to Mexico is sufficient to qualify at least part of *Pilgrim* as a border-as-character film. In *Shorty's Trip to Mexico* the border is much more consequential throughout the film. The border location, the cross-border transactions, and the significance of the border in transforming the lives of the protagonists all mark *Shorty's Trip* as a strong type of border-as-subject film; if the border content were removed, there would scarcely be a film.

Once a film qualified as border-as-subject or border-as-character, I included it for further consideration. After that, questions of a film's message and quality became uppermost in my mind, as measured by a film's narrative power, innovation, performances, aesthetics, and historical significance. Ultimately my final choice of films is personal and idiosyncratic. This should surprise no one, but it might help explain why your favorite border film is not included.

My purpose in part 1 of this book is to identify the characteristics of a set of classic border films chosen from a long list of early classic films, and then to use that categorization as a template for an appraisal of contemporary border film in part 2. *Shorty's Trip to Mexico* and *The Pilgrim* are my basic points of departure. Already they have uncovered two themes that persist in border filmmaking up to the present day: stereotyping and miscegenation.

## IRRESISTIBLE STEREOTYPES

As the twentieth century unfolded, a small catalog of stereotypes quickly emerged in the films of both countries.[5] On the US side, a Mexican male was either a "greaser," or a "Latin lover."[6] The former referred to a duplicitous, conniving, lecherous, lazy, amoral, and violent hombre, who could become a "good greaser" if sufficiently redeemed by diligent accumulation of worthy deeds. The Latin lover was a mysterious, handsome, passionate, and courageous super-stud, epitomized by Italian American Rudolph

Valentino but also portrayed by Mexican actors such as Ramon Navarro and Gilbert Roland, and by notable Anglo actors such as Douglas Fairbanks Jr. Portraits of Mexican females in US films were equally confined. The woman was either a "seductress" with appealingly loose morals, who tended to be both physically and sexually aggressive, which qualified her as irresistible, or she was a beautiful, exotic "damsel in distress," stoically enduring life's indignities while awaiting rescue by a white male hero from *el otro lado*. Minor roles of Mexican lowlifes, clowns, or buffoons featured performers of all sizes, shapes, and genders.

Early Mexican silent films quickly settled into routine characterizations that repeated previous box office successes as a way to guarantee attracting filmgoers.[7] Variations of the "ugly American" male stereotype were a staple. Often he was a boorish tourist with no Spanish, belligerent and disrespectful but also inherently weak, cowardly, or effeminate. In another incarnation, he was invader, imperialist, or colonialist, invariably ruthless and callous, obsessed with making money to the exclusion of all else. Mexican films invariably warned of the threats posed by the country's northern neighbor, while at the same time invoking the superiority of Mexican people, culture, and values.[8] American women were almost always predatory, aggressive, and blonde, endowed with loose morals but also a willful independent streak that added luster to their already blinding sexuality. Characterizations of Mexican women quickly devolved into bipolar portraits of saintly mother or whore. The Mexican term for the femme fatale is *la devoradora* (the devourer)![9] Films that addressed the question of US racism usually reinforced the depiction of Mexico as a nonracist society.[10]

Filmmakers in both countries employed stereotypes as a quick and easy shorthand when introducing characters. The man in the white hat astride a white horse is always a hero, females with blonde or red hair always have dangerous curves, and unfamiliar accents invariably raise suspicions. Once these stereotypes become lodged on the screen (and in your brain), their carapaces are tough to penetrate. And yet in most eras it is not difficult to identify exceptions that supply more nuanced portraits. For instance, one of the greatest Mexican directors of the 1920s was Miguel Contreras Torres, who was the first to consider the complexities of Mexican migration into the US, in his *El hombre sin patria* (1922; The man without a country).[11]

In its brief ten minutes, *Shorty's Trip* delivers a rich portrait of revolutionary border life in the early twentieth century. Shorty himself embodies a popular archetype. He is a capable, resourceful white American male who assists rebels in an honorable cause against a repressive regime during a time of revolution. He is a handsome daredevil intent on rescuing a beautiful Mexican sweetheart (Anita, herself appealingly modest and retiring though not lacking courage). And he is a moral man with the power to bestow the gift of marriage and the rights to US residence upon his beloved. Other Mexican characters in the film rarely rise above the level of crude caricature: the general is a monster of cruelty and corruption, and the rebel leader remains shifty-eyed and untrustworthy despite his revolutionary credentials.

In *Shorty's Trip*, life in the US is presented as infinitely preferable to life in Mexico. The land south of the border is lawless and undemocratic, overrun by venal officials more interested in personal gain than the well-being of ordinary citizens. The backwardness and moral inferiority of its leaders justify Shorty's gun-running intervention into Mexican domestic affairs, with a clear implication that Mexicans cannot manage their affairs without Anglo assistance. Shorty's rescue of Anita reinforces the US claim to be a sanctuary for the world's oppressed, while the migrant's universal American Dream is codified in Anita's passage—through suffering and struggle, romance and betrothal, and climactic entry into the US and citizenship—to claim the honorific "Mrs. Shorty USA."

The boundary line itself has prominent material and cognitive weight in *Shorty's Trip*. (It is also a vital though brief presence in *The Pilgrim*'s final scene.) Crossing the line legally requires diligence, upright character, and the blessing of officialdom; crossing illegally risks arrest, danger, hardship, and even death. Those who succeed in reaching the other side, legally or illegally, may anticipate radically altered rules and conventions of behavior. Such physical and institutional barriers pose enormous challenges but are insufficient deterrents when life on the other side offers infinite rewards: freedom, security, refuge, opportunity and profit, rebirth, and new identity.

These two films also reveal divergent intentions and strategies on the part of the filmmakers. *The Pilgrim* delivers its message through comedy, an irresistible hero-convict, and splashes of sentimentality. It makes a joke of Chaplin's existential choice between the US and Mexico. In contrast, *Shorty's Trip* is nonstop action and drama, inviting viewers to identify with the couple's struggle against an oppressive regime and share in their sweet victories of true love and revolution.

## MISCEGENATION

*Miscegenation* (from the Latin *miscere*, mix, and *genus*, race) is a formal term describing the liaison between Anita and Shorty. This sober-sounding word has acquired pejorative overtones through its historical association with legal statutes prohibiting dalliances between Blacks and whites. The Spanish-language equivalent, *mezcla de razas*, translates as "mix of races," and the related word *mestizaje* refers simply to a mixing of people of diverse racial origins. Despite these linguistic nuances between Spanish and English, both countries celebrate the merging of races and cultures as part of their foundational myths of national origin and identity. Mexican mythology, for instance, refers to *la raza cósmica*, or "cosmic race," to suggest the dynamic convergence of the country's racial and ethnic differences; in the US, the closest equivalent may be *E pluribus unum*, meaning "one out of many." Both characterizations are optimistic in tone, but they are not the same: the Spanish phrase celebrates the positive, creative side of hybridization, whereas the English implies an expectation of assimilation into a single homogeneous identity.

Given the passion and sensitivity associated with this terminology, it is perhaps surprising that the romantic attachment between Anita and Shorty—a brown Mexican female and a white American male—goes unremarked in *Shorty's Trip to Mexico*. The early twentieth century was not an auspicious time for racial harmony in the US. There were, for example, long-standing laws against interracial marriage; and only a year after *Shorty's Trip* was released, D. W. Griffith's *The Birth of a Nation* (1915) appeared. In 1923, Chaplin's *Pilgrim* was savaged by the Ku Klux Klan for its representation of religion. Historically, Hollywood has a reputation for breaking rules regarding screen representations of sex, race, and violence and inventing ingenious ways to circumvent censorship codes periodically imposed on industry leaders by crusading moralists. *Shorty's Trip* simply ignored miscegenation and in so doing normalized it.

Anti-miscegenation laws had been a fixture in US society since the nation's earliest days. In 1664, Maryland passed the first British colonial law banning marriage between whites and slaves. The "abomination" of race mixing was attacked from many sides: by slave owners, racists, religions, and later, supporters of the eugenics movement.[12] Punishments for flaunting the laws were dreadful. The Maryland act ordered that a white woman who married a Black man would herself be enslaved. Moreover, there was no possibility of redemption after the "original sin"; the offspring of a mixed-race union could never return to whiteness through a judicious selection of white partners.[13] Contemporary tracts warned that any offspring of white and Negro was regarded as "corrupted flesh," and no amount of copulation with pure whites over "millions of generations" could breed "the ape" out of miscegenational couplings.[14]

Two and one-half centuries after Maryland, Griffith's *Birth of a Nation* distilled into one monumental film all that was racist about post–Civil War US society. Called by Henry Louis Gates Jr. "one of the most blatantly racist motion pictures ever produced," *Birth of a Nation* was a full-throated assault on interracial marriage, driven by Griffith's conviction that the post–Civil War Reconstruction effort in the United States was a miserable failure.[15] A silent short by Griffith predating *Birth of a Nation* was *Mexican Sweethearts: The Impetuous Nature of Latin Love* (1909), which directly addressed the dangers of interracial sexual encounters, revealing Griffith's fascination with racial and cultural orders, white supremacy, and miscegenation. Rosa Linda Fregoso's archival acumen has uncovered published synopses of about thirty lost films that *favored* miscegenation around that time. They fell into two categories: a rescue fantasy, in which a white male saves a Mexican female from dire personal straits; and a romantic conquest fantasy (including *Shorty's Trip to Mexico*), in which a white man wins a Mexican woman despite competition from Mexican suitors.[16] In both cases, transborder romance between white American males and Mexican women was generally treated favorably, whereas films featuring Mexican men tended to present them as threats to white women.

Griffith's *Birth of a Nation* contained little that would appeal to Black America, and Oscar Micheaux, one of the most prominent African American filmmakers of the early twentieth century, deliberately embarked on an ambitious mission to answer Griffith. Entitled *Within Our Gates*

(1919), Micheaux's film was not universally popular, but nevertheless it was an essential riposte.[17]

By the 1930s, formal production codes adjudicated what could not be depicted onscreen pertaining to miscegenation. Scenes of white women interacting with Negroes were permitted as long as there was no trace of miscegenation. There were no actual guidelines in the files of the Production Code Administration about what exactly was permitted in representations of miscegenation, but there was a file note to the effect that the subject was "taboo."[18] In this heavily moralistic miasma, disputes between censors and filmmakers were rife. Film critic Stuart Klawans described one especially turbulent dispute concerning the film *Duel in the Sun* (King Vidor, 1946), which reputedly conjured up an "atmosphere of sexual frenzy" that even seemed to condone miscegenation.[19]

The miscegenation in Orson Welles's film noir *Touch of Evil* (1958; see chapter 7) takes the form of a recent marriage between a brown Mexican cop and a super-glamorous white American blonde. The onscreen miscegenation again passes without comment, but the two films gesture toward the contradictions involved in screen representations of transborder romance. In both *Touch of Evil* and *Duel in the Sun*, the nonwhite person in a mixed-race couple is played by a white actor in brownface (Charlton Heston in *Touch*, and Jennifer Jones as the biracial Pearl Chavez in *Duel*). In the case of *Duel*, proximity to the indigeneity of the "half-breed" is of more consequence than skin color. In addition, the romanticizing of transborder passions could hardly ever transcend the practices of segregation embraced in film production—regardless of plot indications, the key roles were always assigned to white actors—thereby complicating the portrayals and interpretations of screen representations.

In Mexican films, miscegenation was often approached through the form of the mulatta; mixed-race ancestry is typically discovered through the birth of a dark-skinned child (*Los Angelitos Negros*; Joselito Rodríguez, 1948) or through personal appearance (*La Negra Angustias*; Matilde Landeta, 1949). Such themes were popular in Mexico during the mid-twentieth-century filmmaking boom of the Cardenas era.[20] Both these films are emblematic of the treatment of race and ethnicity in Mexico at that time. The song from *Little Black Angels* still lives as an anthem of racial equality in the US and Mexico.[21]

It was not until 1967 that the US Supreme Court declared laws prohibiting miscegenation to be unconstitutional.

## MEXICO'S MISSING FILMS: *TEPEYAC*, *EL TREN FANTASMA*, *EL PUÑO DE HIERRO*

In 1982, a devastating fire broke out at the Cineteca Nacional, Mexico's national film archive. An estimated 90 to 95 percent of films made between 1896 and 1930 were lost, dealing a mortal blow to the collections that represented Mexico's film heritage.[22] A very small number of feature films were rescued and later restored by the Filmoteca at Mexico's National University, UNAM. The restored films are helpful in piecing together the foundations that later Mexican border films would inherit, even though none of them were focused on border topics.

The oldest of three such films is *Tepeyac* (1917), directed by José Manuel Ramos, Carlos E. González, and Fernando Sayago. Around the time of World War I, the heroine, Lupita, learns that her beloved Carlos has been lost at sea in a German attack. Heartsick, she dreams about the Virgin of Guadalupe and is transported back to 1531, when Spaniards and native Indians coexisted in an uneasy aftermath of conquest. Her dream follows the story of the transformation of the Virgen de Guadalupe into a syncretic spiritual being born of indigenous and Catholic faiths. Lupita awakes to find that Carlos has unexpectedly returned, having survived the wartime attack. The filmmakers promote an indigenous perspective on the creation of the Virgen legend: the church hierarchy is represented as contemptuous and dismissive, and the film is folded deeply into indigenous history, spirituality, mythology, and landscape.

*El tren fantasma* (1927; The phantom train or The ghost train) was made by a leading Mexican silent filmmaker, Gabriel García Moreno, in the style of American thrillers. It is a fairly conventional love story set within an action-packed gangland thriller centered around trains—the antithesis of the contemplative *Tepeyac*. The plot is punctuated by a deluge of shootings, kidnappings, robberies, explosions, heartbreak and betrayal, and even a bullfight. The train sequences are the film's most kinetic, including both the fire-breathing Mexican steam engines and the quaintly coffin-like electric trains that burble uncertainly along urban tracks. (For comparison, Buster Keaton's Civil War train comedy, *The General*, was released in 1926 in the US.) The excitement generated by *El tren* is regarded as proof that Mexico's filmmakers had absorbed the language and style of Hollywood thrillers. Behind its furious action, *El tren* is also testimony to the helter-skelter rush toward modernity in Mexico.

The third restored film, *El puño de hierro* (1927; The iron fist), is something completely different. Released in the same year, with the same director as *El tren fantasma*, the plot hangs on the lives of two couples caught in a web of vice, drugs, and prostitution.[23] Laura is a ranch owner in love with Carlos, who is on the edge of criminality and a recent convert to morphine; Antonio is a gang leader with an affection for Esther, the hostess in a den of vice run by Hawk. Both women are counterstereotypically competent and forceful. In one of the film's gestures to realism, a lecture is illustrated by gruesome real-life images of addicts and their degrading conditions (this kind of borrowing and recycling from other films was typical of the era).

The plot is activated when Hawk persuades Carlos to accept a first needle of morphine. Thereafter, the film's surreal action is a delirious hodgepodge of subplots centered on the vice den.[24] After his first encounter with morphine, Carlos embraces and kisses a small donkey on the lips; a bearded small man endures/enjoys foot tickling administered by a bevy of louche addicts; and in the shady background, a homosexual orgy is underway. A close-up of Antonio and Esther's intertwined ankles is meant to suggest sexual intercourse. Among gang rivalries involving killings and kidnappings, there are comical interventions by a boy who reads Nick Carter stories while dreaming of becoming a detective, clenching an inquisitive pipe between his teeth. In a climactic moment, Hawk opens a trapdoor in the floor of the vice den and starts throwing the bodies of key cast members into a deep well underneath the property. But then Carlos awakens from his morphine-induced stupor. Once again, it's all been a dream.

*El puño* was not popular with filmgoers and was never shown in Mexico City. Today the film is unsurprisingly regarded as a classic of early Mexican silents.[25] Behind García Moreno's exuberant excess lay deep concerns regarding the rapid social dislocation in modernizing Mexico, the changing roles of women, the demise of traditional rural society and rise of large cities, and the violence associated with the proliferation of drug addiction.

## 3  Making Filmscapes

I had my first cigar when I was eight or ten years old. My mother and I traveled a long way to a movie palace in Cardiff (the capital city of Wales) to see *The Robe*, a crucifixion classic. Smoking in theaters was permitted back then, and I chanced to sit next to a large man who spent the entire two hours puffing out sickening clouds of smoke, which wrapped around my head like a World War I gas attack. I watched the film through a veil of nausea and was later unable to recall anything about it.

Later in life, I practiced cinematic devotions in the more sacred spaces of London's National Film Theatre. I also settled into a roofless cinema in Crete, where the stars above competed with onscreen stars (the film was *The Pawnbroker* with Rod Steiger); sat in a car at my first drive-in (*Straw Dogs*, in Washington D.C.); and stretched blissfully on a beach in Playas de Tijuana, watching a jumble of Spanish-language shorts projected inexpertly onto hanging bedsheets. Each venue was a unique filmgoing experience, making the point that *where* one sees a film is a matter of consequence. This simple observation is emblematic of a broad relationship between space/place and film, which is the underlying concern of this chapter and the next.

Two notions of place and space are essential to understanding film.[1] Production *in* place refers to where the film is made, incorporating the physical landscapes and materials of manufacture, such as a studio-based Hollywood production or an independent iPhone shoot in a backyard. Production *of* place refers to the creation of distinctive on-screen spaces, or *filmscapes*, used to render plot, character, and genre conventions involving not only cinematographers but also set and costume designers, writers, musicians, composers, and editors. Production in place and of place come together during filmmaking. An evocative case in film history involves film director Elvira Notari's early twentieth-century Dora film company in Naples, Italy, which shot many films *dal vero* (from real life) using city views and streets. Later, the films were often shown in the nearby Galleria Umberto I, using the town's arcade and adjacent piazza for open-air screenings. The arcade came to be called an *ombrello de pirucchi*, or umbrella for idlers, since it promoted movement, circulation, and social mixing.[2]

Places also connect. When individuals join together to form communities of common interest both near and far, they share friendships, ideas, and projects that over time may develop into established affiliations. Small groups may consolidate into businesses adopting more formal circuits of exchange and alliance that extend across space and time, crossing national boundaries and even going global. Such circuits rely on connectivity and proximity, often exceeding simple geographical adjacency but sustained through processes of digital diffusion and feedback through which ideas and innovations are adopted and transformed by others. When myriad minor places of filmmaking coalesce, they define a broader geographical agglomeration of cultural producers, consumers, and markets that together generate new synergies of creative activity as well as attracting associated cultural industries. This is the process behind the creation of Hollywood.[3]

The US-Mexico border offers an unusual opportunity to examine the in-between spaces where two national film cultures collide and fuse. Tracing the outcomes of these fusions is a principal impetus in this book, offering the opportunity to examine border film as an expression or language of cultural communication and exchange between two nations on either side of an international geopolitical divide. The emergence of filmmaking in the US and Mexico originated in two distinct cultural agglomerations:

one in Hollywood, the other in Mexico City. These clusters evolved from different genetic codes and institutional settings, but over the course of the twentieth century they increasingly became linked through overlapping production, distribution, and financial circuits. The success of such interaction explains how Mexico City in its golden age became known as the Hollywood of Latin America, since it arose out of a process of exchange and learning from Hollywood to the point of challenging Hollywood's domination of global film markets.[4] Today, the film ecologies of international productions in Hollywood and Mexico City are geographically separate but increasingly integrated, involving shared projects, financing, casting, crew, digital effects, and distribution arrangements. In addition, Mexican television programming (the world loves telenovelas!) has a global presence but maintains strong connections with Los Angeles.[5] Many countries in Latin America have recognized the advantages of collaboration and have reformed their national film industries based on their own circuits of international connection and exchange.[6]

## PRODUCTION IN PLACE 1: HOLLYWOOD

I moved to Venice and later Santa Monica, California, in the mid-1980s. By that time, Hollywood Boulevard was visibly the worse for wear, resembling a seedy version of Milton's *Paradise Lost* with Sylvester Stallone in the breakout role of Satan. I didn't recognize many names of the "stars" who had pressed themselves into the sidewalk. Yet the *idea* of Hollywood persisted as a metaphor for a hedonistic dreamworld where forbidden riches and fifteen seconds of fame were the birthright of everyone who stepped into its glare. To understand what it was like at its glorious best (or ghoulish fin de siècle), it's best to turn to Eve Babitz, the perfect Hollywood muse for those times. Eve was a talented partygoer, writer, and film industry player in the 1960s, who possessed an instinctive grasp of the essential synergies between LA the place and "The Industry" (always capitalized in conversations). "Los Angeles isn't a city," she wrote. "It's a gigantic, sprawling, ongoing studio. Everything is off the record. People don't have time to apologize for its not being a city."[7] She loved urban sprawl, dismissing complaints from outsiders while explaining: "It is where I work best, where I can live, oblivious to physical reality."[8] Her sense of Southern California's legendary sunshine was high poetry: "It was one of those blazing LA days when everything seems about to lose its sense of gravity and just rise above the sidewalks."[9] I would happily float around Los Angeles with Eve Babitz in my mind; you can keep lugubrious Joan Didion for yourself.

For the first half of the twentieth century, the history of the US motion picture industry was a story of the rise of Hollywood and the studio system.[10] In its earliest years, the principal base of the film industry was the New York–New Jersey metropolitan area. Its subsequent move to Southern California was, by conventional legend, stimulated by a sunshine-laden climate that permitted year-round filming, but serendipity was also involved. After 1912, an agglomeration of clustered motion picture production companies began to intensify, even though LA remained an offshoot of New York. Then some big industry players, such as Cecil B. DeMille, started to arrive in town, and soon afterward the clusters of film production companies consolidated and grew. The presence of some key talents accelerated Hollywood's rise. For example, Thomas Ince introduced new production techniques that foreshadowed the full-blown studio system, and D. W. Griffith's *Birth of a Nation* (1915) revolutionized expectations about what filmmaking was capable of (a scabrous, racist film, to be sure, but undeniably a technological and narrative pathbreaker).[11]

By the mid-1920s, the name "Hollywood" was being used as a synonym for the US film industry as a whole. This was understandable since the five largest majors (Twentieth Century Fox, MGM, Paramount, RKO, and Warner Brothers) controlled aspects of the three main phases of the film business: production, distribution, and exhibition. The extent of Hollywood's dominance in the industry was such that by 1937, California employed almost 90 percent of the nation's motion picture industry labor force, and New York only 8 percent.[12] Production companies and their soundstages were geographically concentrated in and around Hollywood (Columbia, Paramount, United Artists, and Warner Brothers), with offshoots in Culver City (RKO, MGM), Beverly Hills (Fox), and Burbank (Universal). The presence of Mexican immigrants in Los Angeles after the Revolution significantly influenced the emergence and consolidation of the Hollywood film industry.[13]

Beyond the dominance of the burgeoning studio system, some dazzling demonstrations of cultural fusion and hybridization involved experimental film. In a history of the "minor cinemas" of Los Angeles, film scholar David James illuminated the networks of independent filmmaking in LA, including avant-garde and art cinemas, documentary filmmaking, and pornography. Such activities on the cultural edges consolidated LA's rise over New York City as the preeminent center of film in the US. The avant-garde periphery also forged an emancipatory and progressive film culture.[14] In more recent times, an analogous spin-off generated alternative film and video production in the San Francisco Bay Area after 1945.[15] Both Southern and Northern California revealed how disarticulated urban laboratories for artistic and technological innovation could later nurture global centers for film, video, and new media production.

Still, the gilded age of the Hollywood studio system began unraveling in 1948, when antitrust decisions obliged the majors to divest themselves of their theater chains. The ensuing competitiveness and volatility undermined the grip of the studio system, a trend that was accelerated by the arrival of television in the early 1950s. Steep declines in theater attendance followed. Over the following twenty years, the majors merged with giant media conglomerates (Disney, SONY, Time-Warner, etc.), film-shooting activities broke loose from Hollywood, new markets developed for (re)packaged industry products, and computerized technologies usurped conventional industry practices.[16] By now, new film production facilities were being established far beyond Hollywood, luring "runaway productions" attracted by cheaper labor costs and financial incentives (the many alternatives included Vancouver and Toronto). Yet the inventiveness of the place called Hollywood persisted.[17]

Television's threat to theater attendance diminished when studios realized that television could be adapted to market their film products. Such was the industry's enthusiasm for the new arrangements that after the 1960s, television program and motion picture production facilities combined. The result was a major shift of TV production from New York (its original home) to Los Angeles, which now became the dominant center for TV program production in the US. As a consequence, the same set of multinational firms now dominated both the television and film production industries. The changing structures of the industries were further confused when media deregulation in the late 1970s resulted in an enormous proliferation in the number of TV channels offered to viewers.[18] The agglomeration of entertainment industries in Los Angeles possessed a dynamism that became hugely influential in film, television, music, and politics during the mid-1970s.

In the early 1980s, Hollywood was hit by another tectonic (tech-tonic?) disturbance that sent shock-waves to every corner of the industry. New computer graphics technologies had made it financially and physically possible to produce and manipulate large-scale visual images. By 2002, about three-quarters of the digital visual effects firms in the US were situated in LA, often close to the former studio hubs, Hollywood, Burbank, and Studio City, but also in Culver City, and (the new kids on the block) Santa Monica and Venice. Smaller clusters also existed in Marin County north of the San Francisco Bay Area and in New York City.[19] These firms served local markets for productions of commercials and TV programs, feature films, music videos, computer games, and web design.

The cumulative impact of these structural changes in the film and television industries was that the studios no longer reigned as monarchs of the magic kingdom. The 1980s saw a boom in all kinds of decentralized independent film production, with specialized companies taking over many tasks hitherto performed by studio employees, including preproduction (financing, casting), production proper (the film shoot), postproduction (editing), and distribution. Throughout the freewheeling New Hollywood, former studio employees were replaced by a deep reserve of skilled independent contractors (freelance and temporary) who supported the "Industry's" glitterati and moneybags.

## PRODUCTION IN PLACE 2: CHURUBUSCO, MEXICO CITY

The history of the film industry in Mexico has been very different.[20] For most of the twentieth century it operated in lockstep with cycles of federal government support aimed at promoting a national cinema in Mexico. The cycles of state largesse followed by years of financial deprivation corresponded exactly with periods of perceived successes and failures in the industry.[21] Only in the last quarter of the century did this begin to change.

The first silent moving pictures arrived in Mexico in 1895 and quickly established their popularity among the general public.[22] US producers sought aggressively to deliver their products to proliferating exhibitors in Mexico, and the Mexican public soon came to prefer Hollywood films over offerings by local filmmakers. By 1930, 80 percent of the films shown in Mexico City originated in Hollywood; only four films shown that year were Mexican made.[23] There was no equivalent to *Birth of a Nation* in Mexico. The most famous Mexican film of these origin years was *El automóvil gris* (Enrique Rosas, 1919; The gray car), a twelve-episode serial based on a series of audacious robberies that occurred in Mexico City in 1915.[24] The serial was reedited twice after the advent of sound and condensed into a single feature film. (This is the version I saw.) It is engaging and entertaining, providing an invaluable record of affluent neighborhoods and homes in the city, even though its accumulation of heists tends to become repetitious, reflecting the film's origins as a serial. The climactic execution of the Gray Car criminals used documentary footage of actual executions that director Rojas had filmed during the Mexican Revolution.

The years 1936–56 are generally regarded as Mexico's golden age of cinema. The Mexican film industry matured into a respected art form as well as a source of popular entertainment whose products often idealized Mexico and Mexicans. These films were influential throughout Latin America, and Mexico City became the Spanish-language Hollywood, setting a cultural agenda for Latin America just as Hollywood had done in the rest of the world.[25] Many factors contributed to the dawn of the golden age, particularly a long period of national economic prosperity. Benefits also flowed from connections with the US film industry through the training of Mexican filmmakers who later returned to work on domestic productions in Mexico.[26] During this period, film audiences indulged in a steady diet of quality films with nationalistic themes and Mexican actors. Many films originated in Mexico City's famed Churubusco Studios.[27] As the twentieth century unfolded, film offerings became more diversified, including those with thematic attention to history, social and political issues, and complicated personalities (fewer macho males and more feminists).[28] The preponderant sense of these times was that Mexican audiences were once again able to recognize themselves on the screen.

The life and times of Mexico's film industry for the rest of the century resembled a roller coaster, consisting of alternating periods of crisis and near collapse followed by financial resurgence, usually at the behest of an incoming federal government. The Echeverría presidency of 1971–76 was supportive and gave rise to a second golden age in Mexican cinema, but by now even lean years without state funding stimulated the emergence of independent productions, and interest in commercial cinema revived.[29] Experimental cinema flourished in Mexico and elsewhere in Latin America.[30] Then the release of *Solo con tu pareja* (Alfonso Cuarón, 1991), *Amores Perros* (a striking 2000 directorial debut by Alejandro González Iñárritu), and *Y tu mama también* ( Alfonso Cuaron, 2001; with memorable performances by Ana López Mercado, Gael García Bernal, and Diego Luna) caused critics worldwide to talk about Mexico's New Wave. In 2000 Vicente Fox was elected, the first president from the Partido Acción Nacional (PAN, or National Action Party) after seventy years of rule by the left-leaning Partido Revolucionario Institucional (PRI, or Institutional Revolutionary Party). Fox promptly set about trying to dismantle state involvement in the nation's film industry, but without much success; the new wave was already cresting.

The quality and international success of major New Wave films had a lasting impact on filmmaking in Mexico, but changing methods of financing film productions had longer-term consequences. International coproductions had increasingly become a lifeline for Mexican film productions during lean years of diminished government support. Now they became the subject of everyday dealmaking between US and Mexican filmmakers, production companies, and independents. James Cameron made news in 1997 by shooting *Titanic* at the Fox Baja Studios in Rosarito, Baja California (less than an hour's drive south of Tijuana). And more Mexicans who had worked successfully in Hollywood returned to give back to Mexico's industry.[31] (It is said that Mexican filmmakers preferred to produce films in Hollywood where the money was, but to direct films in Mexico using local talent.)

## PRODUCTION OF PLACE: CREATING BORDER FILMSCAPES AND AUDIENCES

In the first decade of the twentieth century, the US film industry manufactured and exported approximately five hundred fictional films that were set in and along its boundaries with Mexico and Canada.[32] This surge featured a wide variety of genres: Westerns, Indian dramas, Spanish/ Mexican costume pictures, and melodramas (comedy, crime, military), many of which featured border settings. Unfortunately, the majority of Mexican films of that era were destroyed in a catastrophic fire in Mexico City, so knowledge about these films and their reception is limited to newspapers, government documents, and periodicals such as trade journals and early film criticism. Notwithstanding these losses, historian Dominique Bregent-Heald has revealed how films, critical responses, and audiences converge to shape public perceptions of neighboring nations and border regions, and how film spectatorship and practices of theatergoing may alter public life. Needless to say, films never provide entirely accurate reflections of society, but all forms of cultural expression are distortions that can still end up reinforcing or criticizing existing social orders. Over time, the history of filmmaking offers evidence of how popular audience perceptions of the borderlands have shifted and the impact film culture has had on attitudes across an international boundary line.

In the earliest border-oriented films, the iconography of the western landscape dominated filmmakers' visions. They began as idealized notions of borders as *open spaces* where social and interracial encounters flourished (albeit not always peacefully). Later came a more geopolitical understanding of *closed borders* requiring regulation and militarization. The notion of frontier and open space was exploited by transcontinental railroad companies, which sponsored landscape-oriented travelogues to pique the curiosity of settlers and investors. Silent film producers quickly realized the potential of the new medium and moved on to fiction-based features, perhaps most famously *The Great Train Robbery* (Edwin S. Porter, 1903). The moving picture industry was rapidly transformed into an engine for mass entertainment. Film critics and marketing departments fueled audience preferences for Western subjects of adventure with outdoor settings. Another preference, this time for authenticity and greater realism in film portrayals of iconic landscapes, led to more and more location shooting in the American West. One of the most successful films of this era was a remake of *Ramona* (Donald Crisp, 1916), which lasted more than three hours and broke all attendance records at LA's three-thousand-seat Clune Auditorium.

The borderlands became an expansive canvas that lent itself to depicting all manner of human behaviors. It was a kind of petri dish, or contact zone, of in-between-ness that promoted cultural fusions, conflict, crossovers, and social change. One early twentieth-century palette emphasized the porosity of borders and the easy tendency toward hybridization among different groups (including miscegenation and *mestizaje*). Such interactions were encouraged by practices involving mobility, trade, and alliances (e.g., against a common enemy). An alternative palette imagined permeable borders as a threat to national security and public safety. The Mexican Revolution and World War I were surely instrumental in altering US attitudes at this time; Canada was perceived as a friendly, cooperative neighbor, but the threat from the Mexican border warranted policing by the murderous Texas Rangers and later, the US Border Patrol.

In 1991, the Mexican film scholar Norma Iglesias Prieto provided the first comprehensive historical account of the emergence of the border film genre in Mexico.[33] She coined the term "border cinema" to encompass the whole cultural industry of filmmaking as distinct from the actual film product released for public consumption. She also divided the history of border film into three historical periods:

- 1938–69, a period of slow gestation involving an average of two to three border film productions per year;
- 1970–79, when public interest in migration increased and President Luis Echeverría renewed state efforts to revitalize the film industry, increasing the annual rate of border film productions to five; and
- 1980–2000, when border film releases jumped to fifteen per year, most of which premiered in the expanding US film market.

Initially border films emphasized *migration*, the border as a place of transit to opportunities in the US. One of the finest examples (see chapter 6) is *Espaldas mojadas* (1953). Other themes that quickly grabbed audience attention included crime in its multiple manifestations; cultural identity, featuring the border as the place where two national projects clashed; and refuge for those in flight from the law or other criminals.

The popularity of Westerns persisted into the 1970s, but other subgenres began emerging, including drug trafficking and portrayals of the US-based Chicano movement. Both were a consequence of the assumption that Mexican national and cultural identities were under threat in border cultures. Around the same time, and in a lighter mood, musical and comedy films poked fun at *la migra*,—the US immigration and border control authorities. The titles of the so-called *sexy-comedias* were unsubtle and included such temptations as *Mojado . . . pero caliente* (1988), making the point that migrants may be wetbacks, but they're also "hot"/*caliente*, both languages conveying sexual appetite and promise. The Mexican films of the late twentieth century associated with the New Mexican Cinema developed more complex notions of border as refuge, embracing (for instance) the spiritual and existential dilemmas of migrants contemplating border crossings. Two outstanding films from this era are discussed in chapter 14: *El Jardín del Edén* (1995) and *Bajo California: El límite del tiempo* (1998).

The rise of a distinctive Chicano border film offered a significant break from traditional stereotypes in both Mexican and US commercial filmmaking during the last quarter of the century. Films such as *¡Alambrista!* (1977), *Born in East LA* (1982), and *A Day without a Mexican* (2004)—considered in chapters 11 and 13—offered a cultural reaffirmation of Chicano lives. The tendency was even more pronounced in independent filmmaking in Tijuana (using video and super-8 formats), which highlighted the subjective experiences of borderland people and the dynamics of place as captured by images of the city. Prominent examples include *Disneyland pa'mi* (Disneyland for me, 1999) and *Coca-Cola en las venas* (Coca-Cola in our veins, 1995). The former dealt with the desire of a Mexican child to visit Disneyland, and the latter explored border crossing and bicultural sensibilities.

Around the early 1990s, David Maciel offered his English-language view of US-Mexico border films.[34] He noted the early prevalence of Chicano-oriented and drug trafficking themes in Mexican-origin films, but also the rise of feature films relating to border-crossing migrants. On the US side law and order, cops and crime were popular border film themes, often involving heroic feats by the present-day version of the US Cavalry (i.e., *la migra*). Comedy films verging on slapstick were also popular, including the exceedingly silly *The Three Amigos*, "inspired" by *The Magnificent Seven* (which, incidentally, was shot in Mexico). Films from both sides lingered over border landscapes as objects of beauty but also great danger.

Some critics complained about the poor quality of early border films from both countries and cheered the emergence of "quality" independent US productions such as *¡Alambrista!* and *El Norte* (both discussed in chapter 11). Others plausibly suggested that lowbrow films—known as *churros*, or *naco* films—should be taken seriously because they were hugely popular with audiences, even if they lacked artistic, cultural, or socially redeeming qualities.[35] In Mexico, border films appealed to ordinary working people, who were attracted to screen representations that bore a resemblance to their own lives.[36] In Tijuana and San Diego theaters where Mexican films were exhibited, migrant farmworkers in the US welcomed a few hours of escape and contact with their home cultures.[37] So strong were these cross-border film connections that by the 1950s, Los Angeles was regarded as part of Mexico's domestic film market.[38]

The popularity of *churros* was partly a result of the participation by enormously popular stars such as the Almada brothers, Mario and Fernando. In *La banda del carro rojo* (Rubén Galindo, 1976; The red car gang), they played Mexican men struggling to survive in the US. Another box office favorite was María Elena Velasco, known as La India María. She wrote, directed, and starred in *Ni de aquí, ni de allá* (From neither here nor there), which was 1987's top box office success, earning more than $1 million from an investment of $175,000. The film's message was that it was better to be poor in Mexico than earning money in the US. An even more impressive box office was achieved by *Lola la trailera* (Raúl Fernández, 1985; Lola the truck driver). The film cost $175,000 to make and earned $3.5 million in the US and $1 million in Mexico. It is not difficult to imagine what it was about.[39]

Naturally enough the market for Mexican-made, Spanish-language films gave birth to a large industry. In the US the number of screens showing such films in 1941 was 145, growing to a peak in 1951, when there were 683 screens in 443 US cities and towns.[40] This decade of rapid growth was associated with the influx of agricultural laborers; quite simply, field hands became moviegoers (many lacking English). The screens were concentrated in the border states of California, Arizona, New Mexico, and Texas, especially in big cities such as Los Angeles and El Paso, but also in large agricultural zones such as the Lower Rio Grande valley. Nontheatrical presentations expanded the audience base through schools, clubs and churches. Audiences loved abundant singing and action with recognizable stars (especially Dolores del Rio, Pedro Armendáriz, María Félix, and Pedro Infante). Comedies were also popular, along with sentimental gestures to land and country. The movie theater became an important element in the cultural life of many rural communities, where it was often the only source of distraction and entertainment.

The nationwide distribution system for Spanish-language films soon became concentrated in two major companies, Clasa-Mohme and Azteca Films. They were later joined by US-based Columbia Pictures Corporation. In the period 1942–54, Clasa-Mohme's dominance peaked when it acquired the distribution rights for about six hundred Mexican films; by 1955 it had contracts with roughly 450 theaters across the country. But then Spanish-language movie theaters became less popular with the introduction of television and the rise of a younger generation who spoke English and identified with Hollywood films and American culture. Competition among distribution agencies in a shrinking market hurt everyone involved, but it was the introduction of home-based video entertainment that sealed the industry's fate. By 1990 almost all Spanish-language theaters in the US were closed after seven decades of continuous operation.[41]

The pace of US and Mexican border film productions picked up in the late twentieth century. Earlier themes such as migration, romantic comedy, and crime remained popular. However, hyper-violent films about drug cartels and trafficking would soon displace them in audience favor. Many post-2000 films were expensive, star-studded, international coproductions, thematically more diverse and with new emphases on race, gender, and sexuality. By now, the border was one of the most depicted filmscapes in American film, but not everyone agreed that filmmakers were doing a good job in representing borderland lives.[42]

# 4  Using Film as Evidence

DID HOLLYWOOD (AND CHURUBUSCO) GET IT RIGHT?

I confess to an inborn skepticism about film that is traceable to my childhood when I saw *How Green Was My Valley* (John Ford, 1941; adapted from Richard Llewellyn's novel). It was the first time I had seen a screen approximation of my life in a deep valley of small coal-mining towns in South Wales. I was enraptured—that is until the director made two false steps. The first was the scene when coal miners stepped out into the still-dark morning street on their way to work. Ludicrously (for I knew this never happened), they joined in singing together as they walked to the "pit," as the mine was called. The second, even more egregious error was revealed in crudely painted valley scenery, where the winding gear for the mine shaft (where workers were lowered underground to the coal seams) had been placed *on top* of the mountain above the mine. How could this be? The whole point of coal mining in South Wales (which in the early twentieth century produced and exported the world's best anthracite coal) was that the deeply incised valley bottom brought you closer to the coal seams below. Absolutely no one would build a mine shaft on top of a mountain and thereby add hundreds more feet of mineshaft drilling in order to access the coal seams beneath.

I was prepared to overlook the sight of a choir of miners singing in close harmony on their way to a strenuous eight-hour shift of labor in a miasma of coal dust, but I was permanently scarred by Ford's errors of topography and geology that put the pithead on a mountaintop. It made me suspicious of every film I saw thereafter. How pervasive are such cinematic lies and distortions? This is not a trivial query, considering that most people these days imbibe their knowledge of history and current affairs from film and television adaptations and reenactments, leavened occasionally by the stuttering sound bites of cable news.

Filmmakers are known to have a flexible approach to truth, willingly sacrificing authenticity in favor of plot requirements and entertainment value. Occasionally a damp effort is made to alert viewers that a film is "based on a true story." Such avowals are intended to instill confidence in the viewer, but frankly they're better understood as bait; a film can accurately be described as based on a true story when its factual fidelity lies somewhere between a fraction of 1 percent and 99.99 percent. Given such generous margins of error, nebulous reassurances that a film is "based on" or 'inspired by' something or someone give me a headache.

Should I worry about falsification in filmmaking? Would it make things better if I did? Historian Alex von Tunzelmann turned the question around to ask: "What would the history of the world look like if you learned it all from watching movies?" She set out to rate 104 feature films for their historical accuracy. The selection was drawn from international sources, covering various time periods and diverse thematic representations, from the ancient world (e.g., *The Ten Commandments* and *Gladiator*), through the Middle Ages and Renaissance (*The Lion in Winter, Shakespeare in Love*), to modern times (*The Right Stuff, All the President's Men*), and the present day (*Titanic, The King's Speech*).

How reliable were these cinematic representations? The short answer is hardly ever. Only four films scored an A grade for historical accuracy; and fourteen failed outright as representations of fact. The average grade for all films was a dismal C. In practice, it's safer to assume that falsification is the norm and that *all* feature-length films are fantasies. Critic Anthony Lane defended this practice of deception curtly: "Movies live and thrive on irresponsibility."[1]

The fault for inaccuracy and distortion lies not only with the filmmaker. All written histories themselves are imperfect representations of what actually happened in the past because writers are biased and sources are incomplete. What is referred to as "real" or "fact-based" history is but a temporary reckoning of events, subject to constant revision as new information emerges and fresh interpretations displace prior "established truths." Von Tunzelmann doesn't expect this situation to change and recommends that filmmakers take care with the reactions their films are likely to invoke among spectators, urging viewers to "question everything you are told and shown."[2] This seems a heavy burden for the average filmgoer, looking forward to a couple of hours of escape with a fistful of popcorn.

By and large, audiences are unconcerned to distinguish fact from fiction in film; they watch to be entertained. Filmmakers knowingly exploit the viewer's insouciance and even prize *inauthenticity* in pursuit of a required cinematic effect.[3] Nonfiction "documentary" films are just as prone to exaggeration and propaganda. Documentary filmmaker Steven Cantor once said: "Just because the word 'documentary' [is used to describe a film] doesn't mean that everything in it has to be 100 percent truthful."[4] It's worth repeating that in my approach to border film, every portrayal— of fact *and* fiction, truth *and* lies—conveys evidence of ways of seeing the world and imagining one's place in it. This alchemy of occasional truth in combination with manufactured falsehood produces an unstable evidence base that fuels my inquiry.

## CREATING MEANING IN FILM

A film is made by a very large number of individuals, who combine their skills to produce the finished object. Director David Fincher described his view of the experience: "Directing is a bit like trying to paint a watercolor from four blocks away through a telescope, over a walkie-talkie, and 85 people are holding the brush."[5] Still, there is a clear hierarchy in the empire of film. It's made overt in the order in which Oscars are presented at the annual ritual of the Academy Awards. The event's climax is the bestowal of the honor for Best Film (2021 was an exception). This award is given to the film's producers, the people who raised the money, hired the talent, and turned a concept into a product. Earlier in the awards ceremony, the talent is recognized: the best director, actor, and actress are generally regarded as the premier awards, often going to the most glamorous people. Then comes everyone else (writing, editing, costume designer, photography, music, etc.), based on no discernible logic that I can fathom. The foot soldiers in the empire of film (also known as *crew*: the drivers, stunt performers, construction teams, janitors, caterers, and many more) are customarily not recognized at the awards extravaganza (except sometimes after they are dead); a separate ceremony is held to honor technical advances in filmmaking.

The Best Director Oscar carries an almost mythical aura in the film world. A good director is a combination of magician, coach, therapist, visionary, artist, manager, and dictator who occupies the throne at the core of the creative process. It seems appropriate for a film to be identified by its director's name, although not at the price of disappearing other contributors to the enterprise.[6] Lesser mortals on the film set observe this pecking order, but sometimes grudgingly. For example, screenwriter Carlos Cuarón talked candidly about his comfortable partnership with his brother, the director Alfonso Cuarón, when they worked together on *Solo con tu pareja* (1991). The pair often experimented with different versions of scenes, tossing around ideas and so on, but Carlos was always clear that the last word belonged to Alfonso. In the end, Carlos would grudgingly concede, saying: "Yeah, OK. Whatever. Let's move on."[7] Yet film directors rarely have the last word. Producers do, often through contractual devices that require directors to cede authority for the "final cut" to a film's producers. Only very successful filmmakers can avoid such oversight. The arcane struggles waged by directors to realize *their* personal vision of a film are the stuff of many score-settling books.[8]

Once the work of financier and filmmaker is done, the film is ready to be released into the world. It is delivered into the hands of the distributors and offered to audiences, who respond in intensely personal ways that can seem independent of the filmmaker's intentions or craft. In truth, there are as many different responses as there are people watching a film.

Film audiences are rarely innocent neophytes. Over generations, filmmakers have taught them that the content of each film frame is significant: stuff is banished to the edge of the frame because it is less important, the center matters most, and things that do not show up on the screen can usually (though not always) be forgotten. A frame conceals as much as it reveals, and filmmakers endlessly exploit this nexus of trust with spectators, using every tool in their playbook to persuade, tease, and deceive.[9] Audiences respond by willingly surrendering to every kind of cinematic subterfuge. It's part of our viewing pleasure, knowing that we have agreed to suspend judgment, that nothing is as it seems, and that we are watching actors act. Untethered audiences pour themselves into films, expecting to be beguiled and bamboozled; to laugh and cry; to be aroused, repelled, and terrified. Behind the screen, film producers paw endlessly through the entrails of box office receipts gauging the preferences of every known demographic group and then design and market their products accordingly. In this fog of purposeful manipulation and voluntary capitulation, the last thing on the mind of a viewer is whether or not a film is actually true.[10]

What becomes more intriguing is the way audiences come together and create meaning about the films they observe. This returns me to the question of *where* people watch films. It can be described as *consumption in place* (analogous to earlier notions of production in and production of place). Put simply, it makes a difference if you are sitting on a beach watching movies being projected onto hung bedsheets or are ensconced in the gigantic luxury of a movie palace.

Film audience reactions interest many people beyond the headcounters at the box office. Historians, for example, try to fathom how place of consumption will shape memories of a film. During the period 1930–60, six theaters in Laredo, Texas, mostly showed Hollywood films but also offered a program of Spanish-language and Mexican films. There were four English-language theaters clustered downtown within a block or two of one another, with names like Rialto, Royal, and Plaza. The two main Spanish-language theaters (the Azteca and the Mexico) were some distance from the town center, in one case literally on the other side of the train tracks. The Azteca and Mexico attracted older folks who spoke only Spanish, while the downtown hub appealed more to their children and grandchildren, who were brought up speaking English. Going to the movies was virtually the only entertainment option in small-town Laredo. For the

majority Mexican-origin residents, cinemagoing was associated with social integration and adaptation into the new country.[11]

A rather different culture of "going to the pictures" characterized the
mid-twentieth-century small Welsh mining town where my parents lived.
In a town of ten thousand people, there were three cinemas within a quarter mile of one another, mostly showing popular Hollywood imports with
a smattering of British productions. Each night's program was typically a
double feature, a newsreel, a few advertisements, and trailers for upcoming features. During the intermissions ice cream, candy, and soft drinks
were sold from a tray by a person standing in front of the screen. Two of
the theaters doubled as grubby habitats for diverse fauna, but the most
opulent was the Parc and Dare Hall. Named after two local collieries, the
hall was capacious, tall enough for two balconies above the main floor.
The third-tier was so high and precipitous that it was referred to as the
nosebleed section. The least expensive seats were the two front rows right
under the screen on the main floor, from which location I once watched
*1984*, crushed by Edmund O'Brien's colossal, rat-threatened head above
me. Let no one say it makes no difference where you see a film.[12] Funded
by miners' contributions, the Parc and Dare Hall was built in 1892 and
housed a workingmen's library and meeting place. The cinema screen was
installed in 1920. Today the hall is listed as a building of historical and
architectural significance. It still functions as a theater and cinema.

Critics are another species afloat in the ecology that creates meaning from
film. A serious critic delivers more than basic information on recent
releases as a guide for consumers, useful though this may be.[13] Good criticism involves *critique*, a balanced assessment of a film that goes beyond
marketing hype and box office bombast. A critic's duties include commentary on a film's qualities and failings, and when appropriate, insight into
the film as cinematic art. The review may also place the film in the context
of its times or the career trajectory of director or star. Good criticism pays
attention to writing, since the latter requires the ability to render visual
experiences into words and to respect tight word limitations, all the while
fostering a style of "witty compression." Finally, the good critic should possess a "well-stocked mind" that reveals an interest in things beyond film.[14]
Anthony Lane of the *New Yorker* offers his own laconic job description: "A

critic is just a regular reviewer with a ballpoint pen, an overstocked memory, and an underpowered social life."[15]

Over time the accumulated wisdom of the guild of film critics becomes a repository of cultural memory reflecting what was thought about films at the time of their release. (In this way, film historians also play a part in forming public opinion.) The accumulated weight of this rumination adds up to a catalog, or canon, of films generally considered to be of the highest quality and lasting cultural value. The combination of audience response, box office receipts, and critical opinion contrives to manufacture meaning out of film.

In practice, of course, the canon is little more than a popularity contest, engaging cliques of critics who are susceptible to fashion, snobbery, and bad behavior. Every year, the British Film Institute magazine *Sight and Sound* has fun polling hundreds of critics, writers, and academics to ascertain the 100 Greatest Films of All Time. In 2020, the top five films on the list were *Vertigo, Citizen Kane, Tokyo Story, La règle du jeu*, and *Sunrise*.[16] The list does not change very much at the top, and the very big news in 2020 was that *Vertigo* had knocked *Citizen Kane* off its perch at number 1—a position it had held for twenty years! Perhaps this kind of movie trivia caused an editor of *Sight and Sound* to write an essay in 2008 entitled "Who Needs Critics?"[17] The ensuing kerfuffle over what criteria should be used to judge films shifted attention away from celebrating longevity toward a better-defined set of criteria for assessing film quality.

Maybe it's too late to salvage the culture of film criticism? These days, the status of "film critic" is being eroded as the number of self-proclaimed online critics expands exponentially. A surge of new releases from screen and stream has birthed a practice of one-paragraph, "in-brief" reviews. These can be useful and insightful but too often are superficial. Yet even these clips are too burdensome for industry aggregators, who have abandoned reviewing completely in favor of single-number rankings based on averaging scores from murky origins. These are next to useless. Good criticism seems increasingly scarce.

So I am going to stick with an early statement by Siegfried Kracauer from 1932: "The task of the film critic . . . is to compare the illusory world portrayed in . . . films with social reality; he must reveal the extent to which the former falsifies the latter. Briefly stated, the film critic of note is conceivable only as a social critic."[18] These days J. Hoberman comes closest to this directive, frequently chronicling how films intersect with national political events in the US.[19] But if I had to choose just one critic as the inspiration for this book, it would be James Baldwin.

James Baldwin came of age in the mid-twentieth century. He later recollected his childhood filmgoing in *The Devil Finds Work* (1976). The book is a work of film criticism examining Hollywood depictions of Black-white race relations in America in such film classics as *The Defiant Ones* (1958), *In the Heat of the Night* (1967), and *Guess Who's Coming to Dinner* (1967).[20] Baldwin retained a clear memory of the impact of such films on his young mind. One of his earliest (and most striking) filmgoing epiphanies was the realization that he was identifying with the cowboys, not with the Indians. He switched his allegiance, recording the impact of his awakening: "My first conscious calculation as to how to go about defeating the world's intentions for me and mine began on that Saturday afternoon in what we called the movies."[21]

Later in life, uppermost in Baldwin's mind when judging screen portraits of race was *authenticity*, by which he meant the fidelity between actions portrayed on the screen and what he knew from real life, especially what he had witnessed personally. Time and again he interrupts *The Devil Finds Work* to express sentiments like: "I understood *that*; it was a real question. I was living with that question." Not surprisingly, a powerful sense of being-there permeates the book: "Whatever others may imagine themselves to know of these matters cannot compare with the testimony of the person who was there."

In a striking synthesis, Baldwin first contemplates the difference between the cinematic imagination as embedded in *film* and his personal reaction as *witness* to that film. Next he pivots to question the *filmmaker's* original intent: "What do the filmmakers wish us to learn?" From electing to judge film through the prism of his own experience to excavating the traces of filmmaker intentions, Baldwin builds a critique illuminating the condition of racism in contemporary America. It's brilliant. I have decades of experience of the border and border films. I would not presume to emulate James Baldwin, yet I cannot imagine a better teacher.[22]

## THE FLORENTINE METHOD

This book is not a work of conventional film criticism or film theory. Film scholars tend to dispense abbreviated summaries of films, quickly deployed, before proceeding to examine them in the context of some theoretical or philosophical proposition. I do some of that, but usually I linger on the film's own narrative and exposition, letting the film speak for itself before expressing my opinions. Every piece of evidence in film—whether documentary or fiction, truth or lies, present or absent—conveys evidence about ways of seeing and of imagining one's place in the world.

The raw evidence in this book is taken from fictional films that by design wed imperfect truths with creative falsehoods. And because the film sources derive from two different nations, the task of assembling evidence is greatly complicated. How can we bring together these different sources and compare the film/evidence fusions that ensue?

One of the earliest and most consequential instances of cultural fusion and interpretation in the Americas is the Spanish conquerors' desire to accumulate information on Aztec history and cultural practices. The pictorial books, maps, codices, and bilingual translations (on such matters as calendars, festivals, and gods) were the product of collaboration between Spanish authorities and indigenous artists. For the conquerors, they provided information that would speed and consolidate the pacification of the defeated. For those who were conquered, the artifacts represented the only way their venerated traditions could be recorded and kept alive. The consequent documents are regarded as "early forms of cultural hybridity created by contact between Europeans and the Nahua of central Mexico."[23]

The most ambitious of these cultural projects was the *Historia general de las cosas de Nueva España* (General history of the things of New Spain), known as the Florentine Codex (1575–77). It was undertaken by a Franciscan friar, Bernardino de Sahagún, with a team of indigenous grammarians, scribes, and painters.[24] The various "books" of the Codex consisted of two columns of text, the original Nahuatl and its Spanish translation. Two decades later the texts were supplemented with over two thousand painted images.

The Spanish text takes many liberties in rendering the translation from Nahuatl.[25] Common examples include condensing long lists (of fruits, for instance) to make the text move more quickly and eliding sections that were critical of Cortés. Such editorial interventions could not conceal the depravity of the war conveyed by the images. In addition, the Spanish-language version unambiguously attributed the war to indigenous "rebels," whereas the Nahua authors categorically blamed the treachery of the invaders. Sahagún made other radical adjustments of the original Codex in his 1585 revision, casting the war as a Christian act, with Cortés as personification of the will of a Christian god. The revised text ends by celebrating news of the coming of Jesus Christ. In contrast, the original Nahua text ends abruptly with a materialistic Cortés obsessively demanding gold, more gold. The enormity of defeat is conveyed by the absolute emptiness of the Nahuatl narrative: "Finally, the battle just quietly ended. Silence reigned. Nothing happened. The enemy left. All was quiet, and nothing more took place. Night fell, and the next day nothing happened, either. No one spoke aloud; the people were crushed. Nor did the Spaniards move; they remained still, looking at people. Nothing was happening."[26]

What fascinates me about the Florentine Codex and its variations is the way art images were used to mediate the contradictory accounts in the Spanish and Nahua texts; they act as a bridge to confirm, refute, and qualify the relative weights accorded to each text, in this way:

Spanish text -> [*art image*] <- Nahua text

I offer a reformulation that treats border film as the mediating image adjudicating the facts of life in the land between adjacent nations:

Mexico -> [*border film*] <- United States

This is why I begin with the film itself: its images, narrative, and points of view. Then I consider its message about the borderlands and how the message may (or may not) be traced back to real worlds along the borderlands.

This is what I refer to as my "Florentine method." Of course I am not deploying ancient codices but instead using two nations' history and geography as expressed through their present-day cinematic arts. In addition, the photographs of real borderland landscapes, situations, and people that I include are intended to further enrich the process of mediation. I take some pleasure from knowing that these tracks I follow somehow echo the conventions established centuries ago by Nahuatl (and Spanish) scribes and artists.

# 5  Revolution and Modernization

In 1876 Porfirio Díaz became president of Mexico. With its mantra "Order and Progress," his authoritarian and repressive regime lasted thirty-four years until it was overthrown by the Mexican Revolution beginning in 1910.[1] In his push to modernize Mexico, Díaz brought rail connections to the northern frontier, including a transcontinental service to Mexico City in 1884 and to Los Angeles in 1888. He also opened the country to foreign investment, making huge concessions of land that encouraged agriculture, mining, and town development. These initiatives marked a new opening for US influence in the Mexican borderlands and beyond. By 1910, the six Mexican border states had a population of over 1.6 million people (or about 11 percent of the national total), and the four US states had almost 5 million inhabitants (7.3 percent of the US population).

Opposition leader Francisco Madero launched a campaign to unseat Díaz in the 1909–10 election.[2] It failed, and Madero fled to the US, where he called for armed insurrection against the unpopular president. Resistance flared in the border state of Chihuahua and the southern state of Morelos. By May 1911, Madero's forces occupied the border town of Ciudad

71

Juárez, and the ensuing treaty brought an end to the Díaz regime. Madero was elected president, but he faced a country deeply divided between established conservative interests and energized revolutionaries.

In an effort to stabilize his authority, Madero turned to the Mexican army under the longtime command of General Victoriana Huerta. However, by 1913 their alliance had soured. Huerta seized power, arrested Madero, and arranged for his assassination (with the collusion of the US ambassador to Mexico, Henry Lane Wilson).[3] Huerta's coup reignited the Revolution. In the south, the forces of Emiliano Zapata constantly undermined Huerta's authority. In the northern state of Coahuila, an older veteran, Venustiano Carranza, organized resistance, and in Chihuahua, an audacious newcomer named Francisco (Pancho) Villa quickly rose to prominence. An opposition that began as a set of regional uprisings was now congealing into a national movement.

In April 1914, Pancho Villa's Division of the North secured an important victory over federal forces at Torreón. Villa advanced to Mexico City, where revolutionary armies led by Zapata and Álvaro Obregón (the leader of Carranza's forces) were gathered. Huerta resigned in August of that year, but his downfall opened the way for a new "war of the winners."[4] Carranza and Obregón challenged Villa and Zapata for supremacy. US president Woodrow Wilson sided with Carranza, angering Villa, who reacted by leading a minor "invasion" into the small border town of Columbus, New Mexico. Subsequently, a large US force led by General John Pershing pursued Villa into Mexico but failed to apprehend him.

One particular source of irritation between the two nations was Wilson's embargo on arms shipment to rebels in Mexico while allowing General Huerta's army to legally import armaments and munitions from the US. Villa nevertheless shrewdly arranged to obtain arms from the US. The ending of the arms blockade in 1914 was one reason the Revolution shifted in the rebels' favor. Their ability to sidestep the embargo was "made possible by the strong sympathy for the Revolution evident in American border communities, especially their Mexican/Latino populations."[5] Ultimately, a new constitution was proclaimed in 1917, and Carranza was elected Mexico's president.

In Mexico, memories of the Revolution are found everywhere. Even the smallest town has a monument to the popular heroes of the Revolution.[6]

On the US side, the Revolution is largely ignored, an exception being in Columbus, New Mexico, the site of Villa's invasion. This tiny town commemorates the 1916 invasion in a ninety-nine-acre Pancho Villa State Park and two small museums. There isn't much to see beyond a rail station and a few homes. A few locals mention relatives who remember the invasion. Facsimiles of contemporary newspapers feature lurid headlines calling attention to a "blood-mad torch squad of Mexican brutes" shooting local residents. But locals understand that Villa's incursion was the only thing that people remembered about Columbus, at least until March 10, 2011, when the citizens of Columbus awoke to the sound of helicopters and people with guns in the street. Ninety-five years and a day after Villa's raid, federal agents stormed into town, arresting the town's mayor, police chief, and other officials on charges of smuggling guns, ammunition, and body armor across the border to Mexican drug traffickers.[7]

## MODERNIZING MEXICO: *THE WILD BUNCH*

The late 1960s was a time of experimentation in Hollywood filmmaking, stimulated in part by the enormous financial success of Sergio Leone's "spaghetti Westerns." Two—*For a Fistful of Dollars* and *For a Few Dollars More*—are set around the US-Mexico border, and both were released in 1967. Hollywood responded by offering revisionist views and updates of the Western myth in films such as *Butch Cassidy and the Sundance Kid*, featuring the legendary pairing of Paul Newman and Robert Redford, and *True Grit*, with an aging, ailing John Wayne back in the saddle (and on his way to winning the Oscar for best actor).

Sam Peckinpah's *The Wild Bunch* (1969) is set in the revolutionary borderland just before the pivotal Battle of Torreón between Texas and Mexico. It features violent clashes between a gang of US outlaws (the "wild bunch") and combatants on both sides in the Revolution. The story opens just as the influences of modernization are sweeping across the continent, represented in the film by the spreading railway lines, new weaponry such as the machine gun, and automobiles. The shock of the new is contrasted with the obsolescence of the old West, a theme constantly invoked by the words and attitudes of older gang members (many played by stars long past the youthful days of their more dashing screen performances).

The violence of the Revolution as it engulfed the northern borderlands is encapsulated in the film's notorious opening sequence. Disguised as soldiers, outlaw Pike Bishop (William Holden) and his gang ride into town to rob a bank. They pass a small group of children, a mix of brown and white faces, who have imprisoned in a small box a few scorpions with a multitude of rapacious ants. The children laugh as the scorpions try vainly to escape their tormentors. As the disguised outlaws ride by impassively, the children tire of the game, fill the box with straw, and burn the scorpions and ants alive.

The gang members realize that a posse led by bounty hunter Deke Thornton (Robert Ryan) has set a trap to ambush them. In the ensuing gunfight, the carnage is horrific, and director Peckinpah drew much criticism for his slow-motion, almost balletic portrayal of the rapturous bloodletting. The audience's revulsion intensifies in the battle's aftermath, when scavengers quickly descend to strip the bloodied corpses of their valuables. Quickly the depleted gang discovers that the bags they stole from the bank contain only worthless base metal. In the first of a number of border crossings, the gang splashes over the Rio Grande in search of safe haven in Mexico.

A calmer, slower mood descends when Angel (Jaime Sánchez), the only Mexican member of the gang, glimpses his native land along the river bank, exclaiming, "¡México lindo!" (Beautiful Mexico). To which an Anglo gang member replies, "I don't see nothing so *lindo* about it. It just looks like more Texas to me." Angel grins with mock pity, insisting, "Ah, you have no eyes." Eventually, the gang arrives in the village where Angel was raised, where life has been severely depleted by the raids of General Mapache (Emilio Fernández) and his troops. The campesinos offer a warm welcome to their prodigal son and his companions.

An evening fiesta offers respite from the killings and flight. The fundamental decency of hospitality in rural Mexico is conveyed by a village elder, who recognizes that the visitors are outlaws but treats them with respect. In return, he is venerated by Pike, the outlaws' leader. The stoic elder is reminiscent of a similar character in Akira Kurosawa's *Seven Samurai*. He remains unmoved, but warns Pike: "In Mexico, these are years of darkness." And despite the chasm separating Anglo killers from a pacifist rural sage, both sides make common cause around the question of the Revolution. The rebels in the village are described as *puro Indios*, who bravely fight a guerrilla war against superior federal military forces. Later in the film gang member Freddie Sykes (Edmund O'Brien) murmurs his admiration: "*Indios* know how to take care of themselves. They've been fighting Apache for a thousand years."

*The Wild Bunch* culminates in another battle steeped in gore. During a long, almost operatic preparation for the final confrontation, gang members unwind in a whorehouse, then ritualistically dress themselves for combat before slowly marching out abreast to face impossible odds. When a machine gun is unveiled, the mechanized slaughter of World War I is invoked. Members of the Wild Bunch capture the gun and turn it on Mapache's troops. The killing is apocalyptic in scale, though Peckinpah also allows some personal scores to be settled: Pike singles out a haughty German military adviser for execution; and a woman Pike treated kindly in the brothel herself commandeers the machine gun and kills him.

In the mournful aftermath of violence, glimpses of reconciliation and resolution are offered. Deke Thornton, the spent posse leader, sits outside the gates of Agua Verde. He has given permission for his mercenaries to gather up the corpses of Pike and his gang and return them for ransom to the US, knowing full well that the revolutionaries will not permit them to cross the Rio Grande. Freddie Sykes, the sole survivor of the Wild Bunch, arrives with some *Indios*. Sykes and Thornton had once fought together on the same side. Neither can safely return to the US. So Sykes invites Thornton to join him in the cause of the Revolution, adopting classical Shakespearean cowboy talk: "Me and the boys here, we got some work to do. You wanna come along? It ain't like it used to be, but it will do." With a wry grin, Thornton accepts.

*The Wild Bunch* is deservedly famous in Hollywood history.[8] Film buff David Thomson describes it as a "sublime song to disorder and honor."[9] The film is laden with complicated codes of honor that exceed the mere imperatives of survival. The adversaries on three sides (outlaw, posse, and Mexican troops) regard their opposite numbers with wary respect even though they are quick to exploit the slightest sign of weakness. They are experienced warriors who have manufactured distinctive moral universes.

When his right-hand man, Dutch Engstrom (Ernest Borgnine), appeals to Pike to rescue Angel from Mapache's tortures, Engstrom rages: "We ain't nothing like [Mapache]. We don't hang noboby." Yet even though General Mapache is undoubtedly ruthless and corrupt, during a battle against the rebels he is portrayed as a courageous leader, solicitous of his troops' well-being.

Angel, the only Mexican gang member, is the most complex moral character in the film, as befits his dual allegiances. (In contrast, the leading Anglo characters, Deke Thornton and Pike Bishop, are simply serving time and clinging to whatever shreds of self-respect they can muster.) Angel was brought up as a young village farmer in Mexico, but north of the border, he is an outlaw. When he lived in the village, Angel loved the strong-willed Teresa (Sonia Amelio). But after Angel's departure, she too left the village to join General Mapache's retinue, becoming a *puta* (whore) in Angel's eyes. Much later, encountering Teresa behaving flirtatiously with Mapache, an enraged Angel vengefully shoots her. We are, I suppose, meant to understand this horrific act as a matter of honor, and later Angel redeems himself somewhat less ambiguously by pledging to free the farmers from oppression and by risking his life to provide the rebels with guns. If there is any doubt about his ultimate redemption, Angel is obliged to suffer through an almost biblical torture and death at the hands of Mapache.

*The Wild Bunch* was filmed entirely in Mexico, mainly around Parras de la Fuente, a small town in Chihuahua that once was home to revolutionary leader Francisco Madero. Care was taken with the choice of props to convey change and modernization: automobile, train, machine gun, and map. Two central scenes in *The Wild Bunch* involve a train, for instance. Peckinpah's assistant tracked down a dismantled classic locomotive in Mexico City, which was reconstructed and transported to the location shoot. The engine was built in Philadelphia around 1885 and pressed into service in Mexico in 1901. It was active throughout the Revolution and may have transported the victorious Madero to Mexico City, when he assumed the presidency of Mexico in 1911.[10]

The sense of place in the film is strong and surely results from Peckinpah's passion for Mexico, which he regarded as his "adopted second home."[11] After a year at Fresno State University, the young Peckinpah

*Figure 5.1. The Wild Bunch* (1969). Who controls the railroad wins the war.

traveled with friends to study in Mexico City, where he was introduced to Mexican film and filmmakers of the golden age. Much of his early work in television was located along the Texas border, where he met people with whom he would continue working in later years. Peckinpah summed up his attachment this way: "Everything important in my life has been linked to Mexico one way or another. . . . The country has a special effect on me."[12] Such sentiments explain why he knew Mexico so well and took care to ensure the authenticity of his representation of the borderlands.

## IN SEARCH OF GENERAL VILLA:
### AND STARRING PANCHO VILLA AS HIMSELF

As leader of the revolutionary forces in the northern borderlands, General Villa's strategic successes depended on a number of factors: getting money to pay for his war; ending President Wilson's arms embargo imposed on the rebels; and silencing the Hearst newspapers' campaign, which advocated US intervention in Mexico and portrayed Villa as a bloodthirsty bandit. Villa boldly approached the US Mutual Film Company with a deal that would allow the studio to film his actual campaign in return for payments. Mutual planned a silent film with the title *The Life of General Villa* (1914), to be produced by D. W. Griffith and directed by William C. (Christy) Cabanne. It would include appearances by Villa himself and authentic footage of actual battles filmed on location.

The project began life as a short documentary/newsreel that was shown to backers in the US. A feature-length version of the film was subsequently commissioned by Mutual, starring Raoul Walsh as the young Villa. Sadly the film version is now lost, although some fragments and still photographs are said to exist. After its release, the film was credited with helping end the US arms embargo on arms shipments to the revolutionary forces and raising the level of Villa's reputation to such an extent that President Wilson held off from invading Mexico. Villa had proven himself a warrior, but also a shrewd master of manipulating media.

In 2003, a fictionalized account of the collaboration between Pancho Villa and the US Mutual Film Company was released as a television film directed by Bruce Beresford and produced by HBO in partnership with City Entertainment. At the time, it was the most expensive cable movie ever produced. Entitled *And Starring Pancho Villa as Himself*, the film focuses on the convergence of interests that led to the making of the 1914 original, *The Life of General Villa*. It portrays the Mutual Film Company as motivated by profit and Villa by gaining money to finance his war and using the new medium of film to undermine his political enemies in the US. Of the many ways in which US interests intersected with revolutionary and counterrevolutionary forces in Mexico, none matched the sheer bravado of the Villa/Mutual Film pact.

In Beresford's 2003 retelling, Mutual's opportunistic studio head, Harry Aitkin, and his star director, Griffith, delegated the task of working with Villa to Aitkin's inexperienced nephew, Frank Thayer. In *And Starring*, Thayer (Eion Bailey) is spirited across the border to meet Villa (Antonio Banderas). (My Mexican friends often complain about the number of times Antonio Banderas, who is Spanish by birth, has been cast as a Mexican hero, disparagingly referring to him as "Tony Flags," a very approximate English translation of his name.) At first Thayer is intimidated, but he is quickly won over by Villa's directness and charisma. Exactly what Villa thinks about Thayer is less clear. Thayer is obviously naive and inexperienced, yet he holds the key to Villa's battlefield and media successes.

*Figure 5.2. And Starring Pancho Villa as Himself* (2004). Thayer and Villa celebrate signing the contract for making the film with tutti frutti ice cream.

Their first meeting seems like the beginning of what we would today call a "bromance" between the two men. Later, Villa intensifies his charm-siege on Thayer, observing that they share the same first name (Francisco/ Frank) and bestowing on Thayer a pendant that had reputedly belonged to his mother. In thrall to the revolution, adventure, travel, exotic locations, and the proximity of war, Thayer is an easy conquest for Villa.

Thayer is also defenseless against the luster of Hollywood glamour, and he loses himself in a love affair with his leading lady, Teddy Sampson (Alexa Davos). He is impressed by the talented journalist John Reed (Matt Day), who shares his wisdom with the hapless Thayer. And Thayer idolizes Villa's fearless American mercenary soldier, Sam Dreben (played by a peerless Alan Arkin). One has to concede that puppy dog Thayer is ill prepared for the job.

Thayer gets a close look at the many sides of General Villa: his kindness to children, his exercise of justice for a young woman impregnated by a priest, his implacable belief in the cause, and the loyalty he inspires among his soldiers. But Villa is also a general at war. Thayer's tolerance for cruelty is finally exhausted when Villa calms a hysterical woman whose husband he just has ordered killed, first by embracing her, then calmly drawing his revolver to shoot her while she weeps in his arms. Disgusted, Thayer tosses Villa's pendant gift onto the ground and departs Mexico to complete work on the film in Hollywood. Their bromance is extinguished just after Villa secures his critical victory at Torreón and proceeds to Mexico City, where he and his rebel allies secure the Revolution in the north.

In the final scene of *And Starring*'s fictional account of the Villa-Mutual alliance, Frank Thayer is being lauded for bringing *Life of General Villa* to the screen. He is unable to enjoy his success, however, because the finished film has been transformed by Mutual into something less than he intended. Exiting the film's premiere, journalist John Reed consoles Thayer: "The lens is mightier than the sword." But Thayer is broken. Some part of him languishes in Hollywood, but most of his soul is still swashbuckling and romancing across Mexico in the shadow of a charismatic, courageous, and duplicitous Pancho Villa. Thayer has left half his heart and mind on the Mexican side of the border.

*And Starring Pancho Villa as Himself* is an entertaining rendition of an almost unbelievable real-life episode during the Mexican Revolution.[13] Against a backdrop of geopolitical and personal intrigue, the film portrays the emergence of a transborder alliance that—at least for a while—united its protagonists in a common cause. It is also a film about filmmaking, plausibly conveying how the filmmakers' presence complicated the conduct of war, encompassing reenactments of battle scenes and changing battlefield strategy. It demonstrates that Villa's co-opting of Mutual Film Company was itself a revolutionary act. He recognized and took advantage of the potency of the new medium, recognizing it as an instrument of propaganda that could open a second front far from the battlefields, and targeted it toward changing public opinion and federal government foreign policy in the US. (Villa's media coup was no fluke. In 1914, in Mexico City with Zapata, Villa visited the tomb of his hero, Madero, and burst into tears as part of a carefully staged act that was dutifully captured by attending photographers and filmmakers.)[14]

Villa's machinations were greatly helped by the American public's enchantment with movies and keen interest in the spectacle of the Revolution. Large numbers of people north of the border would gather spontaneously along the Rio Grande to observe battles that were underway on the opposite bank. The Mutual Film Company catered to this appetite, transforming a local spectacle into a national entertainment. Mutual was ready to make a hero of General Villa, and the general was a willing coproducer. A character from the HBO film sums up the arrangement thus: the "Mutual and Villa used each other." Yet their collaboration shifted the balance of military supremacy in the Revolution's northern campaign and altered the course of history.

## MANUFACTURING MYTH: *VAMANOS CON PANCHO VILLA*

The portrait of Pancho Villa in the film *And Starring* is deliberately ambiguous. We encounter him as a charming, courageous hero of the Revolution and as an opportunistic, murderous bandit turned general. But what kind of man was he?

This was precisely the question raised in a film entitled *Vámonos con Pancho Villa* (Fernando de Fuentes, 1936; Let's go with Pancho Villa; sometimes Let's ride with Pancho Villa). The film frequently tops the list of Mexico's best 100 films, and director de Fuentes is widely regarded as the most gifted director of Mexico's early sound cinema.[15] The film is unusual because its almost unqualified admiration for Villa is totally undone by an alternative ending that was filmed at the time of the original but released only in 1982, forty-six years later. The paradoxical difference between the hero worship of the original and the desecration in the twelve-minute alternative ending raises the issue of accuracy in filmmaking, already discussed in chapter 4.

*Vámonos con Pancho Villa* is the story of six friends who resolve to join the revolutionary army of General Villa (played by Domingo Soler). They are a mixed bunch, not a wild bunch. They approach war with determination but also with doubts about how courageous they will be. They spend time in friendship and conversations about death and honor. Over time, through their battlefield exploits, they become known as the Six Lions of San Pablo (their hometown), with bravery sufficient to be inducted into Villa's elite, the Dorados (golden ones). By that time three of them have already been left dead on the battlefield. Eventually, only two Lions remain, and the leader, Don Tiburcio (Antonio R. Frausto), is ordered by Villa to cremate alive the remaining Lion, who has contracted smallpox. The disgusted Tiburcio renounces the Revolution and Villa. In the film's celebrated closing shot, we see Tiburcio walking away from the camera along a railway line, carrying his pack, disappearing into the night. Weirdly, he reminded me of Chaplin in *The Pilgrim*.

In the alternative ending, years have passed, and we join Don Tiburcio living happily at his family home in San Pablo. In conversation, he portrays Villa as less than a hero, saying, "He was neither good nor bad." Then Villa arrives, looking like a grubby, ill-mannered bandit, and attempts to persuade Tiburcio to rejoin the struggle. Gesturing toward his wife and daughter, Tiburcio declines, so Villa shoots them, insisting that now Tuburcio is free to join his army. Tiburcio moves to kill Villa, but one of the general's guards shoots him first. The Don's now-orphaned son accepts Villa's invitation to join his army, so the dismal cycle of war and death continues. But Villa's reputation has been trashed.

Unlike Villa, the other populist hero of the Revolution, Emiliano Zapata, has consistently been sanctified for his role in the uprising. Zapata fought mainly in southern Mexico and was motivated by the long-standing suffering of agricultural workers in the state of Morelos. After the dictator Díaz had been defeated, Zapata preferred to return to his southern roots, lacking personal interest in power or politics. This action alone ensured his sanctification by the common people. Zapata was commemorated in Elia Kazan's 1952 biopic *Viva Zapata!*, starring Marlon Brando as Zapata.[16] Posters identified the film as "John Steinbeck's *Viva Zapata!*," and Steinbeck was given writer credit for the film (ten years before he would receive a Nobel Prize in Literature). The historical accuracy of the Zapata portrayal varies among scenes; for example, the circumstances of Zapata's murder were described as "dramatically true" even though details were altered, but Zapata's white horse was traced to Diego Rivera's mural of Zapata and not from real life.[17] Also, he did end up being assassinated, but for over a century Zapata has remained a legendary figure throughout Mexico. In 2005 I came across a small elementary school downriver from the border city of Ciudad Juárez. On either side of the school gate were mural portraits, one of Zapata and the other of Disney's Pinocchio. The title above the mural was Zapata's revolutionary war cry: *Tierra y Libertad!* (Land and Freedom). And today in my neighboring city of Oakland, California, there is an educational building identified as the Emiliano Zapata Street Academy.

I turned to written accounts of Villa in an attempt to reconcile these two films' divergent portraits. Walsh, who played Villa in *The Life of General Villa*, had quickly formed a favorable impression of Villa, observing succinctly, "Here was a man's man."[18] Reed was a renowned US journalist whose political persuasions later led him to become a participant in Mexico's revolutionary struggle. He arrived in Chihuahua City in 1913, where he met Villa. Reed described the general's arrival at the Governor's Palace in Chihuahua to receive a medal, only two weeks before his pivotal victory at Torreón: "He was dressed in an old plain khaki uniform, with several buttons lacking. He hadn't recently shaved, wore no hat, and his hair had not been brushed. He walked a little pigeon-toed, humped over, with his hands in his trousers pockets. As he entered the aisle between the rigid lines of soldiers, he seemed slightly embarrassed."[19]

A more considered viewpoint may be that of Elías L. Torres, who acted as an intermediary between Villa and the government of Mexican president Huerta. Later, in 1931, Torres recorded that Villa was neither the "genius of warfare to whom is owed the triumph of the Revolution" nor a "monster who fills all Mexicans with shame." He was, Torres claims straightforwardly, "one of the most prominent figures of the [Revolution,] . . . who will . . . go down in history haloed in greatness."[20] Torres probably got it right, even if it took over half a century for official Mexico to honor Villa's particular kind of greatness. In 1923, Villa was assassinated at Parral in the state of Chihuahua. It was not until 1976 that his remains were reburied in the Monument to the Revolution in Mexico City.

The improbability of discovering authentic representations in film of the life of General Villa is perfectly encapsulated by the work of Felix Padilla and his son Edmundo, who during the 1930s produced three versions of various episodes in Villa's revolutionary campaign: *El reinado del terror* (1932; The reign of terror), *Pancho Villa en Columbus* (1934; Pancho Villa in Columbus [NM]), and *La venganza de General Villa* (1937; The revenge of General Villa). Their story is best told by Gregorio Rocha, who spent many years searching for the films to use in his documentary *The Lost Reels of Pancho Villa* (2003).[21] The Padillas were itinerant projectionists who traveled throughout northern Mexico and the US Southwest exhibiting silent films rented or bought from distributors in Los Angeles and

Mexico City. They also stitched together three Villa films from newsreels, fiction films, and footage they staged and filmed using friends and relatives. Filmmaker and scholar Jesse Lerner refers to their work as "fake documentary" and places the Padillas in the ranks of "first Mexican-American filmmakers," who just happened to favor the not uncommon practice of recycling their own and others' films.[22]

The Padillas were inventive and promiscuous in their borrowing. For *El reinado del terror* they took from *The Life of General Villa* (1914) but also from a film called *Liberty, a Daughter of the USA* (Jacques Jaccard, 1916). For *La venganza de General Villa,* Edmundo added historical value by incorporating scenes from the film *Historia de la Revolución Mexicana* (Julio Lamadrid, 1928). Filmmaker Rocha described *La venganza* as a precursor of what he called "Border Cinema," not only for the film's geographical locations but also because of the ease with which it crosses boundaries separating fact and fiction, confounds stereotypes, and merges Anglo and Mexican mythologies and meanings.[23]

In *The Wild Bunch,* Peckinpah's different quest for realism extended beyond trains to the choice of location and props and to casting and crew. To cast the outlaws he hired real cowboys, and for the prostitutes, real sex workers from Parras. Of the forty actors credited at the end of the film, twenty-four were Latinos, with all but one being Mexican or Mexican-American. The group included top talent from Mexico. Novelist Manuel Luis Martínez recalled that he'd "never before seen an American movie that portrayed so many Mexican faces."[24] Furthermore, Peckinpah had his characters speak their own languages: English, Spanish, and German. One industry trade paper from 1968 seemed more than slightly befuddled by the film's emphases, leading to the headline: "Phil Feldman Casts Mexican People as 'Heroes' of 'The Wild Bunch,'" as if anticipating that Armageddon must surely ensue. The film's producer, Feldman, observed that "there are many good parts for Mexican actors in the film and no females—except for one small bit."[25] Peckinpah's convictions spread to behaviors behind the camera. Mexican star Alfonso Arau remembered going for lunch on the first day at the Parras shoot only to discover that Anglo and Mexican actors were being directed to separate dining areas. He objected, and Peckinpah ended the practice of segregated dining that same day. In his biography of the film, W. K. Stratton paid tribute to "the indispensable contributions to *The Wild Bunch* made by Mexican and Mexican American film professionals, which, sadly, ha[ve] been largely overlooked."

Today, a half century after its release, *The Wild Bunch* is still remembered for its slow-motion violence and the characters' amorality. Peckinpah explained that he was aiming for realism, and offered: "These things were happening in Mexico at that time."[26]

# 6 The Great Migrations

After 1917, legal migrants to the US were required to undergo a personal inspection (including health and literacy tests) and pay a head tax and visa fees before entering the country. Crossing from Ciudad Juárez to El Paso, for example, migrants would enter a disinfection area where their clothes would be steam cleaned and fumigated, and (if lice were found) their head and body hair would be shaved and bodies scrubbed with kerosene and vinegar. Other cleaning agents included gasoline, sulfuric acid, DDT, and Zyklon-B (later used for exterminating people in Nazi death camps). In 1921, more than 127,000 Mexicans were bathed and deloused at the Santa Fe Bridge crossing alone; in one notorious episode at El Paso jail in 1916, a misplaced match ignited the volatile vapors, and twenty-seven people died. The bathing and fumigating of migrants continued along the Texas-Mexico border until the 1950s.[1]

Around the 1920s, the numbers of crossings made by Mexican nationals increased.[2] Cross-border smuggling became a serious problem, and smuggled goods from the US were so pervasive that some Mexican officials even contemplated building fences around their towns. Facing pressure from

US agriculturalists to ensure their labor supply and an increasingly chaotic border situation, the US Congress passed the National Origins Act on
May 28, 1924, which tightened immigration laws and set aside $1 million
to establish a "land border patrol" which became known as the US Border
Patrol.[3]

The 1924 act transformed the issue of labor migration into a problem of
criminal behavior. Mexico's "migrant" became the US "illegal immigrant,"
leading to an entirely predictable upsurge in recorded illegal crossings as
well as the birth of a lucrative business of migrant smuggling. Mexican
law protected the right of citizens to free entry and exit from Mexico, but
authorities worried about the loss of its citizens through migration. The
Mexican Department of Migration, established in 1926, worked with the
US Border Patrol to curtail unauthorized border crossings.[4]

A massive forced exodus of Mexican and Mexican-heritage workers
during the Great Depression in the 1930s was followed by an acute labor
shortage during World War II (1939–45).[5] In 1942, the US and Mexico
signed an agreement called the Bracero Program, under which the US
government contracted with Mexican laborers to work in agriculture.
Only healthy males from areas in Mexico not experiencing labor shortages were eligible.[6] But the numbers available were insufficient to meet
demand. Domestic food shortages in Mexico stimulated yet more north-
bound migration.

In response to the growing volume of undocumented migration, between 1937 and 1941 the number of border patrol agents tripled, to fifteen
hundred. Most of the new hires were assigned to the southern border,
which became the geographical focus of US Border Patrol operations. In
Southern California, increased numbers of undocumented crossings resulted in a chain-link fence being erected along over five miles on either
side of the All-American Canal at Calexico in 1945, using materials that
had been recycled from a former World War II internment camp.[7]

By now, the principal concern of the border patrol had become removing Mexicans from the US. One of its most successful tactics was to de-
ploy mobile field units near workplaces and transportation corridors. The
success of these mobile units became the foundation for the well-funded
Operation Wetback program in June 1954.[8] Six months later more than
one million migrants had been removed from the US. The ripple effect of

Operation Wetback was widespread. New detention centers were rapidly constructed, but county jails were also rented,—a financially lucrative arrangement for many localities, then as now. Although Mexican authorities collaborated in returning detainees to the Mexican interior, the receiving localities could not cope with the sheer numbers arriving at border towns.

## DEPARTURE: *PURGATORIO*

Migration is a long and complicated sequence of events, whether it is long-distance international or domestic in scale. A variety of push factors explain why people choose to move, typically involving escape from persecution or poverty. Also important are pull factors that describe why people are attracted to a particular destination; these include job opportunities and the desire to reunite with family members. Linking migrant origin and destination is the journey that migrants intend to make, which varies widely in terms of cost, length of time involved, and risk.

Upon arrival at the desired destination, migrants confront new challenges. Successful assimilation and integration into the new homeland usually depend on factors beyond their control. Some places and countries are more welcoming than others. Host community attitudes toward accepting or rejecting migrants are affected by the newcomers' race, ethnicity, class, and immigration status.

Some migrants end up returning to their places or countries of origin. This sometimes happens by choice, but involuntary deportation is often the fate of those without papers, who have committed a crime, or whose application for asylum is denied. The forced return to a former homeland can be life threatening for those who fled for reasons of repression or persecution in their places of origin.

*Purgatorio* (Roberto Rochín, 2008) is a Mexican film based on three novellas by Juan Rulfo, a famous mid-twentieth-century Mexican author. The film is saturated by melancholy and misanthropy. It starts and ends with quotes from Rulfo. The first establishes that all life is a purgatory where each soul is imprisoned within a human body, and the second is a lament: "I wouldn't ask why we die. . . . [B]ut I'd like to know what makes life so miserable." Such existential precision from the outset deflects any later ambiguity on the viewer's part.

The film is set in modernizing Mexico around the mid-twentieth century. The old ways are disappearing rapidly, and the film opens with a delirious montage of Mexico City as a frantic utopia of innovation, technology, and material consumption. It's almost an advertisement aimed at persuading people to forsake the land in favor of city life. In three episodes, *Purgatorio* illustrates the frailty and misery of human lives, especially the illusions of love. The first tale, entitled *Paso del norte* (Northern passage), is a stark portrait of rural poverty in farming communities that directly invokes the impetus for border crossing. Starving families struggle desperately to survive on the land, and some decide to migrate to the city or to *el norte*. The second episode, *Un pedazo de noche* (A piece of the night), is set in Mexico City. A young gravedigger is devoted to a prostitute, but their fumblings toward intimacy are constantly frustrated. "Never love anyone," he advises her, perhaps reflecting Rulfo's personal misery. The final story, *Cleotilde*, concerns an orphaned young woman who enters into a marriage of convenience with an aging aristocrat. She swiftly becomes bored and takes a younger lover, but she is warned that "true happiness is not of this world" just before she is dispatched to the afterlife.

*Paso del norte* is the border episode of most interest here. It introduces an impoverished rural family on the verge of starvation. In desperation, the father, Bonfillo (Eduardo Von), decides to make the journey to *el norte*. He leaves a pregnant wife and two children with his reluctant father, a widower who operates a small fireworks business and harbors deep resentment against his son. Bonfillo soon arrives at a border crossing in the town of Paso del Norte. A nearby official boundary monument receives prominent attention in its role as sentinel. While he plans his next move, Bonfillo observes the humiliations of the immigration process suffered by those who are crossing legally.

Lacking papers, Bonfillo is not eligible for even the most minor amenities. Instead he hires a coyote, who leads a small group of undocumented migrants not to a border crossing but instead into a trap. Vigilante gunfire kills all except Bonfillo, who returns to his village. There his curmudgeonly dad informs him that his wife has run off to Mexico City with a traveling salesman. Bonfillo again leaves the village and his children, this time in search of his wife. The difficulties of coping in the city match those of his former life as farmer and migrant. Reduced to busking on street corners for small change, Bonfillo dies anonymously after being hit by a car at a street corner.

Meanwhile, back in the village, a fireworks explosion kills Bonfillo's children and his father, emphatically signaling the end of rural ways in modernizing Mexico. At least the dead are freed from the purgatory of existence. Modernization and the exhaustion of rural farming traditions fuel desperate migrations by people confronting starvation, who then confront a new universe of perils, humiliations, and dangers during and after their journey. The lives of those who remain behind are equally fraught. *Purgatorio*, released in 2008, seems to have answered Rulfo's question of why mid-twentieth-century rural life is so miserable. It is a chilling film, perfectly modulated as an antidote to happiness and pleasure.

## CROSSING THE LINE: *BORDER INCIDENT*

In 1949 a tectonic shift occurred in US border filmmaking with the release of Anthony Mann's *Border Incident*. Addressing the issue of migrant labor in the period of postwar reconstruction, Mann uses a documentary style, voice-over narration to great effect during the film's opening and closing sequences, lending authenticity to the unfolding drama of vulnerable border crossers. The entire film takes the border as its subject.

The tone is established from the outset by a series of aerial shots of irrigation canals, roads, and mechanized agriculture. A narrator succinctly introduces the film's theme: "'Here is the All-American canal. It runs through the desert for miles along the California/Mexico border. . . . Farming in the Imperial Valley requires a vast army of farm workers . . . and this army of workers comes from our neighbor to the south, from Mexico. . . . It is this problem of human suffering and injustice about which you should know.'"

The screen's display of muscular infrastructure is meant to convey government's ability to turn desert into garden through rational planning, innovative design, large-scale engineering, and dedicated leadership. Such visionary efforts toward economic development are backed by effective law-enforcement agencies utilizing modern technology, machines, weapons, and information.

Behind the outward manifestations of prosperity and postwar recovery lie unpleasant truths about the exploitation of migrants who cross over to work in US agriculture. Many workers at this time would arrive legally as sanctioned guest workers under the auspices of the Bracero Program. Those lacking permits were obliged to seek other ways to cross, often paying to hire coyotes to guide them. Migrants are aware of the dangers they face: the physical and mental endurance demanded by the journey itself and the risk of harm from unscrupulous human traffickers and law officers. They will be exploited on the other side by unscrupulous employers and abused by racists. The Mexican coyotes refer to migrants as "monkeys" or "dumb *paisanos*." When one migrant, Juan García (James Mitchell), complains about low wages, a US smuggler berates him: "You come in here, break our laws, and expect to be treated like one of us." The well-dressed government agents on both sides refer to coyotes as "human vultures."

Early in *Border Incident*, two planes appear on-screen, one flying from the left, the other from the right. They carry representatives from both countries to broker a binational collaboration to improve the lot of migrants by bringing smugglers and traffickers to justice. A cordial alliance is established between Pablo Rodríguez (Ricardo Montalbán), the Mexican principal, and Jack Bearnes (George Murphy), his US counterpart. Agent Bearnes is a decent, upright, efficient, and reliable lawman, so it comes as something of a shock to lose him early in the film. In a nod toward the violence of World War II, Jack is tortured with electrical current and later murdered by a gang member, who drives a heavy agricultural vehicle over Jack's prone body. This scene was shot from ground level and enhanced by using a wide-angle lens, and the screen is filled alternately by the vehicle's churning blades and the terror inscribed on Jack's face. One critic warned: "Normalcy is a condition which rarely intrudes . . . on Mann's bleak vision."[9]

Following Jack's death, audience loyalties are transferred to two Mexican protagonists: the lawman Rodríguez and the migrant Juan García. Pablo is now undercover, infiltrating the smugglers' networks. In the film's climactic battle, Juan leads a group of undocumented migrants through the Cañon de la Muerte, where they are attacked by smugglers. Federal forces arrive too late to help, but the battling migrants have learned to defend themselves. The narrator's voice returns, ominously intoning that nothing will deter migrants from trying to cross into the US. The film

*Figure 6.1. Border Incident* (1949). Binational partners in law enforcement celebrate their success.

closes with a triumphant celebration of the binational collaboration that led to the demise of the gangs, and of the two nations' commitment to protect migrant workers. Accompanied by stirring music, there is much smiling and flag waving by representatives of both sides, including the courageous Mexican lawman, Rodríguez. Sadly, Jack is absent.

*Border Incident* resembles other border films in adopting the passage to modernity as a central theme, this time imagined as a more hopeful mid-twentieth-century rationality based in law and good government. Film scholar Dana Polan refers to *Border Incident* as a "government agency" film demonstrating how effective government can be in reconstructing a war-depleted society. (Polan is less enthusiastic about the border itself, referring to it as "incoherent" and "wasteland" space.[10])

Throughout the film the architecture of public buildings is used to impart a flavor of gravitas and permanence to the institutions and conduct of the postwar government. The Rodríguez-Bearnes summit takes place in the (unidentified) Governor's Mansion in Mexicali, Baja California, a small but imposing Beaux-Arts building that symbolizes rational order.[11] Later in the film, a grand US Post Office building in Calexico, California, emphasizes the importance of communication in modern society. On the domestic scale, images of a beautiful California home emphasize luxury, in contrast to the squalid huts on the Mexican side. However, care is taken to convey favorable images of the traditions of faith and family in Mexico as well as the spiritual, nonmaterial foundations of Mexican society.

Comic relief of any kind is rare in *Border Incident*. We are introduced to a lower order of buffoons when a couple of Mexican badmen visit the beautiful house of a wealthy rancher turned migrant smuggler on the US side. They are overcome by its opulence. Much is made of their inability to fathom the operations of modern appliances in the home. At one point, a frustrated US lawman enters and literally bangs together the heads of the two Mexicans in an effort to instill some sense into them—just what the Marx Brothers or Three Stooges would have done.

Female roles in *Border Incident* are scarce and brief, but memorable. The Anglo rancher turned crime boss has a capable, beautiful, well-dressed, dark-skinned female assistant who is all business. The female gatekeeper who manages the processing of undocumented border crossers on the Mexican side is brittle and authoritarian. The most memorable is the monstrous Bella Amboy (Lynne Whitney), the heartless wife of a smuggler. Blonde, scruffy, and armed, Bella plays the role of a gangster's moll. We understand instantly that she is a person to avoid. At the opposite end of the scale from Bella's murderous vixen is the tearful face of Juan's mother. (She is called María, which seems to be the archetypical name for heroic women in border films.) Her likeness fills the screen in tearful, soft-focus suffering, pleading with her son not to make the perilous border crossing. María was played by Teresa Celli, and the story goes that Mann chose an Italian actress for this role because he needed someone capable of portraying the requisite degree of saintly suffering.

## CRUZANDO LA LÍNEA: *ESPALDAS MOJADAS*

Four years after *Border Incident*, Alejandro Galindo's *Espaldas mojadas* (1953; Wetbacks) was released, soon winning recognition as "the classic Mexican border movie."[12] Even before *Espaldas mojadas* begins, an announcement is screened and read aloud. It's an *advertencia importante* (important warning) intended to discourage Mexicans from attempting to cross illegally into the US: "Our intention is to warn our compatriots of the problems associated with trying to leave the country illegally, which carries with it the risk of awkward and painful situations that could even cause difficulties for the good relations that fortunately exist between our two nations."[13] This well-meant public service announcement was added after the US State Department had delayed the film's release for two years on account of its negative portrait of the US: Americans were obsessively materialistic, observation towers had been erected along the militarized borderline, and border guards shot their guns with intent to kill.

The film opens on Ciudad Juárez, seen from above. A voice-over commentary resembling that used in *Border Incident* underscores the optimistic panorama, this time of a bustling Mexican city. The following shots of El Paso's feature modern architecture and infrastructure, provoking the narrator to make this comparison: "On this side is Mexico, where Spanish is still spoken and the Virgin is sung to with guitars. Over on the other side, the skyscrapers, architectonic symbol of the most powerful country in the world, where everyone has a radio, car, and television."[14]

Dropping down to the street level, the camera encounters Rafael (David Silva), intent on crossing into the US to find work. Lacking papers, Rafael is predictably denied entry and so turns to human smugglers, who will arrange an illegal crossing. A perilous nighttime river crossing ensues. Searchlights and sirens explode on the US side, and gunfire shatters the dark. Most migrants are killed, but Rafael survives and conveys the body of a dead countryman into the river's currents so that it will be carried back to Mexico.

Once in El Paso, Rafael meets Sterling (Victor Parra), who offers him a job laying railroad tracks across the desert. The work is boring and backbreaking, and the employers are racist, cruel, and exploitative. The workers survive the tough work and loneliness by supporting each other: sharing food, telling stories, and singing sentimental songs about their homeland. On one occasion, "comfort women" are brought in to entertain the workers, but Rafael declines to participate.

When one of the rail workers is injured in an accident, Sterling berates him to return to work at once. Rafael intervenes, prompting Sterling to cry out (in English): "Don't touch me, you dirty Mexican greaser!" Faced with arrest for assaulting Sterling, Rafael escapes back to El Paso, where he avoids police pursuit with the help of Mary (Martha Valdés), a Mexican American waitress. In a series of vivid exchanges they discover common ground in their alienation and loneliness. Rafael speaks of "a wheel of loneliness. . . . No-one sees you, no-one hears you. You don't exist!"[15] Mary complains about the prejudice she encounters on *both* sides of the border as a consequence of her Mexican American roots: "I'm not Mexican. I'm a *pocha*. . . . The Mexicans don't like us and the gringos look down on us."[16] She compares the plight of Mexican Americans (rejected in Mexico and the US) with the situation of African American people born in the US: "Our disgrace is worse than the blacks. . . . [T]hey defend themselves. They form groups. They have their dances. They marry and console one another."[17]

The pair decides to return to Mexico. To honor the moment, Rafael addresses her with the Spanish version of her name, María del Consuelo. On crossing, Rafael is detained by Mexican immigration, enabling him to voice sharp criticism of social conditions in Mexico. María waits for him in a Juárez bar, but Sterling arrives. Rafael joins María and gets into a fight with Sterling. Angrily, Rafael and others escort Sterling to the river and order him to swim over to the other side. Sterling reluctantly enters the waters, shouting to the border guards that he has papers, but he is instantly shot by border guards, who mistake him for a wetback. Rafael is consoled by advice that he should not blame himself for Sterling's death, which is a curious morality at odds with the principled Rafael portrayed elsewhere in the film. As they prepare to return to Mexico, María offers Rafael affirmation of her love: "For a woman, there is no world beyond the man she loves."[18]

*Espaldas mojadas* is one of director Galindo's most outspoken films. He is aware of the hypocrisy in the US offer of copious jobs for some migrants and the burden of criminality for others. He is scornful of employers on both sides who abuse and exploit undocumented workers and of the criminal underworlds of both sides that victimize them. Apart from trigger-happy border guards who use migrants as target practice, agents of the law make only one sustained appearance in *Espaldas mojadas*, and that is to pursue Rafael after he has assaulted Sterling, the Anglo railroad contractor.

Galindo's borderland is, however, also a lively melting pot, generously seasoned with observations about identity, tradition, and belonging.

*Figure 6.2. Espaldas mojadas* (1953). A Mexican couple prepare to return to Mexico at a Río Bravo crossing, their American Dreams in tatters.

Sentimental ballads interrupt the film at regular intervals, reflecting on land, family, and tradition. The divide between the cultural traditions of Mexico and the ubiquitous materialism and racism of the US is starkly announced.

Yet as she prepares to return to Mexico, María readily adopts a conventional, subordinate gender role. The film's emphasis on names and name changes reinforces the fluidity of border identities. Starting out in the film as a *pocha* (Mexican American), Mary is reborn as María once her tryst with Rafael is sealed. The train-hopping sage who befriends them has the birth name Luis Villareal, although he introduces himself as Louie Royalville. Later, he declines the invitation to return to Mexico with Rafael and María, preferring instead to journey to Florida. Such mixing and merging of personal identities establishes the border as a space of fusion, a hybrid/ *mestizaje* world where altered identities are the norm, but also where such shifts need not be permanent or immutable. Even though borderland landscapes suggest permanence, human identities—for better or worse—remain flexible, contingent, and dynamic.

*Border Incident*, originating in the US, and *Espaldas mojadas*, originating in Mexico, share a focus on migrants and were released during the time of recovery after World War II. The thematic equivalence of the two films provides an unusual opportunity to compare notes on how US and Mexican filmmakers approached the topic of undocumented migration from Mexico in the 1950s.

Both films present cities as places of extremes, as the locus of modernization and wealth but also of endemic poverty. The urban settings in *Border Incident* are represented as technologically advanced; architecturally distinguished; and modern, well-ordered societies. This assessment is not contradicted in *Espaldas mojadas*, but the latter highlights a more modest Mexican urbanism, preferring to display cultural and traditional family values, especially those pertaining to religion.

An important narrative difference between the two films is that *Espaldas mojadas* forefronts the existential crises of migrant identity and belonging and of loneliness and alienation. On the other side, *Border Incident* adopts a similar plotline but drapes it in the fabric of successful binational policing operations aimed at protecting migrants and destroying the criminal organizations that victimize them. *Border Incident* also hastens the migrants' realization that they must be prepared to fight—if necessary, to the death—in order to secure a place on *el otro lado*. The action in *Border Incident* occurs across the binational land boundary, and in *Espaldas mojadas*, across the river boundary crossing. The films indicate that the struggle to cross is equally fraught no matter where the crossing occurs.

A major difference between the two films is how they approach the matter of policing the line. Bathed in postwar optimism, *Border Incident* begins with a display of technological prowess (the transformation of desert into productive agriculture) and concludes with a celebration of nation-to-nation policing successes. In contrast, *Espaldas mojadas* opens with a stern warning dissuading would-be migrants from attempting the dangerous border crossing. Its climax is the small personal victory of two returning migrants, María and Rafael, which is very different from the climactic celebration of *Border Incident*'s bombastic flag-waving ceremony. In *Espaldas*, law officers on both sides are roundly condemned: trigger-happy US border guards shoot to kill, and local Mexican police are hopelessly corrupt. As one Mexican lawyer comments: "What could one expect in a border town? The police and the snakes are first cousins."

# 7  Border Film Noir

*Film noir* is a French term literally meaning "black film." It refers to a particular style of crime drama that first appeared in the US during the 1940s and 1950s.[1] Noir films from this period possess a distinctive style and conventions: they are typically presented in high-contrast, black-and-white photography, and their convoluted plots have a male private investigator engaging in solving a mystery whose path invariably crosses that of a seductive femme fatale, who may be good or evil, sometimes both. The best noir films have fast-moving, wise-cracking dialogue, often accompanied by the cynical, world-weary voice-over of a narrator, maybe the investigator himself.[2] Noir filmmakers prefer claustrophobic, labyrinthine city settings, with Los Angeles as their favorite dystopia.[3] (In one 1950 film, the "City of Los Angeles" was listed among the cast of characters in the film credits.)[4]

Noir is a style. Unlike the films discussed in preceding chapters (which deal with revolution, modernization, and migration), noir rarely refers to a specific time period or topical focus, preferring instead the generic, such as the "naked city." A film in the style of noir can take place at any time or location and draw its energy from seemingly unlimited origins and themes. (Think, for instance, of the animated characters and mayhem in

*Who Framed Roger Rabbit?*, 1988.) The noir films introduced in this chapter include the perils experienced by a vacationing family, encounters with a serial killer, a private investigator settling a personal score, a rekindled romance, nightclub sleaze, political intrigue, and more. In addition, by now noir has been around long enough for specialized branches to have developed beyond the "classic" noir of the past; *neo-noir* refers to the films of the 1970s and later (*The Long Goodbye*), and *future noir* to films with a science fiction or fantasy setting (*Blade Runner*).

The border in classic noir is usually represented as a transitional, in-between place where louche types seek refuge, sticky conflicts may be resolved, or ordinary Americans find trouble simply by putting one foot into Mexico. In virtually all border noir, crossing over the line is a sign of pending material and cognitive dislocation. The barren terrain becomes a canvas for representing not only the natural beauty of the borderlands but also the murderous themes and passions about to burst onto the screen.[5]

## BORDER FILM NOIR: *BORDERTOWN*

*Bordertown* (Archie Mayo, 1935) was an auspicious early contribution to border film noir. Johnny Ramírez (Paul Muni) is an ambitious Mexican American in Los Angeles who opens a law practice after graduation but is soon disbarred by racist establishment lawyers who control the profession. Denied his American Dream, Johnny heads south to Mexico, where he gains respect and money through working at the Silver Slipper casino. The casino owner's wife, Marie (Bette Davis), falls hard for Johnny, even murdering her husband to ease Johnny's path to her bedroom. But Johnny is infatuated with Dale Elwell, a society playgirl (Margaret Lindsay), who cruelly rejects his overtures even though she is attracted to his physicality. Using her favorite nickname, Dale warns him that they will never marry: "Because you belong to a different tribe, savage." She literally runs from Johnny, only to be struck and killed by a passing car. Chastened, Johnny returns to his mother's home in LA, planning to open a law school. He reassures his mother (and a priest) that he is "back where I belong . . . with my own people."

I enjoyed *Bordertown*'s reversal of expectations that sent Johnny back to Mexico in order to realize his American Dream. Yet despite his success

*Figure 7.1. Bordertown* (1935). Who is the predator?

as a casino owner, he is laid waste by an upper-crust white woman. She appreciates the zesty mongrel in him but would never countenance marriage. In contrast, Marie, the bored wife of the casino owner, is flagrant in her desire for Johnny's carnal company, even killing her husband as a declaration of her independence and availability. These sexual permutations permeate *Bordertown*, but they are strangely invoked in the marketing of the film. The box containing my DVD copy of the film includes a cartoon sketch of Bette Davis, brooding languidly, very white, and sparsely dressed. Behind her looms the figure of a Mexican man (presumably Johnny) whose complexion is much darker than actor Paul Muni's. He is gazing at her with open lust, his hand outstretched to grab. A dark-skinned male threatening a white woman is one of the oldest stereotypes in cinema, but in *Bordertown*, the film's murder is actually motivated by a white woman's desire for a brown male. I imagine that some DVD purchasers were startled by the film's reversal of the natural order of things.

Another early noir film in which border crossing mattered is the splendid *Out of the Past* (Jacques Tournier, 1947). This film sets a high bar for the kind of wise cracking that audiences came to relish in noir films. The male leads are Kirk Douglas in only his second role and Robert Mitchum in his first performance as a "heavy." The on-screen femme fatale is Jane Greer. The film is set mainly near California's Lake Tahoe and Mexico's Acapulco. Night scenes occupy about two-thirds of the film. Mitchum and Douglas are simply superb together, and Mitchum's relationship with Jane Greer is pure Hollywood Shakespeare. On first seeing her in a Mexican bar, his voice-over recalls: "Then I saw her coming in out of the sun." Soon after, he recollects an equally evocative rendezvous: "Then she walked in out of the moonlight." Mitchum was clearly impressed, but later in a bitter break, he snaps at her: 'You're like a leaf that the wind blows from one gutter to another." (The screenplay is by Nicholas Musuraca.) The riches in *Out of the Past* are so plentiful that James Ursini built a catalog of almost twenty key noir characteristics gracing the film's baroque world.[6]

Many noir films featured plotlines conveying that crossing the border into Mexico was inherently risky. In *Jeopardy* (John Sturges, 1953), a couple with a young son drive across the border at Tijuana and pass immediately into a spooky realm. Driving south to Ensenada through an increasingly desolate and apparently uninhabited landscape, they come to a gas station, which the wife (Barbara Stanwyck) refers to as the "last stop in civilization." After that, the paved road becomes nothing more than "dirt and desolation . . . [in] shifting sands and bruising rocks." That's when diverse unpleasantnesses emerge to threaten the family.

A similar hysteria undergirds the desert noir *The Hitch-Hiker* (Ida Lupino, 1953), generally identified as the first truly noir film directed by a woman. (Lupino was also a famous actress.) Two old friends, middle-aged men out on a fishing trip, decide to pick up a hitchhiker, who turns out to be a serial killer. Making it clear they should cooperate if they want to stay alive, he forces them to drive across the border into Mexico and then south to Guaymas, on the Gulf side of the Baja California peninsula. The road trip is set in a spectacular, harsh desert landscape (actually filmed in the US). It features sympathetic portraits of Mexican people, including friendly locals and competent, attentive police officials. The Spanish language is used frequently in the Mexican scenes but, in a bold move, the film had no English-language subtitles.

The use of border crossings as markers of transition carried over into a neo-noir era in the 1970s and after. In Robert Altman's remake of *The Long Goodbye* (1973), for instance, Eliot Gould expertly plays a perpetually stoned Philip Marlowe, mostly concerned about feeding the cat. His laconic response to most distractions is to concede: "It's OK with me." But underneath, the real Marlowe harbors a deep devotion to the private eye's code of honor. He agrees to help his (special?) friend Terry escape from a snarl in Los Angeles by driving him across the border into Tijuana.[7] Later, when he discovers that Terry betrayed him, Marlowe decides that this time it's definitely not OK with him. So he returns to Mexico and executes Terry, restoring harmony to his gumshoe universe.

## BORDERTOWN TRAP: *TOUCH OF EVIL*

Tijuana never really outgrew its twentieth-century reputation as a "sin city." I doubt it really tried. By 1950, the city had swollen to almost sixty thousand people, triple the number from just ten years earlier. This was the cheeky, upstart border town in which Orson Welles chose to set his classic film noir, *Touch of Evil*, a benchmark in border noir.

*Touch of Evil* was originally released in 1958. Forty years later, in 1988, a revised version closer to the director's intentions was issued. Today the film has lost none of its fascination and impact. With a star-studded cast (including Welles himself), a propulsive music score (from Henry Mancini), and stunning black-and-white photography (by Russell Matty), it defines the classic film noir with the border as its subject. Film historian David Thomson described *Touch of Evil* approvingly but also inaccurately: "Its Mexican-American border was a new place in American movies, rancid and risky."[8]

The film's trailer warns us to expect a "story of a border-town trap" in a place called San Robles, which is rife with violence and corruption. (Welles could not get approval to film in Tijuana. Instead, the film's emblematic sidewalk arches and backyard oil derricks were shot in Venice, California.) If your skin is white, crossing into Tijuana and back requires little more than a casual wave from the border guard. Once across the line, the adjacent town is a tight, complicated maze of corrupt cops and a criminal underworld hiding in plain sight. No one seems sure of the foundations of their fragile existence.

*Touch*'s much-admired opening scene is a long single take that quickly establishes mood and focus. A bomb explodes in a car that has just crossed over from Mexico and been parked on the US side. The aftermath is witnessed through the eyes of Mexican lawman Miguel "Mike" Vargas (Charlton Heston, in brownface) and his American wife, Susan (Janet Leigh), who are returning from their honeymoon in Mexico. In the ensuing confusion, Vargas tries to calm Susie and excuse his country, explaining: "This isn't the real Mexico, you know that. All border towns bring out the worst in a country." Vargas is ready to define San Robles—and border towns more generally—as exceptional places in Mexico, where everyday standards of behavior and policing are provisional, inexplicable, and out of the ordinary.

In a reversal of conventions, Vargas the Mexican cop is more upright and honorable than any lawman on the US side. In seemingly perpetual darkness, the elegant street arcades are pockmarked by rotting bars, brothels, and burlesque joints serving a toxic brew of sex, vice, and narcotics. (Such accessories would become all but mandatory signatures in subsequent border noir.) In one scene an exuberant saloonkeeper is played by Zsa Zsa Gabor, the mistress of lascivious burlesque performances; another den shelters the indelible Marlene Dietrich, playing Tanya, madame of a house of ill repute.

Standing astride the border town is police chief Hank Quinlan, the Colossus of San Robles, played by Welles himself. In pursuit of his idiosyncratic vision of justice, Quinlan breaks laws with impunity, plants evidence on suspects, murders as necessary, and terrifies the locals on both sides of the line. His default facial expression is suspicious contempt, occasionally seasoned by the stink of violence in the breeze. Quinlan generously slathers contempt on Vargas, who is (a) Mexican, and (b) an honest cop, and thereby twice cursed in the Quinlan universe. Everyone becomes smaller when confronted by Quinlan's enormous bulk. He epitomizes the worst kind of bullying, ugly American, armed with badge and pistol. He quickly arrests a man named Sanchez in connection with the car bomb, but only after planting incriminating evidence in his apartment.

The principal dramatic axis in *Touch of Evil* is defined by Vargas and Quinlan, the honorable versus the corrupt complicated by brown-white racial antagonism. The second axis orbits around Susie Vargas and her antithesis, Tanya the brothel queen.[9] The war between Quinlan and Vargas is the film's driving conceit. For Tanya, the universal force is straightforward: sex is a paying proposition. Susie carries a heavier weight, balancing sexuality and wholesomeness, courage and victimization. Truth be told, Susie is the most intriguing character in *Touch of Evil*. She is Vargas's new wife, and it is through her that we experience the various shades of border underworld. There is no doubt that Susie will be placed in jeopardy, and the only mystery is how intense her suffering will be.

We meet Susie Vargas returning from Mexico in a flashy convertible with her new husband, whom she calls Mike (Heston). She is every inch a smashing blonde Hollywood heroine. Heston is his usual rugged self, except that he has on dark makeup to look more Mexican (thankfully, he does not adopt a Mexican accent). In quick succession Susie is terrified by the car bombing, accosted by Mexican thugs, and led across the border alone and at night. There she meets the Mexican crime boss Uncle Joe Grandi (Akim Tamiroff). Susie confesses to Grandi that he frightens her, but she still stands up to him. On learning of Susie's solitary nocturnal perambulations, Vargas is concerned for his wife's safety. His surprising response is to sequester her in a small, isolated motel owned by Grandi in the middle of the desert on the US side. She is the only guest at the motel except for a malfunctioning desk clerk with blatantly odd habits (think of Norman Bates in *Psycho*, 1960). Mike reassures Susie that she'll be safe.

Susie impatiently awaits Mike's return. Her sleep is disturbed by noise emanating from an adjacent room. After she hammers on the wall, a gang of slimy neighbors invades the room. They are Mexican and Anglo males, some tough-looking butch females, and a sprinkling of crazies. In a still-shocking scene, she is drugged and apparently raped (the action

*Figure 7.2. Touch of Evil* (1958). American police chief prepares to murder Mexican crime boss.

occurs off-screen). Susie is then delivered back to a San Robles hotel, where Quinlan plans to murder Grandi and blame senseless Susie for the crime. When Susie recovers, the first thing she sees is a close-up of the eye-popping face of Grandi's corpse! Her fall from grace is complete when she is jailed by Quinlan and charged with Grandi's murder.

Meanwhile, Vargas is barging around San Robles in macho mode. He has misplaced his spouse, dammit, and cannot find Quinlan or Grandi. Petulantly, he demolishes a bar and most of its patrons before getting answers that lead him to Susie. In a prison cell, she remains in a state of shock, but Mike reassures her that all will be well. He tenderly tucks a blanket around Susie, then promptly abandons her once again to continue his vendetta against Quinlan. The border is certainly bringing out the worst in this Mexican lawman.

Sadly, Susie now slips from the narrative. She's done the heavy lifting of plot motivation and suspense. All that remains is the Sanchez-Quinlan face-off.

It's blacker than night. The landscape is industrial, with fragile wooden walkways over dark waters. Quinlan and his partner discuss their predicament while Vargas trails after them, recording their conversation because

Quinlan's partner—tired of his boss's corruption and killing—is wearing a wire. But Quinlan catches an echo of the recorded conversation. Realizing that his partner has betrayed him, Quinlan shoots him before turning to confront Vargas. A gun is fired, but it's Quinlan who falls, shot by his partner who has finally tired of his boss's ways. Familiar honky-tonk piano music drifts over the waters, signaling the return of Tanya (Dietrich). Gazing enigmatically at Quinlan's corpse, she offers the bleakest of eulogies: "He was some kind of man. What does it matter what you say about people?" She is referring to Quinlan but is also offering a wry comment on border towns.

Having escaped death, Vargas now races away from the murder scene. (We wonder, where on earth is he disappearing to this time?) He reaches the convertible automobile, where a saintly Susie waits like a wan invalid. "It's all over, Susie, I'm taking you home," the gallant Mike reassures her as they resume the journey that opened the film. I'm not sorry to see Vargas go. Susie suffered a lot because of his macho behavior and careless neglect. Their future together looks bleak. It's best to remember them as the biracial couple whose marriage passes without comment in a film that warrants its reputation as a superior example of the border film genre.

## MEXICAN NOIR? ELENA GOES CLUBBING: *AVENTURERA*

What about film noir in Mexico? Historian Carl Mora argues that there is no such thing: "There was never really a Mexican *film noir*, although some laudable attempts had been made."[10] So many noir styles had surfaced in diverse Mexican films after 1945 that it might have seemed superfluous to invent a separate noir tradition in that country. Traces of noir are indicated by the choice of private eye and femme fatale as protagonists; the fondness for dimly lit urban settings; and plotlines that involve murders to be solved, mobsters to combat, corrupt cops to avoid, and irresistible (but terribly dangerous) dames.[11] In Mexico, noir traces were already prominent in the homegrown *cabaretera* genre, which attracted some of the industry's greatest talent. These films had lots of music and dancing and were often centered on a "bad" girl with a heart of gold, working as a prostitute or *fichera* (hostess) in a dance hall, brothel, or nightclub, which served as a microcosm for the wider male-dominated Mexican society. The *cabaretera* films drew attention to the limited options open to women in the years following the Mexican Revolution by contrasting the life of the *fichera* with that of an idealized "good" woman (meaning she who stays home and cares for family and is subordinate to a man in her life).[12] Two of the best *cabaretera* films reveal how US film noir may be equated with Mexican *cabaretera*.

*Victimas del pecado* (Emilio Fernández, 1951; Victims of sin) has a well-deserved reputation as the grimmest of the *cabaretera* films. The plot is simple. A dance club favorite named Violeta (the athletic Ninón Sevilla) rescues an abandoned baby from a trash can. She confronts the baby's father, who responds by forcing her into a life of prostitution. The overwhelming bleakness of this situation is offset by the film's lively dance numbers and music based in Afro-Cuban rhythms and drums, with quieter interludes for maudlin love ballads offering cautionary wisdom, such as "Don't Sell Your Heart." The very dark-skinned musicians join in lascivious dancing with the very white Violeta, mostly played for laughs. There are moments of comic relief, including pugilistic buffoonery and a fart joke. It's easy to understand why people loved these energetic melodramas (as well as their descendants, the telenovelas). At its heart, director Fernández's tale is about social change and dislocation in modern Mexico. The trains clanking past the nightclub tantalize the trapped with the opportunity to leave.

Julio Bracho's *Distinto amanecer* (1943; Another dawn) is one of the most famous of Mexican *cabareteras*. Julieta (Andrea Palma) works as a *fichera* in order to support herself and her husband. She rekindles her affection for a former flame and arranges to elope with him. Yet at the train station on the morning for departure, Julieta relents. Asked why she is crying when the train departs the station without her, Julia replies, "I would have cried even more if I'd left."[13] The film's oft-noticed similarity to *Casablanca* (1942) only adds to this *cabaretera*'s pleasures.[14]

A *cabaretera* film that easily qualifies as border noir is *Aventurera* (Alberto Gout, 1952; Adventuress). Its special distinction as a border film is that not one of its characters mentions crossing over into the US. Everything the characters need or want is available in Mexico: refuge, recovery, reinvention, community, security, money, and (perhaps) love. This is something new for us: a border film in which the protagonists' motivations are purely homegrown, having no reference to what exists on *el otro lado*.

The film's heroine is Elena (Ninón Sevilla again), a wholesome young woman living with her well-to-do parents. Her life is upended when her mother leaves with a lover and her father subsequently commits suicide. Orphaned, Elena departs for Ciudad Juárez, a border town with a sleazy reputation. There she is introduced to Rosaura, the head of a local brothel. Elena is drugged by Rosaura and forced into a life of prostitution. She is an excellent singer and dancer, skills that provide extra income.

She meets Mario, a rich young lawyer from Guadalajara, who proposes to her. He is impressed by her performance of the song "Chiquita Banana" (smitten, as was I, by the tower of bananas clamped onto her head). The betrothed couple return to the family home in Guadalajara, where Elena meets Mario's mother, who happens to be . . . Rosaura, who finances her luxurious Guadalajara life with proceeds from her Juárez brothel! Elena determines to destroy Rosaura and her sons. She marries Mario, delivering her first attack on the family's reputation by performing a provocative dance during her wedding reception. Then one night she enters the room of her brother-in-law, intending to seduce him. Rosaura interrupts, and she almost succeeds in strangling Elena before Mario arrives to separate the two women. In the face of defeat, Rosaura retreats to Juárez, but not without leaving instructions to have Elena murdered.

Elena now promotes her dancing career. Mario arrives in Juárez, begging her to come back to Guadalajara. Instead she leads him to Rosaura's brothel, where he grasps the full enormity of his mother's crimes against her. Elena and Mario hug in what may be an act of reconciliation.

The songs are the key to the *cabaretera*. This film is bookended by a number called "Aventurera." It is first performed by a solo male singer, then near to the film's end by a female-male duo. The song is a cynical ballad about life and love whose principal refrain is "Sell your love dearly, adventurer." (In *Victimas del pecado*, the refrain was "Don't sell your heart.") Elena understands the import of this message better than most. As played by Ninón Sevilla, she is the brains and heart behind the film, able to project youthful innocence and adult toughness, a volatile anger and melting sadness, skillful seduction, and murderous strength. And always she is a magnetic dancer and singer.[15] Ultimately Elena kind-of wins, but her future is uncertain.

I must record that *Aventurera* is not universally admired. Ana Y. López loudly chastised the film's excesses, epitomized by Ninón Sevilla's "exaggeratedly sexual glance, over-abundant figure, extraordinarily tight dresses, rolling hips, excessive laughter, and menacing smoking."[16] A contrary view of Elena is that she offered a place of sexual and economic liberation for women on and off the screen. Critic Paul A. Schroeder Rodríguez suggested that Elena "will never be a traditional wife, and will instead go on to be a liberated woman in charge of her own sexuality and her own livelihood." He also quotes Gilberto Pérez: "Elena may not be a philosopher but she is certainly a warrior, and *Aventurera* celebrates her invincible spiritedness."[17] I concur.

The place of the border in *Aventurera* sets the film apart. After her mother's departure and father's death, the young Elena flees northward to Ciudad Juárez, a borderland sin city, but she never crosses over the line. In Juárez she suffers the indignities of male harassment in every situation she encounters and is forced into a life of prostitution. The scheming Rosaura herself has an intriguing relationship with the border: she practices business with ruthless venom at a Juárez brothel in order to provide money to support a rich lifestyle in Guadalajara. The hypocrisy and cruelty involved in this arrangement explain why Elena is intent on destroying every vestige of her empire and family. One essential irony in *Aventurera* is how tainted money from Juárez, the sin city, finds its way to an opulent, "decent" family in Guadalajara. The film also complicates the role of Juárez: it is a place to profit, as when Elena leaves Guadalajara to start her independent career in Juárez, but also a place of refuge and restoration where a bruised Rosaura returns to gather strength for her final assault on Elena. Migration to the Juárez border is enough to satisfy most needs without the necessity of crossing to *el otro lado*.

*Touch of Evil* and *Aventurera* leave indelible traces on noir/*cabaretera* border film. Both feature women protagonists who, in different ways, dominate the film and determine its outcomes. In *Touch*, Susie Vargas is fearless and strong from the outset, although ultimately she is undone by the border. Elena's story, in *Aventurera*, follows a reverse logic; she begins by losing everything and only then rebuilds her life, through a driven self-will laced with courage. Elena draws power and freedom from the border, never once evincing interest in an American Dream. The supporting women in *Touch*, Zsa Zsa Gabor and Marlene Dietrich, build their own lives in Mexico.

## THE EMERGENCE OF BORDER FILM

From the earliest days of silent film, the US-Mexico borderlands were popular settings for filmmaking, largely due to the appeal of Westerns, which featured sweeping, visually splendid landscapes that could accommodate all manner of themes and genres. Romance, adventure, and comedy films were especially popular, but socially aware filmmaking was encouraged by governments seeking to promote a sense of national identity and belonging.

After the advent of sound, border-oriented feature films engaged prominent historical themes, especially the Mexican Revolution and the modernization of Mexico. Films from both countries offered rich commentaries on cross-border cultural differences, the exhausted authoritarianism of Mexico's dictatorship, and the plight of ordinary people confronting modern machines and warfare. Mexican productions celebrated the country's revolutionary heroes, including Pancho Villa and Emiliano Zapata.

An enduring theme emerging in early border film was cross-border migration by Mexican workers in search of employment in the US. Long-distance domestic and international movements were portrayed largely as a consequence of poverty and depopulation in rural Mexico and available work in the US. The films of both countries were elegies of disappearing rural ways of life and the devastating upheavals of modernization.

By the mid-twentieth century a second major theme in border film was based on vice, narcotics, sex, and corruption and their entanglements with public and private institutions of policing and law. The border was almost always treated as a dark place of danger where criminal depravity flourished on both sides of the line.

By mid-century, the border had become one of the most photographed landscapes in film. The borderlands' on-screen presence had been established as a tangible geography, as an attitude of mind, and as a place of permanent collision and fusion.

PART 2 Fusions

We wonder
how two cities are split, how they swell. Watch how they collide.

—Natalie Scenters-Zapico, "Crossing," *The Verging Cities*

# 8  Borderlands before Borders

The most telling and necessary way to open a conversation about border film is through films that portray ancient history. They are not truly border films by definition. How could they be? Nothing like the present-day boundaries existed at the times being portrayed on-screen. Yet the films inhabit places that would become our contemporary borderlands and are evocative of the ancient empires and their peripheries. Through consideration of this deep past, we glimpse a people's origin myths, the stories they tell, and their legacies for the present.

In prehistoric times, before the US and Mexico existed, the vast continent of North and Central America was occupied by empires of indigenous peoples. Strong north-south connections existed across what was to become the US-Mexico border, which were the principal axes for trade, migration, and conflict.[1] First came the Olmecs, who constructed an impressive urban culture on the Gulf of Mexico (near present-day Veracruz) between 2500 and 400 BCE. Next to rise in prominence were the Maya, who occupied the Yucatán and parts of today's Guatemala from 1800 BCE

113

to 925 CE. These groups were subsequently overtaken by the aggressively militaristic states of the Toltecs (1000 BCE–1200 CE), and later the mighty Aztecs (from 1200 CE until the Spanish entrada in 1521). Nothing in the territories now occupied by the US matched the size or splendor of the Aztec Empire. Nevertheless, the Southwest Pueblo cultures (primarily Anasazi, Hohokam, and Mogollón) developed sophisticated settlement systems that reached a pinnacle of cultural brilliance in the late ninth and early tenth centuries CE. They were connected by trade to Mesoamerica via the Chichimeca region of the Sierra Madre, the entire subcontinent an integrated landscape in perpetual motion.

In 1521, the Spanish swept into Mexico and stayed for three hundred years.[2] When the Pilgrims landed at Plymouth Rock in 1620, there were already "over 400,000 Spanish and over 30,000 Portuguese . . . living on the far side of the Atlantic, alongside indigenous inhabitants, peoples of mixed race, and a rapidly growing population transported from Africa to provide a labor supply." As historian J. H. Elliot tartly noted, the Pilgrims' "discovery" had in fact been claimed by Spanish and Portuguese monarchs a century before. He continued: "From the vantage point of the 1620s, it may well have seemed that the hemisphere's future lay with people of Iberian stock."[3] This was not to be, but it is something to remember when Anglo immigrants lay claim to the past.

The Spanish conquerors had difficulty pacifying the northern peripheries of Nueva España. They often encountered resistance and revolt that obliged them to adopt more pragmatic arrangements for government. Nevertheless, by the late 1700s Spanish forts (presidios) and missions had penetrated deeply as far as Alta California (the present-day US state of California). Another element in Spain's pacification strategy was a program of town building that provided the foundation for many settlements in today's borderlands. This included a discontinuous string of presidios extending along the Río Bravo almost to the Gulf of California, following a path that was close to what would eventually become the US-Mexico border.[4]

Spain's northward progress was also hindered by strong resistance from hostile indigenous tribes that extended from the Appalachians to the Pacific Ocean. These tribes frequently fought among themselves to extend their territory and influence, but once the Comanche had defeated the Apache in the early eighteenth century, their hegemony was so complete that "the eighteenth and early nineteenth-century Southwest was unequivocally a Comanche creation, an indigenous world where intercolonial rivalries were often mere surface disturbances on the deeper, stronger current of Comanche imperialism."[5]

By the early nineteenth century the territorial sway of the Comanche sprawled to include deep raids into present-day Mexico. The Comanche knew no frontiers. Demands from Euro-American colonial powers were often simply rejected, modified, or ignored. Indigenous peoples (some of whom came to be known as "Mexicans"), together with assorted white immigrants (known later as "Americans"), were obliged to coexist in one vast melting pot, a constantly changing tapestry of alliances and bloody wars that persisted for over a century.[6]

Prior to the Mexican-American War of 1846–48, the history of pre-Columbian settlements in Central America was gathered behind closeted archives in Spain. Lacking conclusive evidence, archaeologists freely mythologized about the provenance of fabled ruins. In efforts to forge links between the present day and the glorious past, many explorers' sketches from life were distorted to the point of falsification.[7] We may scoff at such hubris today, but it is worth remembering that Spain had once sought to trace the origins of Mesoamerican architecture and art to precedents from classical Rome.[8]

Thus it was that between 1839 and 1843 American writer and amateur archaeologist John Lloyd Stephens and British architect Frederick Catherwood collaborated on producing two volumes devoted to Maya architecture. Stephens surprised (and pleased) sponsors and readers by concluding that the architectural wonders were evidence of a superior race whom he claimed as ancestors of Americans owing no allegiance to European origins. So enamored was Stephens of his conjectures that he schemed to ship the Mayan ruins from the Yucatán ruins to a nineteenth-century "theme park" in the US, where, gathered together on a single site, the exhibits would testify to a seamless evolution from Mesoamerica to the present day.[9]

The Mayan grip on contemporary imaginations extended beyond the explorer and the exploiter. John Lloyd Stephens's contemporary Joseph Smith, founder of the Church of Jesus Christ of Latter-day Saints, also nurtured a desire to co-opt the rich archaeological record by proposing that the Americas had been settled by members of the lost tribes of Israel. Later, in the 1870s, it was the turn of French émigré photographer Augustus le Plongeon and his wife Alice to suffer overheated imaginations while traveling in the Yucatán. Le Plongeon made important archaeological finds but doctored his photographs of the Mesoamerican sites to prove their remote origins and significant links to the foundation of Freemasonry. Inspired by his assertion that world culture originated from the Americas, Le Plongeon nominated himself and his wife as reincarnated monarchs of a former "Kingdom of Móo," which had supposedly flourished more than one thousand years before their arrival.[10]

I was also misguided, though not to such a preposterous degree. Having always been enthralled by Mesoamerican archaeology and architecture, on my first trip to Mexico in the 1970s I went to Uxmal and Chichen Itzá in the Yucatán. Like others before me, I was perplexed by the inexplicable "collapse" of a lost civilization. When I asked a local resident what had become of the Maya, he squinted at me suspiciously. "What do you mean?" he asked. "I am Maya. The Maya are still here." I learned that day something important about uninformed presumptions made in the present and the obligation to pay careful attention to other peoples' history.

## CONQUEST: *LA OTRA CONQUISTA*

*La otra conquista* (1998) relates the immediate aftermath of the Spanish entrada. Director Salvador Carrasco expressed his purpose as recovering the history and perspectives of conquered indigenous peoples.[11] The film reveals how the twin dynamics of military power and spiritual assault clashed with indigenous beliefs to produce a warped hybrid of Euro-American identities. It begins horrifically, portraying the devastation wrought by the 1520 Spanish massacre of indigenous people at the Great Temple of Tenochtitlan (in present-day Mexico City). The lone survivor of the carnage is Topiltzin (Damián Delgado), an illegitimate son of the former Aztec emperor Moctezuma. Revered by his brother as the last human receptacle of Aztec traditions, Topiltzin is devoted to the Aztec Mother Goddess, spending his days reconstructing narratives of codices that had been systematically destroyed by the conquerors.[12] His painstaking toil to reconstruct the remnants of Aztec civilization is an affront to the new colonial order being imposed by Spain.[13]

In an effort to consolidate his position and create a new empire in Nueva España, Hérnán Cortés (Iñaki Aierra) has shrewdly taken Tecuichpotzin (Elpidia Carrillo)—Moctezuma's daughter and successor—as his mistress and interpreter. She subsequently adopts the Spanish appellation Doña Isabel, but also reveals that Topiltzin is her half brother. Cortés spares Topiltzin's life but insists that he receive instruction in the Catholic faith. The slow process fails to produce the desired result, so Topiltzin is subjected to barbaric torture known as "forced conversion." As he recovers, the first object he sees is the face of a statue of the Virgin Mary. Subsequently renamed Tomás, he is confined to a monastery, his hair tonsured, and is obliged to speak Spanish and wear the blue habit of a novice.

The second part of *La otra conquista* is more personal and intimate, as director Carrasco lingers on the fates of the "cultural orphans" forcibly severed from their faith by Spanish dogma and cruelty. Mexican intellectual Octavio Paz characterized the subsequent emergence of the cult of the Virgen de Guadalupe as a spiritual response to the orphan status that indigenous people acquired after the conquest.

Despite receiving instruction from Father Diego (José Carlos Rodríguez), Tomás follows his own path, seeking to reconcile his reverence for the Aztec Mother Goddess with his devotion to the Catholic Virgin Mary. The situation deteriorates when Diego discovers that in an act of resistance, Tomás and Doña Isabel are forging Cortés's signature on letters they have written to the king of Spain. Soon after, he overhears the sister and half brother in an act of incestuous lovemaking motivated by a desire to perpetuate their race. Months pass, and the now-pregnant Doña Isabel is isolated and imprisoned while Tomás slides toward madness.

Though weakened by his malaise, Tomás engages Diego in spirited debates about their different faiths, insisting at one point: "You and I share the same belief." He is unforgiving about the devastation caused by the Spanish, passionately accusing Diego: "You turned my people into ashes!" Father Diego is moved by these exchanges and turns inward to examine his own soul: he is not losing his Catholic faith, but feels an obligation to rebuild it from the roots. In a visually striking moment, Diego and Tomás

*Figure 8.1. La otra conquista* (1998). Meeting of the minds? Father Diego and Topiltzin/Tomás.

*Figure 8.2. La otra conquista* (1998). Syncretism through death? Diego, Topiltzin, and the Virgin Mary statue.

face each other in full-screen, close-up profiles (reminiscent of Ingmar Bergman), epitomizing the confrontation of white European high church Catholicism with brown indigenous American mysticism.

Tomás is not eating and is losing his grip on reality. In a vision the Virgin Mary is revealed to him as the Aztec Mother Goddess. Fatefully, a statue of the Virgin Mary is delivered to the monastery, a gift from Cortés to Father Diego. Tomás becomes obsessed with her. He resumes eating, rebuilding his strength with purpose. The last quarter hour of the film is almost wordless. Music takes the place of speech. As described by director Carrasco, all the musical styles in the film (indigenous, ancient, and modern, J. S. Bach's choral music, etc.) are now fused into hybrid compositions representing a thrilling newness.

Tomás is ready. He dresses carefully as a warrior and goes to meet the Virgin Mary. He penetrates the sacristy where her statue is located and carries it up to the topmost window in the tower. Climbing through the window, he tugs the statue after him. As he struggles, the Christ child in the Virgin's arms is shaken loose and symbolically drops back into the sanctuary. In his final action, Tomás removes the Virgin's crown and grasps the statue before plunging to his death. He imagines the Aztec Mother Goddess waiting below for him. Tomás smashes into the ground, greeting the Mother Goddess, before immediately absorbing the crushing weight of the Virgin's statue onto his body. Through this fatal concussion, the symbolic fusion (or syncretism) of Tomás's two faiths is achieved.

In the quiet aftermath, Father Diego arranges the body of Tomás alongside the statue of the Virgin. This time, three faces fill the screen in a triangle, resembling the holy Trinity of Christian faith with Diego at its apex. In the tranquility, Diego mouths "Unum deum" (One God), but his face betrays uncertainty about who this new god is that the fusion has wrought. Part of the victory is Topiltzin's, who "canonized" the Aztec Mother Goddess in the form of the Virgen de Guadalupe. The Catholic Church itself has been transformed through its merger with the spiritual forces of the indigenous inhabitants of the conquered lands. Father Diego is rightfully perplexed about where such cultural collisions will lead.

## THE UNAVOIDABLE RECIPROCITY OF FUSION: *CABEZA DE VACA*

Spanish explorer Alvar Núñez Cabeza de Vaca was shipwrecked off the coast of Florida in 1528, then spent the next eight years walking across the continent to the Pacific coast, and thereafter to Mexico City.[14] His journey included parts of the preborder borderlands, including today's Texas and

Mexico's northern territories. Along the way he and his companions were enslaved and survived many near-death encounters, but they were also aided by many indigenous groups whom they encountered. By the time de Vaca was reunited with his countrymen, he well understood the negative consequences of the Spanish occupation, realizing that he had come to the Americas expecting to conquer an alien culture, but instead the culture had changed him.

A cinematic version of Cabeza de Vaca's journey was very popular in Mexico, even though it reportedly took considerable liberties with the historical facts.[15] The film was entitled *Cabeza de Vaca* (1991) and was directed by Nicholas Echeverría, with director of photography Guillermo Navarro and special effects/makeup by a promising newcomer named Guillermo del Toro.

During de Vaca's walkabout, when he is not being caged, cruelly abused, or prepared as someone's evening meal, he practices magic-tinged healing rituals based in a rudimentary knowledge of Western medicine supplemented by local knowledge. He slowly gains a reputation as a healer and begins attracting devoted followers. Many years pass. On hearing that there are Spanish horsemen nearby, de Vaca destroys his heathen accoutrements and dismisses his indigenous followers, whom he knows the Spanish will enslave. He and three other surviving colleagues are discovered by a small group of Spanish slavers on horseback, riding toward them like a shimmering mirage ready to be vaporized.

De Vaca's reabsorption into Spanish company is almost as strange as his first experiences of arrival in the Americas eight years earlier. At the encampment, a Spanish captain is forcing slaves to build a cathedral. De Vaca is horrified by the cruelty of his countrymen, how they deliberately murder and enslave indigenous people and destroy their treasured culture and artifacts. To appease them, de Vaca tells tall tales about imaginary cities of gold even though he has encountered no such thing. He also attempts to broker a truce between the invaders and the original inhabitants. This effort fails, and the film ends with a desolate image of scores of slaves laboriously shouldering an enormous cross of silver across the desert salt pan, accompanied by a single soldier beating the rhythm of the march on a drum.

Later in his real life, after returning to Spain, de Vaca continued to seek the favor of the Spanish court and at one point led an authorized

expedition to the Rio de la Plata region in South America. It was not successful, and upon returning to Spain he was imprisoned. Historian Andrés
Reséndez portrays de Vaca as a tragic figure: "an orphan, a self-made man,
a visionary, a fervent Catholic, and a consummate survivor who had overcome the most adverse circumstances while holding fast to his ideals."[16]
The real Cabeza de Vaca may have been all these things. His cinematic
portrayal is of a prototypical borderlander who brought wisdom, patience,
friendship, and fortitude to his new land, and whose ideas about his land
of origin were utterly transformed by his experiences. The film is a compact classic of cultural hybridization after postconquest contact.

## COMPULSORY CHRISTIANITY: *YO LA PEOR DE TODAS*

*Yo la peor de todas* (María Luisa Bemberg, 2003; I the worst of all) is the
story of how the most brilliant woman in seventeenth-century Mexico
was persecuted to death by the Catholic Church.[17] The opening sequence
depicts a meeting between two men, a Spanish viceroy and a newly elected
archbishop of Nueva España. They are discussing how to realize an alliance ordered by the king of Spain. The opulence of their clothing and the
table at which they sit are highlighted because the screen surrounding
them is entirely black. This framing device is frequently adopted throughout Bemberg's film, heightening the painterly quality of the film's visual
compositions and costumes but also suggesting the cocooned isolation of
the protagonists and the opacity of powers governing the lives of ordinary
people. As representatives of state and church, both men are powerful: the
viceroy is a practiced diplomat, aware of his superior edge as the representative of the Spanish king, but the archbishop's polite deference is tinged
with ambition and resistance, even traces of cruelty. Any alliance between
them will be fractious and vindictive.

The viceroy and his wife, Doña María Luisa (Dominique Sanda), visit
the convent in order to meet Sor Juana Inés de la Cruz (Assumpta Serna),
in real life an astonishingly accomplished scholar and thinker. Born in
1648, Sor Juana is a prolific writer and philosopher, whose works extend
from light verse to theological disquisitions.[18] At the convent, she is favored
by having a private study and access to books and scientific instruments.

However, the archbishop regards the convent that shelters Sor Juana as little more than a bordello. Intent on replacing the Mother Abbess with a stricter leader, he arranges to meet co-conspirators from the convent who have their own reasons for wanting the Mother Abbess deposed. After their visit, the archbishop uses incense burners to cleanse his residence of the smell of women.

Doña María, the vicereine, becomes a more frequent visitor to the convent, and a strong attraction develops between her and Sor Juana. She equates her viceregal crown with Sor Juana's veil because both signify the confinement and subservience of the women who wear them. In what first appears to be a kind of courtly foreplay, the vicereine asks Sor Juana to take off her veil. "All of it," she insists. Pause. Then comes the threat: "It's an order." Sor Juana reluctantly obeys, as Doña María removes her ornate hat. Enthralled, the vicereine whispers: "This Sor Juana is mine, only mine." They kiss. (This scene is an invention. Consensus is that the deep affection between the two women was real, but not carnal.)[19]

Unknown to both women, the poems written by Sor Juana to Doña María are being copied and delivered to the archbishop with the misogynistic sinuses. He disparages the poems as lascivious since they were written by a woman to a woman. Doña María is aware of the threats posed by their relationship, and she promises Sor Juana that while she and the viceroy are in New Spain, they will protect Sor Juana.

Now Sor Juana becomes a pawn in the struggle between state and church. All too soon, the viceroy and vicereine are called back to Spain, after which the church-inspired attacks on an unprotected Sor Juana escalate. Her former confessor, Father Miranda (Alberto Segado), abandons her. When she teaches convent pupils that "intelligence has no sex," she is ordered by the new Mother Abbess to focus instead on giving singing lessons. Increasingly isolated and persecuted, Sor Juana is tricked into writing a critique of a theologian who is much admired by the archbishop. Her downfall is assured once the essay is published. Father Miranda voices approval on seeing Sor Juana reduced to the role of washing floors at the convent and is unsympathetic to her defense of her relationship with vicereine Doña María: "The more I loved her, the closer I felt to God," she pleads. Sor Juana promises obedience but does not understand what the church expects from her. The vindictive Miranda advises: "a different Juana."

*Figure 8.3. Yo la peor de todas* (2003). The natural order of things.

*Figure 8.4. Yo la peor de todas* (2003). Displacing identity.

Coldly and without mercy, Miranda imposes a sadistic auto-da-fé (a cleansing ritual of penance) upon Sor Juana. She must surrender all her worldly possessions and attachments. Miranda's demands are punctuated by acts of extreme cruelty that are not portrayed in the film, but they are described in Mexican author Octavio Paz's testimonial to Sor Juana,

*Las trampas de la fe* (The traps of faith).[20] What is presented on-screen is enough: the emptying of her convent quarters, the pillaging of her treasures, confiscation of her books and instruments, the preordained 'guilty" verdict at her stage-managed trial, and a confession that she signs with her own blood: *Yo la peor de todas*, I the worst of all. Sor Juana spent the remainder of her short life attending to her ailing convent sisters, until a virulent plague claimed her life.

## THE CRUEL LEGACIES OF SPAIN

For most of the three hundred years of Spanish occupation, the fulcrum of exploration and settlement along the northern borderlands was the valley of El Paso del Norte (present-day Ciudad Juárez). It was first traversed by Franciscan friars from Spain in 1581 on a mission to impose and enforce Christianity on the Pueblo Indians of New Mexico.[21] In 1598, a Mexican-born conquistador, Don Juan de Oñate, led a party of settlers from Mexico to the upper reaches of the Rio Grande/Río Bravo valley, thereby establishing the first European settlement west of the Mississippi. He was fiercely dedicated to the colonizing mission but was also counted as a cruel man. His legacy remains controversial to this day, but he is acknowledged as a pivotal figure in borderlands history.[22]

Among Oñate's most despicable exploits was to order the destruction of the seemingly impregnable Acoma pueblo in 1599. The pueblo inhabitants had been hard-pressed by demands from Spanish invaders desperate for food and clothing. They retaliated by killing twelve of their oppressors, one of whom was Oñate's nephew. In response, Oñate dispatched seventy-two soldiers who labored for three days to destroy the pueblo, slaughtering five hundred men and three hundred women and children and taking eighty men and five hundred women and children captive. Oñate subjected the captives to a formal trial in which all were found guilty of murder. Everyone between the ages of twelve and twenty-five was sentenced to twenty-five years of servitude, males over twenty-five had one foot severed (this was one of Oñate's signature punishments), and children under twelve were removed from their parents and placed in the custody of the Franciscan order. Don Oñate later wrote to the colonial viceroy about the Acoma incident: "As punishment for its crime and its treason against his Majesty, . . . and as a warning to the rest, I razed and burned it [the pueblo] completely."[23] There was no mention in the letter of those who had died, were mutilated, or were enslaved as a consequence of his brutality. Only much later was Oñate prosecuted in Mexico City for his regime of terror, found guilty, stripped of his titles, and exiled from New Mexico.

Such sickening violence was the universal tool of Spanish conquest throughout the Americas and was well-known even before the time of the Acoma assault. Yet history remains a fickle companion, favoring the "winners," and some reputable US historians persisted in referring to the Acoma campaign as a "miraculous" and "brilliant" victory for Spain.[24] A decade ago some white people I talked to in Texas and New Mexico tended to remember Don Oñate as the architect of European-style government in a region of barbarous savages. People with indigenous roots, however, remembered only his hateful cruelty. Somewhere in between, local Chicanos and Mexicans found little to admire in the man but grudgingly conceded his significance in history.

Today commemorative statues of the conquistador Juan de Oñate are still being built in south Texas and New Mexico, but not without opposition. In Alcalde, New Mexico, during the 1997 celebrations of the four hundredth anniversary of the first Spanish settlement, opponents disfigured a towering statue of Oñate by sawing off its foot, boot, spur, and all. Antipathy again resurfaced in 2017, when the same statue's left foot was painted red and the words "Remember 1680" (the year of the Pueblo revolt) were splashed on an adjacent wall.[25] Around the same time, at El Paso international airport a small statue of don Oñate on a horse was retired from its glass case inside the main entrance of the terminal and replaced outside by a twenty-six-foot high statue of the murderous don belligerently astride a rearing horse. I cannot foresee a time when this stain will be erased. In 2020 a new wave of protests surfaced in New Mexico when a demonstrator in favor of removing an Oñate statue at the Albuquerque Museum was shot by a member of a right-wing militia. The monument was ordered removed by the local mayor as an "urgent matter of public safety."[26] This action occurred during a summer of anti-racism sentiments generated by the Black Lives Matters movement, which included opposition to statues and other monuments celebrating disgraced

historical figures, as well as other symbols of oppression such as the confederate flag.

Sor Juana has been canonized as a brilliant thinker and writer, a proto-
feminist warrior, and prominent lesbian from Mexico's seventeenth-
century history. *Yo la peor* is punctuated by flashbacks that illuminate Sor
Juana's preconvent origins and identity. (Quotations from her poetry and
other writings are also skillfully deployed to demonstrate her character
and rhetorical skills.) The first remembrance establishes Sor Juana's intellectual powers. As a young woman, she was interrogated by an assembly
of (male) scholars and churchmen, who peppered her with a wide range
of questions relating to science, philosophy, and theology. She successfully
answered all the questions, and the film replays an ovation she received
from her audience. The second flashback provides insight into Sor Juana's
sexuality. It recalls that as a child, she would dress as a boy even though
her mother gently asked her to desist. Later, Sor Juana reflected on her
personal motivation: "Since I couldn't dress as a man, I dressed as a nun."
To my knowledge the oral examination is part of the historical record, but
the acts of cross-dressing are not.

The piquant subject of her sexual orientation will continue to fascinate
because the historical evidence on this matter falls somewhere between
exceedingly sparse and nonexistent. I discovered a shred of anachronis-
tic "evidence" on the box containing the DVD version of *Yo la peor*. It is
comically over-the-top, teasing us to watch "Lesbian passion seething behind convent walls." Well, not really. Sor Juana and Doña María share a
fictional kiss on-screen, but I observed no other evidence of uninhibited
seething. (Except one scene in the film in which a small group of nuns
dressed in full habit play handball in a somewhat agitated manner.)

The two most unforgivable acts of the Spanish conquest are the genocide
directed at indigenous people and the crusade to eliminate the culture of
the conquered. Mexican anthropologist Guillermo Bonfil Batalla has
given us a language to describe the continuing legacies of these actions in
the present day. He distinguishes between a *México profundo*, that is, a
world view deeply situated in the cultures and traditions of Mesoamerican
indigenous peoples, and a *México imaginario*, an imagined Mexico based
in Spanish and European sensibilities. In his view, "The recent history of

Mexico . . . is the story of permanent confrontation between those attempting to direct the country toward the path of Western civilization and those, rooted in Mesoamerican ways of life, who resist."[27]

Present-day *mexicanidad*, or "Mexican-ness," is a consequence of the unpredictable fusion of indigenous prehistory with a legacy of Spanish/European intervention. Bonfil Batalla was of the opinion that Mexico's future depended on recovering the traditions of *México profundo* rather than continuing to revere the colonial residues from Spain. It's a persuasive characterization, even though both mental maps may already have been overlain by a third, a *México global*, referring to Mexico's absorption of contemporary practices connected with globalization.

The three films in this chapter suggest how the fusions of *profundo* and *imaginario* have played out through successive stages: conquest, genocide, and extinction (in *La otra conquista*); fusions both positive and negative, purposeful and accidental (*Cabeza de Vaca*); and the repression or erasure of cultural differences (*Yo la peor de todas*).

As mentioned, Salvador Carrasco, the director of *La otra conquista*, intended to recover the history of the conquered peoples, and the second part of *La otra conquista* lingers on the fates of "cultural orphans" forcibly severed from their faith by Spanish dogma and cruelty. But consider again Topiltzin's half sister, Tecuichpotzin, daughter of the Aztec emperor Moctezuma II. After the conquest she became the consort of the conqueror Cortés and took the name Doña Isabel (sometimes Isabel Moctezuma). She also gave birth to Cortés's daughter and later prospered in both Nueva España and Spain. Although her later life is not part of *La otra conquista*, Doña Isabel is an early example of an elite *mestiza*: a powerful woman who emerges from the fusion between Mexico *profundo* and Mexico *imaginario*.

During his exile, Cabeza de Vaca was confirmed in his empathy for indigenous peoples and their spiritual and material customs. He never abandoned Catholicism but instead constructed a personal syncretic hybrid of faiths that he maintained for the remainder of his life. He renounced the cruelty and venality of the Spanish conquerors but remained loyal to the Spanish Crown, at the same time he championed the interests of indigenous peoples in Central and South America. The quintessential proof provided by *Cabeza de Vaca* is that when civilizations clash, both victors and vanquished are altered.

Sor Juana de la Cruz died in 1695 at the age forty-seven. She was tortured and neglected to death by the Catholic Church and its corporate subsidiary, the Inquisition, even though it took a plague to dispatch her corporeal self. The film dramatization of her life, *Yo la peor de todas*, is forthright in linking her name to so many issues in the present. Today Sor Juana is highly regarded as a leading Mexican poet, essayist, playwright, and forward-looking intellectual, scholar, and theologian. Her reputation in the English-speaking world has flourished since translations of her works have become available.[28] My hope is that the towering legacy of Sor Juana will not be subjected to the same kind of bowdlerizing and commodification that smother other icons of Mexican culture such as Frida Kahlo.

These three preborder films convey legacies that should be carried forward to the present: the insanity of total war, genocide, and cultural destruction; the violence and repression in the name of diverse faiths; the fragile truths of rationality and scientific reasoning; the pervasive depths of anti-intellectualism and humanity's deference to authoritarianism; and the risks and bounties of fusions and difference.

# 9 From Final Girl to Warrior Woman

In the ten years following 1993, more than 430 women were murdered in the state of Chihuahua, and hundreds more simply disappeared, mostly in and around Ciudad Juárez. One-third of the victims had been sexually assaulted; others had been mutilated or showed signs of torture, their bodies dumped in desolate places. No one was sure what caused the epidemic that came to be called "femicide." Criminologists suggested that it began as the work of a serial killer or copycat killers, but so large was the number of victims that organized crime in the form of drug cartels or human trafficking gangs was blamed. As the crimes continued, the explanations became more outlandish, referring to international sales of human organs or to interventions by religious and satanic cults. From the outset, members of the Juárez police department were implicated in a growing catalog of malfeasance that included failure to investigate the killings, torture of suspects, and the assassination of witnesses and lawyers involved in related criminal proceedings. The uncontained violence was partly the fault of the police and judicial systems in Mexico.[1]

129

Even before the femicides Ciudad Juárez had a reputation as the most dangerous place in Mexico because of drug cartels.[2] In the five years after 2006, 40,000 people were murdered in Mexico, a national murder rate of 14 per 100,000 inhabitants. In Ciudad Juárez, a city with a population of 1.3 million, the murder rate was 189 per 100,000.[3] After years of living with different kinds of death, Juárez suffered from depopulation, business closures, and housing abandonment. One-fifth of its population (about one-quarter million people) left the city over a three-year period. Many moved across the border into El Paso, where local businesses enjoyed a mini-boom in consumer services such as shopping and dining.

Another factor that changed Juárez radically in the period leading up to the femicides was the rise of the maquiladora (assembly plant) industries, which attracted migrants in large numbers in search of work, especially young women.[4] Located just across the border in Mexico where labor costs were relatively low, the *maquilas* imported raw materials and components from the US, assembled them into complete products, then returned the goods to the US for distribution and sale. In the early 2000s, migration to *maquila* towns was boosted by new housing construction and mortgage financing that promoted homeownership.[5] Several women I met moved to Juárez and Nogales mainly to gain a foothold in the property market.

Although slow to start, by 1979 *maquila* production accounted for one-quarter of Mexican manufacturing exports. In subsequent decades, two-thirds of all Mexican *maquilas* were established in just three border towns: Tijuana, Mexicali, and Ciudad Juárez. (Tijuana became famous as the television assembly capital of the world.) Later, smaller clusters of *maquilas* in other border cities joined the boom. In 1965 there were twelve *maquilas* along the border; by 1996, the number had grown to over fifteen hundred, employing over one million Mexican workers. Women formed the majority of *maquila* workers until about 2006, when the gender share became more equal.

Suspicions arose that young *maquila* women were being targeted by the murderers. Initially, dead bodies were discovered in remote locations outside the city limits of Juárez, often mutilated and crudely buried in shallow graves. Then in 2001 eight bodies were discovered inside the city. I knew that place. When I visited the site, eight tall pink crosses bearing the first names of murdered women had been erected. Two bus drivers were arrested in connection with the crimes. They were not hardened criminals. In 2002, the attorney of one driver was shot by police after he became too critical of the lack of progress in their investigations. The police officers were exonerated for acting in self-defense. The second driver's attorney complained about the violations of his client's rights; four years later, he too was assassinated on a Juárez street. The murders of Juárez women continued, but the crimes were nudged from the headlines by an epidemic of cartel-related violence.[6]

## LAST WOMAN STANDING: *MISS BALA* AND *MISS BALA* (REMAKE)

The representation of women in border film during the early decades of the twenty-first century underwent a remarkably swift evolution. First the woman was a stereotypical "Survivor," one who stoically outlasts her trials and torments; then she morphed into something more powerful: a "Final Woman," who reaches beyond survival to cause demonstrable changes in her condition and surroundings; and finally she is transformed into "Warrior Woman," a strong, skilled combatant capable of premeditated actions involving courage and leadership in situations of great risk. This evolution in border film is bookended by a 2011 film called *Miss Bala* (2011; *bala* is bullet in English), a Mexican film directed by Gerardo Naranjo, and a 2019 remake of the film with a different director. (For clarity's sake, I refer to these films as *Miss Bala* 1 and *Miss Bala* 2, respectively.) The heroine in the *Miss Bala* 1, rated R, is a survivor who ends up miraculously still standing after a series of abuses and humiliations. In the remake only eight years later the heroine of *Miss Bala* 2 (rated PG-13) is now a mercenary who kills for cause and an appropriate fee. How did this transformation unfold on the screen?

On a path to self-advancement, a young woman named Laura (Stephanie Sigman) plans to enter the Miss Baja California beauty competition in Tijuana. She is unlikely to win because she is not tall, blonde, and light-skinned, but she hopes to attract attention and opportunity. Things start unraveling after Laura inadvertently witnesses a gangland attack at a nightclub in which several murders are committed. She escapes, but in her panic she approaches a law officer who promises to help. There is a saying in Mexico that if you approach a police officer for help with a problem, you immediately acquire two problems. This officer delivers her to members of the same gang who were responsible for the nightclub murders. Using threats and promises, the gang leader Lino (Noé Hernández) coerces Laura to work for the Las Estrellas gang as a driver and "mule" (a cross-border smuggler). He sweetens his demands by promising to use his influence to advance Laura's progress in the Miss Baja competition. Meanwhile, agents from the DEA begin pressuring Laura to help them track Lino and his gang. One night, after an ambush, a badly wounded Lino turns up at Laura's home. Instinctively she tends to his wounds, and in gratitude Lino spares the lives of her father and brother, whom he had earlier threatened to kill.

The day of the pageant arrives. Laura surprises everyone by winning, because Lino has fixed the result. One of Laura's obligations is to provide sexual favors to a prominent military general. Lino plans to use the access Laura will gain as an opportunity to kill the general. The day Laura is delivered alone to the general's bedroom, she is aware that the Estrella gang will soon attack. Terrified for her own survival, she warns the general of the plot. He swiftly alerts his guards, and as the ensuing battle subsides, she spies Lino talking with the general in a conspiratorial manner. Before she can make sense of their connection, Laura is grabbed and beaten by the general's guards, then forced to attend a press conference where the capture of the Estrella gang is announced. She is paraded alongside the surviving gang members and thereby implicated as a co-conspirator in the attack.

As the film draws to a close, Laura is dumped from a van onto an anonymous Tijuana street of warehouses and factories. She has survived, at least up to this moment. She intuitively grasps the imperative to get away from this exposed situation and reflexively begins walking down the street.

The 2019 American remake transforms Laura into a vengeful killer. *Miss Bala* 2 has a female director (Catherine Hardwicke); a Latina lead, now called Gloria (Gina Rodríguez); and a predominantly Latinx crew. The remake replays the beauty competition and nightclub killings, but the on-screen violence in *Bala 2* is much more muted, in keeping with the film's PG-13 rating (the original was rated R). But after that, *Miss Bala 2* is transformed into a fable of female empowerment: Gloria survives, but she becomes an avenging angel. Seen through a constant drizzle of glamour, Gloria and the gang leader Lino (Ismael Cruz Córdova) almost flirt their way toward a Stockholm-syndrome kind of romance. He takes Gloria to his architecturally significant hideaway in the picturesque Valle de Guadalupe wine region north of Ensenada. With impeccable manners, he introduces her to family members at a local restaurant. And in a token of dawning devotion, he teaches Gloria to fire a machine gun (spoiler alert!).

The climactic shoot-out begins as it did in *Bala 1*. Gloria has been crowned Miss Baja California, and she is transported to accommodate the general. What happens next reveals a complete abdication of the original plot. Gloria fires a gun, wounding the general, then steps aside while Lino finishes him off. Then she fires again, this time to kill Lino! As the gunsmoke clears, Gloria departs not to a press conference but instead to swanky digs, where she meets her Central Intelligence Agency (CIA) handler. He flatters her; the agency needs someone like her to help wage the war on drugs. Gloria seems to relish this prospect much more than a beauty competition crown. The film credits roll, incongruously backed by a cheerful collection of tourist images of downtown Los Angeles. (I took this non sequitur to be a threat that a sequel is in the offing.)

In *Men, Women and Chain Saws* (such a title!), Carol Clover makes a case that the most enduring image of the young threatened female in the slasher films of the 1990s was that of a survivor, she who does not die. Clover calls her the "Final Girl."[7] In early versions, the Final Girl was portrayed as bookish, solitary, watchful, and intelligent, but resourceful when goaded by extreme circumstances to defend herself. Later versions are more grown-up; the Final Girl no longer visits haunted houses or buys tickets for those dangerous prom-night dances. Yet she is the one left standing after protracted conflict. By my account Laura, in the first *Miss Bala*, is a resilient woman who ventures beyond Survivor status, performing acts of great courage and emerging alive. In contrast Gloria, of *Miss Bala 2*, is represented as a prototypical Woman Warrior, almost a superhero who runs toward danger. The question in this chapter is:

What exactly happened during those intervening eight years, when border women shifted from being Survivors to become superheroes, Woman
Warriors? It could not possibly have been the enticement of a corner office
at Langley.

## GENERATIONS: *COMO AGUA PARA CHOCOLATE,* *HOW THE GARCÍA GIRLS SPENT THEIR SUMMER*

There must be a special place in film heaven for *Como agua para chocolate*
(1992, *Like Water for Chocolate*). Adapted from an enormously successful
novel by Laura Esquival, the film was directed by Alfonso Arau, one of
Mexico's most prominent actors and filmmakers. The phrase *como agua
para chocolate* refers to emotions that are reaching boiling point. The film
is largely confined to the hothouse atmosphere of a multigenerational, all-
female household just as the Mexican Revolution was getting underway.
The four women in the household represent archetypes of the revolutionary era: Doña Elena (Regina Torné) is the stern matriarch, steeped in old
prerevolutionary ways; Rosaura the eldest (Yareli Arizmendi) is accustomed to privilege; Gertrudis (Claudette Maillé) is the rebellious middle
daughter, destined to fight alongside Pancho Villa; and Tita the youngest
(Lumi Cavazos) is weighed down by family obligations but loves to work
in the kitchen with Nacha, the cook (Ada Carrasco).

Tita and Pedro (Marco Leonardi) are deeply in love, but when he approaches Mama Elena for Tita's hand in marriage, he is rudely rejected.
As consolation, she offers Pedro the hand of her eldest daughter, Rosaura,
pointing out that Tita, her youngest, is duty bound to remain unmarried
and care for her in old age. Pedro accepts the hand of Rosaura because it
will allow him to remain close to Tita.

Brokenhearted, Tita diverts her passion into cooking. One day her tears
get mixed into a dish she is preparing, and everyone who partakes of it
suffers devastating anguish over lost loves. Tita senses her extraordinary
power, so when she seasons some food with rose petals that Pedro brought
her, all who partake experience amorous urges. The consequences for Gertrudis are far-reaching. While taking a shower, her body gives off so much
heat that the wooden walls of the shower burst into flame. Far away, her

aromatic musk reaches a rebel soldier, who impulsively quits the battle-field and rides out to find her. He scoops the naked Gertrudis onto his horse and together they gallop away.

Still suspicious of Tita's lingering affection for Pedro, Doña Elena banishes him and his wife Rosaura to a different town. Tita eventually finds affection with John Brown, an Anglo doctor from Eagle Pass (who has a Kikapu Indian grandmother). When Doña Elena dies, Pedro and Rosaura return. The passion between Tita and Pedro is rekindled, becoming so intrusive that Tita's planned wedding to Dr. Brown is called off. The ailing Rosaura dies. That same evening, Tita and Pedro ecstatically make love, after which he dies from too much happiness. Tita swallows matches, setting the house on fire.

The women in *Como agua* offer stark contrasts regarding the changing roles of women after the Mexican Revolution. Representing prerevolutionary society, the matriarch Donña Elena is dead by the film's end, symbolizing the emergence of the modern era. Her first daughter, Rosaura, is a transitional figure: her attitudes and expectations remain rooted in prerevolutionary traditions, but her corporeal existence in a revolutionary era renders her adrift, unsettled, weak, and ultimately dead. Tita, the youngest, is doomed to perpetual service, obliged to refuse marriage in order to care for her mother. Nevertheless Tita, the bruja (witch), is combustible, surrendering to passions, engaging magic powers, and extinguishing herself and her lover by fiery desire.

Gertrudis is a creature of the future. She breaks the grip of family and tradition by marrying a soldier. He carries her away to be reborn into a world of revolution, freedom, and desire. She is transformed into a general in Pancho Villa's Northern Army; later, she returns home, arriving in a chauffeur-driven Model T Ford; she smokes and drinks alcohol; and she dresses fashionably. In *Como agua*, Gertrudis is the most compleat Warrior Woman, the embodiment of a modern woman and her era.

Fresh portraits of girls and women appeared on-screen in the early 2000s, and names of female directors began featuring in the credits. A milestone film encapsulating these trends is *How the García Girls Spent Their Summer* (2005), directed by Georgina García Reidel. The plot focuses on a female-only Chicana household. The head of the family is a crusty and willful grandmother, Doña Genoveva (Lucy Gallardo). Lolita, her divorced daughter (Elizabeth Peña), is the family's principal breadwinner, and her teenage granddaughter Blanca (America Ferrera) confronts the abyss of graduation from high school the next year. The lack of men in the household becomes a central issue in this tender comedy of manners. The women experience this absence differently and rise to its challenge in their own ways.

The film is set in the sunbaked desert borderlands, a setting of some consequence. The smallness of the town and the vastness of the surrounding landscapes diminish the human presence. Opportunities for paid labor in the town are scarce, and the only real jobs (those paying wages) lie elsewhere. The material physicality of the settlement reflects the cognitive mindsets of its residents; and the film is unafraid to convey the sheer boredom of everyday life for women in an isolated, fly-speck border town.

The principal nucleus of the community is the local *carnicería* (butcher shop), where Lolita works. It is a meeting place where the town's women gather most days to shop and gossip. Lolita is much admired by the handsome butcher, and she is attracted to him but is cautious about men since her divorce. The other place of congregation in town is a set of public benches where a handful of old men meet and hold court. They're a diverse, chatty group, greeting everyone who passes by and recounting oft-repeated stories about cars and women recalled from a distant youth. Both the *carnicería* and the park benches serve as stages where local Greek choruses comment on town life (an engaging device that pulls viewers into the plot and personalities).

It's summer, and while Lolita is taking her time about considering the butcher's polite advances, the family matriarch Doña Genoveva has decided she's ready for radical change. She buys an old car without knowing how to drive and engages her gardener to provide driving lessons. The gardener is an older man who sometimes gazes wistfully at her, but she has no use for a man in her life. Meanwhile teenage Blanca is bored out of her skull at the border. She hangs out with a girl gang and flaunts convention by taking rides on the back of a motorcycle belonging to a town rebel.

As summer wanes, Doña Genoveva finds happiness (and more) with her gardener/driving instructor. Lolita allows the butcher to kiss her (and more). Blanca loses her virginity, quits her gang, and focuses on graduation so that she can leave town for college. Grandmother, daughter, and granddaughter are equally outraged by the spirited sexual behavior of the other family members. The most deeply shocked is Blanca, who exclaims, "Grandma is a whore!" But soon all three adjust to the altered family equilibrium.

*García Girls* knows its limits, is witty, and is delightfully realized. The film is a romantic comedy, but its focus on the closed world of three generations of females makes one acutely aware of the tedium of time and limited horizons at the rural edges. Each woman resists such confinement, albeit through conventional ways: grandmother and mother find love and affection with honorable men, and daughter puts away childish things to pursue college entrance anyplace else.

## DIFFICULT WOMEN: *JULIA, FROM DUSK TIL DAWN, BORDERTOWN*

Julia is a hard person to like. In the noirish eponymous film (Erick Zonca, 2008; *Julia*), she is played by the versatile Tilda Swinton. Julia is sexually promiscuous, alcoholic, and untrustworthy, with a capacity for premeditated violence. As the film opens, she has lost yet another job. Her friend Mitch (Saul Rubinek) pleads with her to attend an Alcoholics Anonymous session. There she meets Elena Gonzales (Kate del Castillo), who explains that she plans to kidnap her son Tom (Aidan Gould), who was taken from her by the boy's grandfather. Desperate for the $50,000 that Elena offers, Julia agrees to kidnap and transport the boy to Mexico to be reunited with Elena.

The kidnapping does not go smoothly. Elena goes missing, and Julia is stuck with a boy she just kidnapped. She and Tom reach an uneasy truce and set off in search of a safer, more secluded desert hideaway. Julia independently contacts the boy's grandfather, who agrees to pay a $2 million ransom to ensure Tom's safe return.

The plot then pivots around a dramatic nighttime scene in which Julia's car attracts the attention of a border patrol helicopter. She ignores instructions to stop and instead turns off-road in a reckless attempt to escape. The screen and soundtrack explode in blinding clouds of dust stirred up by car and helicopter and a deafening cacophony of engines mixed with megaphone instructions emanating from above. (I learned this terror, as described in chapter 17.) The swift appearance of the looming border fence disallows evasive action by Julia. Propelled by its momentum, the car smashes head-on through the fence and into Mexico. The helicopter abandons its pursuit, and in the stunned silence Julia calmly restarts the stalled engine and creeps the last few feet that takes the vehicle completely over the line. The remainder of *Julia* unfolds in a starkly different world.

Waking the following morning in Tijuana, Julia is elated to learn that her friend Mitch is en route to Tijuana with the grandfather's $2 million ransom money. To celebrate, Tom and Julia leave their motel for some food and relaxation with someone called Diego, whom she had just met. But the next morning, Tom has disappeared. Julia and Diego are informed by a cab driver that Tom has been taken by professional kidnappers who use Tijuana as a hunting ground. The cab driver refuses to help Julia locate Tom, so in panicked anger she shoots him. Then Julia follows a woman who leads her to the place Tom is being held, but she is overpowered by the two kidnappers. Questioned about how she found their hideout, Julia blames Diego, who is dragged in and summarily executed. Julia saves herself by offering the $2 million ransom money to the kidnappers. They agree but insist that Tom stay with them while Julia gets the money from Mitch at the Tijuana airport. There Mitch reveals that Elena is not Tom's mother but is part of a scam to trick Julia into kidnapping Tom. Lacking options, Mitch agrees to give Julia the $2 million to buy Tom's freedom.

The film's dramatic climax takes place alongside a busy four-lane highway in nighttime Tijuana. On one side of the highway Julia is parked with the ransom money; on the opposite side, the two kidnappers hold Tom in their car. Between them lie four lanes of speeding traffic and blinding headlights. The ensuing tussle involves a dangerous dance among swerving vehicles. Eventually the kidnappers leave with the money, and Julia recovers the traumatized Tom. Together they stand at the roadside, exhausted. Hugging Tom tightly to her, Julia recovers her resolve, telling him, "OK. I'm taking you to your mother."

*Julia* is a tough, taut, and intricately plotted thriller. The film is anchored by Tilda Swinton's performance. She is rarely absent from the screen and is deliberately introduced as an unpleasant, unstable, but alluring "good-time girl" who participates in a deceitful kidnapping scheme. Julia's worldview shifts when she crashes through the border wall into Mexico. In a spiraling sequence of events, she schemes to secure a $2 million ransom from the boy's grandfather, murders a man, tracks down the thugs who rekidnapped the boy she originally kidnapped, and swaps $2 million in exchange for his life. Mexico had transformed the noir archetype of an amoral femme fatale into a warrior.

Robert Rodriguez is a favorite among border film fans.[8] His *From Dusk til Dawn* (1996) transforms a petulant teenage girl into a vampire killer. Two fugitive bank robbers, Seth and Richie Gecko (respectively, George Clooney and Quentin Tarantino) are on the run and heading for the Mexican border. Along the way, they kidnap the vacationing Fuller family, father Jacob (Harvey Keitel), teenage daughter Kate (the splendid Juliette Lewis), and son Scott (Ernest Liu). The Geckos commandeer the family's RV and instruct Jacob to drive across the border to a remote tavern where the brothers plan to meet someone. If Jacob drives them to the rendezvous, the family's lives will be spared.

This unlikely alliance succeeds in crossing into Mexico and by nighttime arrives at the tavern, with the evocative name Titty Twister. Neon lights promise *chicas calientes* (hot girls), and there seem to be an awful lot of bats flitting around. Seth and Richie insist that the Fullers join them for celebratory cocktails. Inside the establishment, things are calm until Santanico Pandemonium (Selma Hayek) appears.[9] She is the featured artiste at the Titty Twister, with an impressive routine involving sparse clothing and a gigantic blond python (or boa constrictor?). Either way, Santana is definitely striking. She climaxes her burlesque by biting Richie Gecko, who promptly bleeds to death before returning to life as a vampire. As clouds of bats storm into the bar, it seems that *everyone* in the Titty Twister is undead. A chaotic battle ensues, with the Fullers and Seth Gecko as the prey. Daddy Fuller is bitten and is transformed, and son Scott is devoured by a whole herd of vampires. Seth Gecko and the Fuller daughter Kate reveal extraordinary prowess and imagination in slaughtering the lusty undead. But they are hugely outnumbered, and their end seems nigh as slivers of dawn slice through the Titty Twister, forcing the vampires to withdraw.

*Figure 9.1. From Dusk til Dawn* (1996). Titty Twister bar atop a Mesoamerican temple (plentiful free parking).

Outside the saloon, vampire killer Kate is still standing. She was tested and did not yield. She and Seth Gecko part company. In the early dawn light, the camera pulls back from the battle zone, revealing that the foundations of the Titty Twister tavern rest on a pyramid of Mayan or Aztec origin. Its foundation is strewn with haphazardly dumped cars of previous patrons, who presumably had no need for car keys after converting to vampirism. It's unclear what director Rodríguez intended by this reference to classical architecture and indigenous traditions. Perhaps it is a complaint about excessive partying by vacationing Americans in the land of Mesoamerican culture?[10]

Gregory Nava takes a passionate stand against the Júarez femicides and the absence of progress in prosecuting any culprits in his film *Bordertown* (2006). The film begins and ends with stark visions of Juárez neighborhoods engulfed in flames. A crusading editor of the newspaper *El Sol de Juárez*, Alfonso Díaz (Antonio Banderas), scoffs at the official estimate of murdered women (375), claiming the number is closer to 5,000. He is joined in his pursuit of justice by an outsider from Chicago, a reporter named Lauren Adrian (Jennifer Lopez). She is motivated to help a young woman, Eva (Maya Zapata), a maquiladora worker who was abducted, raped, and buried alive by a bus driver hired to return workers to their homes after late-night shifts. Miraculously she survived, and she turns to Lauren for help.

Lauren decides to impersonate a maquila worker to lure the attacker into the open. With her hair dyed black and pinned up Mexican-style, she's good to go. (She mentioned earlier in the film that she spoke no Spanish, but no matter.) One night, Lauren gets on a bus with the same driver who assaulted Eva. Police officers have already gathered at the same site where Eva was attacked, but the driver takes Lauren somewhere else. Fortunately, Lauren is able to fend off her attacker and escape.

*Bordertown* now focuses on the corruption on both sides of the border that inhibits the prosecution of Eva's attacker. A voice-over has warned "No-one listens!," and the persistent efforts of Lauren and Alfonso culminated in his assassination (unfortunately a common fate of too many journalists in Mexico). The trail to the driver is cold. Lauren is offered an attractive new posting, which is a bribe to buy her silence. Outraged, she quits her job in Chicago and replaces Alfonso as the crusading new editor of *El Sol de Juárez*.

The *Bordertown* crew ran into difficulties during filming in Juárez. The crew was harassed by local police, threats were received, and camera equipment was stolen. Most of the principal photography was subsequently transferred to other locations, in the US. Despite these complications, *Bordertown* remains a courageous, landmark border film that addresses head-on a shamefully neglected topic. And for the record, when I was in Juárez in the 2000s, the city certainly was on edge, and nighttime streets and restaurants were devoid of people. But this was the worst of times. On later visits I found Juárez to be an absorbing, dynamic, attractive, and historically significant place, with wonderful people who care enormously about their city. It also benefited from strong support emanating from El Paso.

## WOMAN WARRIORS: *SAVAGES, GO FOR SISTERS, LA MISMA LUNA, SIN NOMBRE*

Selma Hayek, in Oliver Stone's *Savages* (2012), plays Elena Sánchez, head of a drug cartel, a self-made crime lord, and ruthless Warrior Woman.

*Savages* is a violent film featuring two best friends, Chon (Taylor Kitsch) and Ben (Aaron Taylor-Johnson), who happen to be in a relationship with the same woman, Ophelia (Blake Lively). The two men operate a lucrative marijuana business in Laguna Beach, Southern California. Ben is a UC Berkeley graduate in business and botany who uses his scientific and business skills to raise and market a superior product. Chon contributed the seeds acquired during his military service in Afghanistan. Reflecting Ben's Berkeley connection, the pair naturally devote a percentage of profits to philanthropic work in Africa and Asia. Ophelia looks beautiful (stoned or sober) and easily manages to keep both her men happy.

Chon and Ben's success is noticed by Lado Arroyo (Benicio del Toro), a CEO who works on behalf of Elena, *la señora del narco*. She proposes to take over their business while leaving them in charge of production. They politely decline. But as "negotiations" continue and the situation deteriorates, Elena's toughs kidnap Ophelia and take her to Tijuana in order to put pressure on the partners, who understandably go seriously bonkers.

In the final shoot-out Chon and Ben deliver the ransom money and grab Ophelia from the narcos, while somewhere above a DEA helicopter (carrying agent John Travolta) hovers, ready to pounce. Gunfire crackles, and Ben is mortally wounded. In a gesture to *Romeo and Juliet*, Chon administers fatal overdoses of poison to Ophelia and himself. But wait! It was only a dream! So the final scene is replayed, quickly substituting a happier ending. Elena gets thirty years in prison; Lado opens his own business in the vacuum left by Elena's departure; the corrupt DEA officer grabs the ransom money and disappears; and our ménage à trois retires to a beachfront property in Indonesia. As they stretch out lazily with afternoon cocktails, Ophelia worries that they are living like "savages." She seems to be referring to the simpler life they now lead in Indonesia, but to me, this seemed a more apt description of the trio's previous business model.[11]

Mother and child separations provide fertile ground from which Warrior Women emerge. In *Go for Sisters* (John Sayles, 2013) one woman is prompted to rescue a son kidnapped in Tijuana. The film has leading roles for two African American women: Fontayne (Yolanda Ross), who has served prison time, and Bernice (LisaGay Hamilton), her probation officer in Los Angeles. Twenty years earlier, they had been students in high school, so alike that they could "go for" (i.e., pass as) sisters. Bernice has learned that her estranged son is a possible murder suspect, and she seeks to enlist Fontayne's street skills to find him. They also tap into the local knowledge of Freddy Suarez (Edward James Olmos) a myopic, aging ex-police officer, who has been fired without pension for solving crimes that implicated his superiors. The trio soon discover that Bernice's son is involved in cross-border people smuggling and is now being held hostage by a Chinese gang. They decide to cross over into Tijuana (and later Mexicali) in search of Bernice's son.

Freddy offers a short orientation and training exercise for Fontayne and Bernice, including words of wisdom, "Border towns—you get real good people here, but you also get the worst of both sides," and he underscores the exceptional nature of border towns: "This isn't Mexico. This is like a theme park for bad behavior." In fairness, Freddy is an equal opportunity stereotyper, blaming Americans who come to Tijuana to do the stupid things they cannot do at home. (This is a familiar lament about ugly Americans in Mexico, who offer the exculpatory defense: "I left my brains at the border.") The Chinese ("Chinos") in Go for Sisters are regarded with suspicion by Mexicans and Americans. Says another character: "We don't know about the Chinese, and they won't tell us anything."[12]

The mix of racial and ethnic diversity in Go for Sisters is one of the film's most appealing aspects. Its interracial alliance between the two black women and the brown ex-cop is engaging and unusual. (Director Sayles has a deserved reputation for realizing racial diversity in the casts of his films.) Fontayne, Bernice, and Freddy do not get in one another's way during the investigation but regularly come together to share information and collaborate on more complex tasks. In one fine moment, Freddy has just finalized a deal with the cartel bosses for the return of Bernice's son, after which he is dumped out onto a gritty nighttime Tijuana street. It's late, the traffic is bad, and the neon-lit street is noisy and garish, causing problems for Freddy's failing eyes. He pads his way uncertainly along the sidewalk before being spotted by Bernice and Fontayne. They stop and carefully corral him into their car and then drive off. It's an unhurried, touching moment addressing Freddy's frailty, even though all three of them will soon be involved in a contretemps with drive-by assassins.[13]

Another mother-child separation saga is the independent Mexican American production La misma luna (Patricia Riggen, 2007; Under the same moon), which features Rosario (Kate del Castillo), who deposited her nine-year-old son Carlitos (Adrián Alonso) with her relatives in Mexico while she leaves to work in the US. As the film opens, Carlitos has decided to go in search of his mother at the same moment that Rosario plans her return to Mexico. Their separate journeys are spiced with songs, comedy, and toxic levels of sentimentality. Several times Carlitos is rescued by kindly souls, including the famous musical group Los Tigres del Norte, who sing the refrain: "And so for love, I will cross the border without fear." After many adventures, mother and son reunite on a street corner in East Los Angeles (a real place, where a mural was subsequently painted to commemorate the film's fictional happy ending).

The dangerous northward journey of Central American migrants and their victimization by predatory gangs is the subject of *Sin nombre* (Cary Joji Fukunaga, 2009; Nameless). A Honduran family—father, daughter Sayra (Paulina Gaitán), and uncle—plan to join relatives in New Jersey by riding illegally on a train known as La Bestia (The Beast). The real-life train used to travel regularly across Mexico from the Guatemalan border to Reynosa, the crossing point into Texas. Casper (Edgar Flores) is a member of the Mara Salvatrucha (MS) gang who preys on train riders. He recruits a boy named Smiley (Kristyan Ferrer). Together with the frightening gang leader Lil Mago (Tenoch Huerta Mejía), they terrorize and exploit the migrants. Mago intends to rape Sayra, but Casper intervenes to kill him, after which Smiley is given orders to assassinate Casper.

Early in the journey, there are optimistic moments when migrants talk about their plans for the future. Local residents gather around the slowed or stopping train and offer food to the riders. But as the train approaches the border, the mood sours; local residents turn mean, hurling rocks and insults at uncomprehending riders. Casper has hidden on the train as it winds northward, shunned by fearful migrants, who scheme to throw him off the train. Sayra warns him of the danger, and as the train slows, they both jump off it, leaving her father and uncle to continue the journey separately. Later she learns that her father has been killed and her uncle arrested.

Finally, Sayra and Casper arrive at the river boundary between Mexico and the US. Casper arranges with a coyote to transport them across the river in an inflatable raft, which can only carry one of them at a time. Casper insists that Sayra go first. When she is halfway across, MS gang members descend on the riverbank and seize the waiting Casper. Sayra watches as he is summarily executed. She has endured many traumas and now confronts a new test in the dawn's early light: an endless parking lot devoid of life attached to a giant shopping mall, emblematic of her fading American Dream. Yet resolutely she places a telephone call, stoically mustering the courage to begin the next stage of her turbulent journey, alone.

The dramatic emergence in border film of empowered women is one of the most prominent characteristics of turn-of-the-century filmmaking. It was a long time coming and certainly reflects contemporary trends toward advancement and equality for women in countries around the world, including the US and Mexico. Equally clear is that much remains to be done, that the gains made are uneven and come without guarantees of permanence. However, the early prototypes of saint and sinner discussed in part 1 have been displaced by a richer catalog of courageous female characters. In this chapter alone, we met a vampire killer, a narco queen, a revolutionary, a street fighter, a hustler, overachieving grandmothers, assassins, and crusading journalists.

Other factors favoring the growth of women in film relate to changes in the film industry after 2000. The increasing number of border-related films allowed more opportunities for filmmakers to experiment. In addition, films of the new century included several blockbuster productions with big talents behind and in front of the camera. These are clues that are leading me to suggest that we are entering a golden age of border film.

# 10  Narco Nations

During the first decade of the twenty-first century, a long-brewing war among Mexican drug cartels erupted into plain sight, with devastating loss of life and social upheaval. The traditional cause of conflict among cartels revolved around who was in charge of what territories (known as *plazas*). This time, however, the tense balance of power was greatly exacerbated by disruptive interventions by the Mexican federal government.

After 2000, the seventy-plus years of one-party PRI rule were ended by the election of the conservative PANista Vicente Fox who, with the support of the US, authorized determined actions to curb the power of the cartels. In 2006, Fox was succeeded by another conservative, Felipe Calderón, who opened his six-year term of office by prioritizing an all-out war against the cartels. The Mexican military was called in to capture drug lords, clean up corrupt local governments, and when necessary eliminate opposition and execute criminals.

Such actions only intensified inter-cartel rivalries because established balances of power were destabilized by the federal interventions. The widespread violence spilled over to affect the population at large as waves of conflict spread across the nation, from the Pacific cartel heartlands in the state of Sinaloa to Veracruz on the Gulf of Mexico. In the north, a succession of turf wars surged tsunami-like out of Tijuana along the entire border region, engulfing Ciudad Juárez and northeastern states.[1] Federal troops routinely cleaned up one plaza before moving on immediately to the next. The *federales'* cleanup operations were reputedly as bloody and merciless as the inter-cartel wars.[2] So pervasive was the penetration of the cartels that Mexico came to be called "narcolandia" (drugland).

The violence peaked around 2008 in Tijuana, and later in other border *plazas*. Ciudad Juárez became famous as the most dangerous city on the planet. The cartel wars had claimed over two hundred thousand lives in Mexico. Aggressive interventions by police and military quieted the border for some years, and residents moved successfully to reclaim their damaged communities one block at a time.[3] However, cartel-related violence once again rose—this time to record levels—during the presidencies of Peña Nieto and his successor since 2018, the left-leaning AMLO.

## THE NEW NARCO FILM: *TRAFFIC*

There was an upsurge of films about the US-Mexico border after the year 2000, a predictable consequence of the binational expansion and influence of Mexican drug cartels and related police efforts. The release of *Traffic* in 2000 was a benchmark event in the move toward blockbuster, big-budget films concerned with Mexican drug cartels. Previously, low-budget films in both countries had featured drug trafficking, but *Traffic* signaled that Hollywood was in step with current issues (however belatedly) and alert to the box office potential of films addressing the epidemic of drug-connected violence in Mexico.

*Traffic* is a stylish, tense, and absorbing film, boasting a talented cast and setting a high bar for all films that followed. It won Oscars for directing, supporting actor, editing, and adapted screenplay. Directed by Steven Soderbergh, the film version of *Traffic* was closely based on a potent British television mini-series called *Traffik*, which aired in 1989. Both versions had complicated plotlines dealing with the global mechanisms of law enforcement and drug production, distribution, and consumption. However, Soderbergh's film version was simplified by the deletion of one of *Traffik's* most original themes concerning the role of poppy growers and suppliers in Afghanistan and Pakistan. Three other plotlines were retained in *Traffic* but were adapted to a US setting.

The action in *Traffic* takes place in Tijuana, Washington, D.C., and Southern California. The three plots increasingly overlap, and different color tones were adopted for each setting in order to clarify audience comprehension. The Tijuana story concerns rivalries among corrupt law enforcement agents and military personnel engaged in Mexico's fight against the drug lords. The conflict is encapsulated in two figures: Javier (Benicio del Toro), who plays a Tijuana cop with a flexible moral compass who is drawn into the orbit of Salazar (Tomas Milian), a deeply corrupt general who is secretly working to assist the Ciudad Juárez cartel in its bid to displace the Tijuana cartel.

The Washington, D.C., plot occurs against the backdrop of US federal government efforts to devise more effective drug policy. The hero is Robert Wakefield (Michael Douglas), the nation's newest drug czar, who is motivated to the point of evangelism to find solutions. He is rudely awakened when his interventions are blocked and he discovers that his daughter has descended into addiction.

The Southern California plotline features Drug Enforcement Agency (DEA) officials who are building a case to prosecute a local drug lord. DEA officer Montel Gordon (Don Cheadle) is successful in placing narco Carl Ayala (Steven Bauer) in prison to await trial. But then Ayala's wife Helena (Catherine Zeta-Jones) emerges unexpectedly from the background to defend her husband, renegotiate terms with the Tijuana cartel suppliers, and eliminate her family's enemies.

Time and again, *Traffic* returns to the existential and moral dilemmas confronting individuals who have, for whatever reason, been drawn into an underworld dominated by the perverse logics of cartels. A basic foundation of amorality is established early in the film, when a rogue agent characterizes law enforcement as an "entrepreneurial activity." Salazar, the general sent to clean up the Tijuana cartel's mess, is the film's prime example of a player who is on the surface a representative of law and order but underneath is a crook in pursuit of personal gain. He can be charming when necessary, but Salazar is otherwise a malevolent dealmaker and killer.

Javier, the Tijuana cop, is more richly realized. He has a distaste for cartels but is not above making extra income through illicit side dealings. He is drawn accidentally into Salazar's orbit, but after his partner is executed by Salazar, Javier determines to betray Salazar to the DEA. For this service, Javier receives assurances of US protection plus a promise that his local baseball diamond in Tijuana will be connected to electricity in order to give kids an alternative nighttime activity not involving cartels. Told by a DEA agent that he should feel good about betraying Salazar, Javier mutters: "I feel like a traitor." In another revealing moment, Javier visits his deceased partner's wife. She is immobilized by grief but desperately seeks reassurance that her husband died honorably. Javier looks into her eyes and lies, vowing that he has told her "*la pura verdad*" (the plain truth).

The leaders of the Tijuana cartel have dreamed up a "project for the children'" that involves fabricating dolls made of pure cocaine, making it easier to smuggle the product into the US and market it to young consumers. In Washington, D.C., Robert Wakefield has learned a simple truth: that the drug wars are unwinnable as long as demand for the product remains so high in the US market. When Wakefield prompts his staff—"The dam is open for new ideas"—not a single staffer responds to his challenge. In another futile initiative, Wakefield meets with Salazar, now appointed drug czar for the Mexican government on top of his employment by the Juárez cartel. Salazar is predictably hospitable and cordial, but nothing substantial comes from their pleasantries.

Wakefield's family life is fractured when he discovers that his daughter is a drug addict. As her descent accelerates, he takes to the streets to find her and resigns from the charade of anti-drug policy making. He is a broken man but finds redemption in a crusade to save his family. We last encounter him with his wife and daughter at a Narcotics Anonymous meeting, humbly introducing himself by saying, "We're here to listen."

An unexpected protagonist now rises to prominence in *Traffic*. This is Helene (Catherine Zeta-Jones), wife of Carlos Ayala, the kingpin of drug distribution in Southern California. Inexplicably unaware of her husband's involvement in the drug trade—or possibly wantonly oblivious—Helene is shocked when her husband is arrested by the DEA. She intervenes forcefully after their son is threatened by the Tijuana cartel as a way of purchasing her silence. Efficiently and competently, she sets about engineering Carlos's release, renegotiating the terms of his contract with Tijuana suppliers, and eliminating his enemies. She morphs decisively from being a proud mother to an acting drug lord, motivated by a simple desire: "I want our life back!" (Helene is definitely a late-flowering Warrior Woman.)

As the film ends, Helene is victorious, Salazar has been eliminated, and Javier sits contentedly on the benches of his newly floodlit neighborhood baseball field.

*Traffic's* portrayal of the border is rich and detailed. The borderline is a place of open exchange, a fluid, porous space where crossing over is routine for ordinary people, smugglers, and legitimate commerce. The film cuts swiftly from one side of the line to the other, underscoring the frequency of cross-border connections. As one character attests: "The border is disappearing," due in part to the NAFTA agreement, which facilitated the movement of trucks laden with exports (including contraband) across the line. Border expert Tony Payan made the case that the borderline itself was the determining factor in Juárez politics and economic development over the past forty years. The city relied on the advantages conferred by its border location to such an extent that weaknesses in its economy, social and cultural fabric, and political organization were papered over. When stressed by cartel wars and economic downturn, the social order of the city collapsed.[4]

Another central message in *Traffic* is that cartel life and logics have diffused way beyond the borderline. The narco industry is now global in its organization and reach. Governments in the US and Mexico (and beyond) collaborate to interdict cross-border trafficking and to prosecute drug lords, but corruption is ubiquitous at all levels in every nation. By comparison, the small-time operators in *Touch of Evil* seem like a mom-and-pop arrangement, and the optimistic cross-border collaboration of *Border Incident* an improbable pipe dream.

The circuits of interaction that characterize cross-border cartel-cop interactions in *Traffic* are illegal and immoral, but also form a perverse adhesive forging binational integration. The north-south-north exchanges of money, guns, and drugs are the most tangible evidence, but so is human trafficking and other illicit exchange. *Traffic* illuminates how subtle the circuits of influence and connection can be. In one scene, the evil General Salazar meets a victim he has tortured into submission. Over a lush meal of food and wine, he tries persuading his victim to switch sides and betray friends. Salazar no longer issues threats. Instead, he flatters his victim by emphasizing their common background—both had been educated in the United States.

Real-world campaigns to control drug cartels in Mexico have tended to employ an iron fist and distinctly extralegal methods. Following the appointment in 2008 of former lieutenant colonel Julián Leyzaola Pérez as Tijuana's secretary of public security, Leyzaola's first action was to move his family out of Mexico. In confrontations with cartels, he was fearless and brutal. He avoided a number of attempts on his life using intelligence provided by US law enforcement agencies. He banned the popular band Los Tucanes de Tijuana from their hometown because they performed *narcocorridos* that glorified local drug lords.[5]

Leyzaola's attack on Tijuana's cartels was followed by a large-scale *depuración* (purification) of rogue officers in the local police force. Many simply disappeared into local army bases and were never seen again; some were transported to distant federal prisons and tortured; and others were exposed as cartel employees, dismissed from the force, and left to fend for themselves (which was tantamount to a death sentence).[6] The corrupt cops were not missed by local residents (*tijuanenses*), who had endured years of police brutality.

Local businesses regarded Leyzaola as a hero, and he enjoyed a great deal of personal impunity. Community watchdogs were less happy, worrying about the abrogation of civil rights under his watch. Conspiracy theorists suspected that he was cleaning up the *plaza* for the benefit of the local drug lord, known as El Chapo, and cynics claimed that Leyzaola had been hired simply to produce *un espectáculo* (a show) for the US agencies funneling money into Mexico's anti-drug efforts. However, even a respected local newspaper, *Zeta*, whose courageous coverage of the narcotics industry had previously marked their staff as cartel targets, named Leyzaola Man of the Year in 2009.[7] Subsequently, Leyzoala moved on to become police chief in Ciudad Juárez, after which Tijuana's murder rates started to inch up once again.[8]

Ciudad Juárez attracted considerable financial assistance from a federal government anxious for victories of any kind in the drug wars.[9] President Calderón came to Juárez in 2010 with a list of social programs to aid the stricken city. Conceding that a military solution to cartel violence would not work by itself, Calderón sought to combine policing with judicial reform and social programming—an approach favored by the U.S.[10] A year later, Calderón was back in Juárez for his fourth visit since the violence began, celebrating the one hundredth anniversary of the Mexican Revolution. Announcing a change in the city's name to the honorific Heroica Ciudad Juárez, Calderón touted the benefits of his program Todos Somos Juárez (We are all Juárez), which in one year had pumped over $250 million into restoring the city's bruised fabric.[11] The number of violent deaths in the city fell to 142 for the month of April 2011, down from its peak of 359 in the previous October.

One reason crime statistics improved in Juárez was police chief Julián Leyzoala. Fresh from his cleanup in Tijuana, Leyzoala adopted a strategy straight out of his Tijuana playbook: within a year, the number of murders in Juárez was reduced by one-third, about two hundred rogue police officers had been purged, and complaints about human rights abuses had increased.[12] As happened in Tijuana, residents gave their police chief a lot of leeway to conduct his business; Leyzoala again banned a prominent musical group (Los Tigres del Norte) on the grounds that their music glorified drug traffickers.[13]

## METASTASIS: *NO COUNTRY FOR OLD MEN*, *THE LAST STAND*, *PÁJAROS DE VERANO*

During the early decades of the twenty-first century, the metastasis of narco culture in the real Mexico was simultaneously infecting Hollywood film. One of the earliest examples was *No Country for Old Men* (2007), a noir Western directed by the Coen brothers, who also wrote the screenplay from a novel by Cormac McCarthy.[14] *No Country* is a direct descendant of *Traffic*, which delved more deeply into the penetration of Mexican cartel violence *north* of the border. Out hunting one day in West Texas, Llewelyn Moss (Josh Brolin) stumbles across the bloody residue of a drug deal gone wrong (abandoned trucks, dead dogs, dead men, dying men). He steals a case containing a large sum of money left by one of the narcos and subsequently spends the rest of the film running for his life. His principal pursuer is the monstrous Anton Chigur (Javier Bardem), who is characterized by another assassin as "a psychopathic killer."

Local Sheriff Ed Tom Bell (Tommy Lee Jones) is reluctantly drawn into the war between Llewelyn and Chigur, who has orders to recover the money and dispatch Llewelyn. On the edges of this maelstrom is Carla Jean Moss (Kelly Macdonald), Llewelyn's wife, whose affection for Llewelyn provides some normalcy in the film. One of Chigur's last acts in *No Country* is to dispatch Carla Jean into the good night; he had promised that if Llewelyn did not return the stolen money, he would kill his wife. Llewelyn didn't, and Chigur delivered on his promise.

Tommy Lee Jones's Sheriff Bell exists as the moral center of *No Country*, an old-school defender of his community. Once in a while, Bell pauses to reflect on his career as a lawman and how cartel violence is altering his world. Exhaustion and incomprehension are etched into his face as he announces his decision to quit, stating: "I feel over-matched." His father, himself a former lawman, offers small consolation: "This country's hard on people. Can't stop what's coming." *No Country for Old Men* makes clear that what's coming in the borderlands is a terrifying war without limits.

The clash of cultures also manages to evoke humor. In the small border town featured in *The Last Stand* (Jee-Woon Kim, 2013), Arnold Schwarzenegger growls and glares his way back into film after taking time off to perform as governor of California. He plays Sheriff Ray Owens, a former LAPD narcotics officer now approaching retirement. His peaceful existence is shattered by news that a fugitive narco, Gabriel Cortez (Eduardo Noriega), will soon pass through his county, fleeing at high speed en route for Mexico. The flinty Sheriff Ray vows: "I'm not going to let that guy come through my town without a fight," and he hurriedly assembles a ragtag gang of "deputies" (in the manner of John Wayne in *Rio Bravo*). There's lots of small-town satire.

At the very last moment, on a bridge crossing into Mexico, Sheriff Ray succeeds in capturing Cortez (well, he is Arnie, after all). There follows one of those timeless exchanges between victorious lawman and a vanquished opponent. Not understanding why a small-town sheriff would risk everything to stop him from crossing into Mexico, Cortez asks: "You let thousands of illegal immigrants into the US every day. Why worry about one who's going back?" Sheriff Ray scowls at him with contempt: "You give those immigrants a bad name."

What happens if the metastasis of narcoculture is unstoppable? The consequences for isolated indigenous communities are nowhere better told than in the Colombian film *Pájaros de verano* (Cristina Gallego and Ciro Guerra, 2019; Birds of Passage). The film is divided into five episodes relating the history of the north Colombian drug trade from the late 1960s to the early 1980s and its impact on a group of Wayuu indigenous people in one settlement. Before the cartels, the local language and culture were intact, having survived (through isolation) both the Spanish entrada and the modernization of Colombian society.

The Wayuu are mostly farmers and ranchers, whose long-established way of life begins to unravel when a couple of locals start trafficking in marijuana. Their success draws others into the business but also introduces an alien morality into the community, encouraging interfamily rivalry, murder, rape, and the betrayal of sacred ties. The central symbol of this disruption is a grand, white mansion built in glorious isolation by the local cartel boss on a barren tract of land. Untethered from the traditional order, the villagers descend into war. Tragically, they are aware of their descent but powerless to stop it. As one character remarks, "We've lost the soul," and a vengeful eye-for-an-eye morality has taken its place. The Wayuu's original sin is diagnosed as too much contact with *alijuna*, Spanish-speaking Colombians. The mansion is destroyed as an act of war, becoming a ruin commemorating the extinction of a culture.

## DOMESTICATING VIOLENCE: *600 MILLAS*

The imposition of cartel law on local people became a popular theme of border films. The best example was *600 Millas* (2015; 600 miles), a Mexican production written and directed by Gabriel Ripstein that focuses on gun running from the US to Mexican cartels, known colloquially as the Iron River.[15] We meet Bureau of Alcohol, Tobacco, Firearms, and Explosives (ATF) agent Hank Harris (Tim Roth) patiently monitoring local gun shows, checking sales receipts, and following leads. His suspicions are aroused by Arnulfo (Kristyan Ferrer), a young and naïve cartel foot soldier. When Arnulfo is pulled over one day by agent Harris, he impulsively kidnaps the ATF agent and transports him to Mexico, hoping to curry favor with his uncle Martin, who is a local cartel chief. The long drive into Mexico gives Hank the opportunity to calm the hyper-agitated

*Figure 10.1. 600 Millas* (2015). Breakfast time in Mexico: Arnulfo and cartel leader Uncle Martín.

Arnulfo. When their road is blocked by a rival cartel checkpoint, Hank quietly reassures the pistoleros of his high-level cartel connections, and they are allowed to pass. Hank later explains to Arnulfo that the ATF and cartels sometimes "help each other out."

Uncle Martín is amazed by Arnulfo's stupidity in delivering an ATF agent right to the heart of his operation. In the family kitchen, Martín deposits his breakfast dishes in the sink and orders his nephew to kill Hank, but Arnulfo cannot bring himself to do this. Furious, Martín prepares to do the deed himself, but before he can act the frightened Arnulfo shoots his uncle.

The situation spirals out of control. Arnulfo appeals to his mother, who lives nearby. She is more fearful of her brother Martín's wrath and orders Arnulfo to leave. Two *sicarios* (one of them his godfather) arrive with orders to kill Arnulfo and Hank, but Hank manages to escape with Martín's gun. The *sicarios* argue about where to execute Arnulfo, because his mother insists they cannot do the deed in her house. Out of nowhere Hank returns and with surprising efficiency, he executes the pair. He and Arnulfo escape together. Arnulfo had saved Hank's life, so Hank may be returning the favor, or he may be taking Arnulfo as hostage; whichever it

*Figure 10.2.  600 Millas* (2015). Breakfast time in the US: agent Hank and spouse.

is, they are once again together on the road, this time with shared fates. The slow, almost dialogue-free drive north to the border mimics the fugitives' earlier journey into Mexico, except that Hank is now in the driver's seat, literally and figuratively.

It's early morning, and Arnulfo is sleeping on the back seat. Driving off-road in the middle of nowhere, Hank stops the vehicle and motions for Arnulfo to get out. Half asleep and puzzled, Arnulfo complies, whereupon Hank quickly drives away, abandoning Arnulfo without food, water, or weapon. The bemused young man faces almost certain death in the desert, either from the elements or at the hands of vengeful family members.

The full enormity of Hank's betrayal of Arnulfo is revealed in the film's preternaturally quiet finale. The action opens on another domestic scene, this time breakfast in Hank's home, where he leisurely discusses the upcoming day with his wife. It's impossible to reconcile the banality of this scene with the violent acts Hank had committed a few hours earlier. The screen credits begin to roll, but we still hear the sounds of dishes being cleared and fragments of conversation. The Harrises appear to have a busy day ahead of them.

*600 Millas* is no blockbuster, but it is an essential twenty-first-century border film. Through Arnulfo we learn how gun trafficking is an essential part of cartel operations and how cartel incursions into everyday life on both sides of the line are normalized. Through Hank, we understand that corruption exists on both sides of the border. At every level—individual, family, and community—daily life is dominated by fear and uncertainty. Especially vulnerable are young people, for whom criminality is sometimes the only route to advancement and survival. Most important is that *600 Millas* reveals how cartel culture has become "domesticated." The ease with which gun purchases are made is chilling. Orders to assassinate are served up along with breakfast. Arnulfo's mother is so fearful of her "family" that she abandons her son to cartel killers; an assassin sent to kill him is his godfather. Corruption on both sides of the line allows Mexican cartels and the ATF to move guns along the Iron River. The boundary line separating the two nations has no more significance than a traffic light.

The realization dawns that Hank is not a rogue agent; his behaviors are normal, at least for the bisected ATF body. He is a capable executioner, morally slippery, and treats his mistress as a throwaway item. Yet in his other guise, Hank is well-known in the community for diligently performing the daily tedium of monitoring purchases at gun shows. As a family man, he enjoys commonplace table chatter with his wife, though it's doubtful she has read the fine print in his job description.

## "IN THIS WAR, THERE ARE NO BORDERS"/"EN ESTA GUERRA, NO HAY FRONTERAS": *SICARIO*

A second benchmark border film was released in 2015, fifteen years after *Traffic*. *Sicario* (Denis Villeneuve, 2015; Assassin) took narco films deeper into the problems of policing the border line in another big-spending, award-winning production, with a top-drawer cast and crew. The film grabs audience attention with a tense raid on a cartel safe house in Chandler, Arizona. There Federal Bureau of Investigation (FBI) agents discover a literal charnel house, with large caches of corpses individually wrapped in plastic and stuffed behind the interior walls. (The accompanying score by music director Johan Johansson is stomach churning.) Moments later, a bomb explodes outside the house and two investigators are killed. An agent involved in the raid, Kate Macer (Emily Blunt), subsequently seizes an opportunity to strike back at the bombers by joining a special operations team. This is a determined act by a Warrior Woman, soon to meet her match.

Kate discovers that the team she has joined has a murky provenance. She first meets the man in charge of a drug war special ops unit, Matt Graver (Josh Brolin). Matt is untidy, flip-flop wearing, and long-haired, not at all the standard issue suit-and-tie FBI agent. He enjoys reminiscing about the good old days in Medellín, Colombia, when there was only one cartel to combat. He tells Kate that was "the kind of order we could control," not like now, when too many cartels and too many law enforcement agencies clutter the battlefield, each vying for small gains in territory and dominance. No one believes the drug war will ever be won, and all improvise their own opaque and malleable rules of engagement. Matt tells Kate that his job is to "dramatically overreact" and "shake the trees and create chaos," because in those moments his enemies are exposed and mistakes are made.

Kate's other partner is Alejandro (Benicio del Toro), an enigmatic former prosecutor who quit his job in South American law enforcement to pursue Fausto Alarcón (Julio Cesar Cedillo), a cartel leader who murdered his wife and daughter. Now deeply inserted into US covert ops, Alejandro's sole purpose in life is to execute Fausto. Kate resembles his murdered daughter, and Alejandro is unexpectedly protective toward her—sometimes. He lowers Kate's expectations about the dirty swamp she now inhabits: "Nothing will make sense to your American ears. And you will doubt everything that we do. And in the end, you will understand nothing." (The edgy screenplay is by Taylor Sheridan.)

Alejandro and Kate are both lusting for vengeance in a world where moral codes are atrophied and flexible. In a short scene when Alejandro crosses paths with a former Medellin colleague who offers sympathy for his loss of wife and daughter, Alejandro stoically accepts the condolences but right away enters a room to torture his next captive. When Kate seeks reassurance that the Matt+Alejandro tag team is acting within the limits of the law, her former boss deflects her concerns: "If you fear that you're operating out of bounds, you're not. The boundary's been moved." Hardly encouraged by this nonclarification, Kate nevertheless proceeds with her new assignment, manifestly ill prepared for what comes next.

Arriving in Ciudad Juárez, Kate's first job is to help transport a witness from Juárez to El Paso. As they approach Juárez, Alejandro gestures dramatically: "There she is—the beast—Juárez!" Entering the city, they spot naked corpses strung up on a freeway overpass, some missing heads or limbs. Seeing Kate's distress, Alejandro offers practical advice: "Watch out for the state police. They're not always the good guys." This does not calm Kate. Inevitably, the mission runs into trouble. Returning to El Paso with their witness, the convoy is stalled in traffic on a bridge, and a spectacular gunfight erupts. People die, but Kate is told not to worry because the news won't even make tomorrow's newspaper in El Paso. (Many residents in the real Juárez were outraged by the portrayal of their city in this film.)

During a pause in the tension, Kate gains a different perspective on Juárez. A colleague offers to show her something cool. From an El Paso rooftop, the pair witness flashes of gunfire and explosions on the other side. Kate's companion explains: "This is what happens when you cut the head off a chicken," meaning that when you eliminate one drug lord, others will rise up to battle for succession.

*Sicario* moves toward a climactic nighttime battle intended as a pretext distracting attention from Alejandro's entry into Mexico in order to confront Fausto Alarcón. It's dawning on Kate that she is involved in this operation solely to provide legal cover for illegal covert operations on Mexican soil. During the raid, Kate confronts Alejandro about this duplicity. In response he shoots her in the chest. (She is wearing body armor and so survives the attack.) Later, when the mission is over, a traumatized Kate refuses to go along with the subterfuge, yelling at Matt: "I'm going to tell everyone what you did!" After a brief pause, Matt replies coldly: "That would be a major mistake."

Left behind in Mexico to pursue his independent mission, Alejandro has reached Alarcón's hacienda. After executing everyone in sight, he joins the Alarcón family at their dinner table. Alarcón tries to persuade Alejandro that the murder of his wife and daughter was nothing personal, merely business. Alejandro is unmoved, saying: "Para mí es personal" (For me it's personal). He then shoots Alarcón's wife and two children before dispatching Alarcón himself. Mission accomplished.

In *Sicario*'s denouement, a recovering Kate is hiding in an anonymous motel, staring vacantly from a balcony. Alejandro arrives, and with a remnant of solicitude suggests: "I would not recommend standing on balconies for a while, Kate." He has brought papers that need her signature, certifying that their cross-border raid was undertaken legally and by the book. At first she refuses, until Alejandro thrusts a pistol under her chin and commands: "Sign it." Then she does.

Preparing to leave, Alejandro is unable to resist offering a final piece of advice, advising Kate to disappear into a small town with law and order, because "this is the land of wolves now." Out there are many packs vying for dominance, and Alejandro is a member of one. As he walks across the parking lot, Kate returns to her balcony and prepares to shoot him. Sensing her intention, Alejandro stops and turns to her with open arms, offering himself as a defenseless target. The defeated Kate cannot bring herself to pull the trigger. Agent Kate Macer is an impressive Warrior Woman, but I doubt she would ever find a safe suburban haven. The two wild and crazy guys, Alejandro and Matt, will no doubt pick up fresh assignments, since every nation needs ingenious combat-ready killers. Indeed, Brolin and del Toro reprised their roles in a 2018 sequel called *Sicario: Day of the Soldado* (soldier). The whole effort was an unimaginative, routine cops-and-robbers runabout.

Cartel films reveal a hermetically sealed narcolandia composed of drugs, guns, cops, and violence, nurtured by an atmosphere that feeds corruption. Cumulatively, the films convey how narcolandia works at varying geographical scales. *Traffic* deals with cartel ops and policing on a global level, necessitating interventions by national governments and international policing agencies. *Sicario* is submerged in a quagmire of never-ending regional trench warfare inhabited by cartels and universally corrupt law enforcement in which small victories one day become tomorrow's defeats. And *600 Millas* reveals cartel penetration and integration at everyday levels of community and family, a chilling sedimentation of evil representing the domestication of violence.

The cartel culture does not rely solely on intimidation and extreme violence. In film and real life it actively promotes a positive image among the communities it controls, since it is part of the cartel's tactical tool kit to pacify conquered communities instead of implementing a state of permanent total war. So cartels will pay musicians to produce corridos (popular ballads) about heroes who are portrayed as Robin Hoods helping people in poor communities. The same culture simultaneously demonizes the local police and degrades government as functionally incapable of providing for the people's needs. Neglected by governments and corrupt law enforcement and terrified into submission by cartels, traditional institutions of civil society atrophy and collapse. Autonomous local militias sometimes organize for purposes of self-defense, demonstrating that some communities are prepared to resist even to the point of death.

Drug cartels are present throughout Mexico, although their influence is far from total in large metropolises such as Mexico City. When a cartel sets up operations in rural areas, control is often swiftly imposed and absolute. Drug lords pay special attention to places of strategic importance where defenses are vulnerable (such as border ports of entry) or where there are facilities or infrastructure essential to their operations (e.g., transportation networks). The atlas of narcolandia would also indicate that the influence of Mexican cartels extends deeply into the US, beyond the border zone and into cities that represent the cartels' major markets. The new narco films provide vivid demonstrations explaining why it is difficult to imagine ways to dislodge or defeat such entrenched and virulent criminality.[16]

# 11   Lives of the Undocumented

IMMIGRATION REFORM UP TO 9/11

There is a moment of intense anguish in Gregory Nava's *Mi Familia* (1995), a multigenerational saga of an immigrant family who arrive in East Los Angeles in the 1920s when the border is "just a line in the dirt." Jimmy (Jimmy Smits) and Isabel (Elpidia Carillo) sit together in their room at night. Confronting Jimmy's mask of impenetrable stoicism, Isabel breaks down, wailing tearfully: "No-one knows me [in this country]." Jimmy responds with tears of his own: "I know you." It is a tragic moment when they recognize the common challenges facing immigrants: alienation and rejection.[1]

The foundation of contemporary US immigration policy was established by the 1965 Immigration Reform Act, also known as the Hart-Cellar Act, after its sponsors. It abolished the country-of-origin quotas that had controlled immigration up to that point, installed family ties and needed skills as the principal criteria for entry into the US, and increased the overall number of migrants permitted to enter the country. The newcomers were mostly people from Asia, Latin America, and the Caribbean, much different from the predominantly European stock of earlier generations. Over time many new immigrants took advantage of the law's provision allowing unification of families of permanent residents.[2]

The 1965 act also placed quotas on legal immigration into the US, capping it at 120,000 persons annually. This was way below the number demanded by the US labor market, and in combination with hard times in Mexico, the numbers of unsanctioned crossings into the US ballooned. The 1965 act classified anyone arriving after the quota was exceeded as a criminal, thus creating a problem of "illegal immigration." Border apprehensions escalated from one hundred thousand per year in 1968 to half a million by 1973.[3]

In a fresh attempt to stem the flow of undocumented migrants from Mexico, President Ronald Reagan signed the Immigration Reform and Control Act in 1986. It provided general amnesty for undocumented migrants who had been resident in the US since 1982, special entry provisions for migrant agricultural workers, and sanctions against employers of workers without papers. As a consequence, more than three million persons in the US became legal residents by the early 1990s, while sanctions on employers who hired undocumented workers were rarely enforced. Undocumented immigration from Mexico continued.[4] By the mid-1990s, the US began building fences designed to deter illegal border crossings in El Paso, Texas; San Diego County, California; and Nogales, Arizona.[5] Landing mats from the Vietnam war, used for temporary aircraft runways, were now recycled as border fences. The new fortifications pushed migrants toward more remote desert and mountain regions to cross. Deaths from drowning, heat stroke, and hypothermia increased.[6] As crossing became more hazardous, migrants turned for assistance to human smugglers known as coyotes and found themselves unwittingly caught in a fog of criminality.

The election in 2000 of Presidents George W. Bush in the US and Vicente Fox in Mexico seemed to promise joint action on immigration reform. However, after the attacks of 9/11, the US adopted a more belligerent stance on matters of national security, creating the DHS in 2002, which incorporated agencies dealing with immigration, customs and border control, terrorism, and drug trafficking. During Bush's second term, comprehensive immigration reform was again promoted, but it failed in 2007, largely because opponents of reform rejected any actions that could be construed as "amnesty" for the undocumented. Subsequently, the Bush administration shifted to more hostile immigration measures emphasizing enforcement, including deporting people already in the US illegally.

## FORCED DEPARTURE: *YA NO ESTOY AQUÍ*

Few films better convey the experience of forced migration than *Ya no estoy aquí* (Fernando Frías de la Parra, 2019; I'm no longer here). The film won ten Ariel Awards (the Mexican equivalent to the US Academy Awards) and was nominated for an Academy Award.

Ulises (Juan Daniel García Treviño) is a style-conscious teen with indigenous roots who lives in the northern Mexican city of Monterrey, two hours south of the border. He dresses with panache and styles his thick black hair into swatches, with peroxide blond highlights, buzz-cutting the rest. He is a spectacular advertisement for himself, a free spirit, and natural leader—inevitably the qualities that attract the wrong kind of attention from the Los Pelones gang, which rules the barrio.

Ulises's days consist of hanging out with his small dance troupe, known as Los Terkos (*terco* means stubborn or obstinate; the film's use of the letter k in Spanish is deliberate). They are devotees of *cumbia*, a Monterrey specialty that involves dancing in ways that reflect indigenous dance moves blended with traces of hip-hop. (The effect, including costumes, is entrancing.) The troupe's main work is raising enough money to buy the latest MP3 mix of killer *cumbia*.

The Los Pelones gang serves the community by occasionally delivering food and consumer goods, accompanied by loudspeaker messages informing residents that these are gifts, and they should not rely on police or government to provide for them. The gang enforces neighborhood allegiance through terror: they show the Los Terkos kids a video in which a disobedient youth is beheaded and warn Ulises to keep off the street and cease dressing as he does. Soon after, four members of Los Pelones are killed in a drive-by shooting; Ulises is blamed, and he realizes he must flee to protect his life and the lives of his family.

McAllen, Texas, lies two hours north via a fast toll road from Monterrey. Regular bus service is provided between the two cities, as a lure to Mexican shoppers. Ulises crosses the border illegally, hidden underneath one of these buses, and travels on to the borough of Queens, New York City. He is befriended by Lin (Angelina Chen), who is fascinated by his strangeness (it's the hair), which is exaggerated since neither speaks the other's language. Intensely lonely, Ulises is showing little sign of adapting to New York, and Lin tires of him. He tries dancing *cumbia* for money under an elevated section of the train track but is told he needs a permit to perform. A friendly cop tells him where to pick up a permit, but Ulises experiences this exchange as one more setback.

Ulises calls his mother in Monterrey, but she warns him: "Don't come back. They'll kill you." He wanders into a club where he meets a *fichera* (hostess, possibly more), herself a migrant, who confirms that life in America is hard. She invites him to rest at her apartment. In an effort to raise his spirits, she advises: "No steps back, even to gain momentum!" But it is too late. Ulises cuts his hair (his major mode of self-expression) and loses himself in drugs. Predictably, he is picked up and agrees to deportation. His final view of the US is from inside an ICE detention center.

Returning to Monterrey, Ulises discovers that Los Terkos have disbanded. One former member is dead, and another has found God. There are riots in the barrio where Ulises is hiding from Los Pelones. In the background, a speech by Mexican president Andrés Manuel López Obrador (AMLO) warns that drugs and guns are the sources of all evil in Mexico. As swarms of police cars gather to impose order, a solitary Ulises listens to *cumbia* and tentatively begins once again to dance.

## ON THE OTHER SIDE: *EL NORTE*

Gregory Nava's *El Norte* (1983) was released almost four decades before *Ya no estoy aquí*. It built a reputation as the canonical history of forced departure, crossing over, adaptation, alienation, and tragedy emblematic of migrants fleeing from oppression and persecution.

Rosa and Enrique (Zaide Silvia Gutiérrez and David Villalpando) are sister and brother in flight from death threats received in their Maya village in Guatemala. The film straightaway adopts a dense cosmology meant to lift it out of the ordinary and into the realm of the universal by drawing on legends and traditions that emphasize the epic nature of the siblings' saga. Primarily, Nava invokes the classic Quiché Maya creation account entitled the *Popul Vuh* (Book of the People).[7] The Hero Twins in this legend, Hunahpú and Xbalanqué, are children of the gods who travel to the Underworld and perish after a long journey and many trials, then magically arise to defeat the lords of the Underworld.

*El Norte*'s classicism is emphasized by its formal division into three acts. Act 1 is set in Guatemala, where the suffering of exploited indigenous coffee plantation workers is painfully revealed. The father of Rosa and Enrique is murdered; soon after, their mother is disappeared. Preparing to depart from Guatemala, Rosa sets aside her *huipil* (a colorful indigenous dress) in favor of something less "Indian" for the trip through Mexico. She and her brother learn that copious outpourings of vulgar language will help them pass as Mexicans, and that if they are challenged, they should claim origins in Oaxaca, since Mexicans believe that all Indians look alike.

The second act involves the passage to the Tijuana border crossing. The border zone is described as *como la guerra* (like a war zone), and Tijuana as the anus of the world (the language used in the film is more vivid). Rosa and Enrique's first attempt to cross the border ends abruptly when they are abandoned by an unscrupulous coyote. Next, they elect to cross through tunnels, where they are attacked by voracious rats. Finally, exiting the tunnel at night, they pause to gaze north toward San Diego, stretching before them like a jeweled magic carpet.

The long final act is the story of the hero twins in *el norte*. Their tiny, grubby apartment is nothing like the manicured single-family home they'd seen in the pages of *Buen Hogar* (the Spanish-language *Good Housekeeping*), though it does have a flush toilet and electricity. After taking English-language classes, Enrique secures a job in an upscale restaurant, first as a busboy and then as a waiter; Rosa joins Nacha, a helping angel (Lupe Ontiveros), providing house-cleaning services to rich Anglo homeowners. Rosa has difficulties operating a washing machine. Rather than reveal her ignorance, she washes sheets by hand and hangs them out to dry in the afternoon sun. Her brittle, coiffed employer is baffled and shocked by such primitive customs.

*El Norte* reaches a summit of adaptation when Enrique arrives home one evening proudly wearing the "uniform" of a restaurant employee and confronts Rosa, dressed in gringa-style clothing and makeup. He

*Figure 11.1. El Norte* (1983). Rosa and Enrique celebrate their new identities.

complains half-seriously that she looks like a "clown." It is a key moment: the newcomers have donned their disguises, but each is made uneasy by the visible evidence of change in the other. The ever-optimistic Enrique encourages his sister: "In this country you work hard, but you can get somewhere. . . . Nothing can stop us now!" Which we know cannot be true.

The ongoing fusion of twin cultures is now displaced by a devastating moral dilemma. Enrique is offered a job in Chicago that comes with the promise of legalized status in the US. His elation is short-lived, because Rosa falls ill with typhus, traced to the rat bites she sustained in the Tijuana tunnels. She delayed seeking medical care, fearful of arrest due to her undocumented status. Rosa's health deteriorates, and she lapses into fantastical reveries heavy with foreboding. Desperate to obtain legal papers, Enrique pleads with Nacha to look after Rosa while he departs for Chicago. She is appalled that he would even consider abandoning his ailing sister, saying, "Rosa may be dying, but you are already dead." Enrique realizes that ambition is eclipsing his homeland traditions of obligation to family. He abandons his dreams of Chicago, job, and green card. Later, when a failing Rosa awakens in hospital, she sees Enrique calmly watching over her bedside. With the violins of Samuel Barber's mournful Adagio in

the background, Rosa voices her terrible realization that they do not belong on either side of the line:

> "Life here is very hard, Enrique. We're not free. . . .
> In our own land, we have no home. They want to kill us. . . .
> In the north we aren't accepted. When will we find a home?"

Rosa dies. Enrique once again pulls out his day-laborer clothes, wearing what may be his father's hat. On as street corner, he calls out to pro-
spective employers: "I have strong arms!" He will not be denied, but deep
down Enrique knows that his American Dream has failed: his sister is
dead; like his father before him, he began life as a peon in Guatemala, and
he remains a peon in the US. Lest we forget what drove our Hero Twins
from Guatemala, the film closes with a full-screen silhouette of his father's
decapitated head, black against a blood-red background.

## GOING BACK, CHICANO CINEMA: *¡ALAMBRISTA!*, *THE BALLAD OF GREGORIO CORTEZ*

In 1977 Robert Young's *¡Alambrista!* broke new ground by depicting the
trials of undocumented migration from the migrant's perspective. Young
was an experienced documentary filmmaker who believed that fictional
film had more to offer than the "objective" viewpoint of documentary
films. The film's title refers to a tightrope walker (*alambre* means wire
in English) and metaphorically to an illegal immigrant.[8] The film opens
in the Mexican state of Michoacán, where Roberto Ramírez (Domingo
Ambriz) and his wife, baby daughter, and mother are eking out a fragile
existence. Desperate for money and greater security, Roberto decides to
cross into the US to find work. His father had done so years earlier and
had not been heard from since. Roberto's mother unsuccessfully pleads
with him to stay. After a long bus trip, Roberto crosses the border, which
at that time was little more than chicken wire topped with razor fencing.

Once in the US, Roberto meets a work crew from Mexico and gains
steady employment. His closest companion is Joe (Trinidad Silva), who advises him to act *con confidencia* when meeting gringos. He teaches Roberto
a few English words, the most useful of which is "hameggscoffee" spoken as

a single word. Joe also teasingly pushes Roberto to offer the waitress a little kiss, but Roberto chastely protests: "But I am married." The duo set off to Stockton, California, riding underneath the railroad cars. One morning Joe is no longer present, having fallen from his precarious perch under the train. Disconsolate at the loss of his friend, Roberto enters a diner, where he orders hameggscoffee from Sharon, an Anglo waitress who acts kindly toward him. Every waking moment of Roberto's life is spent working in the fields, but he also sells his blood for cash and is ecstatic when he lands a job directing crop-spraying helicopters to fields needing treatment. He is proud of his working uniform and wage increase but cannot avoid being soaked by chemicals and is being sickened by the work.

One night, Sharon the waitress intervenes to prevent Roberto from being robbed on the street, after which she takes him to an apartment she shares with her little brother and infant daughter. Sharon teaches him English and she learns some Spanish; together they attend energetic evangelical religious services that Roberto cannot comprehend. Eventually they become lovers, even though Sharon knows that Roberto is sending money to a wife in Mexico. Their affection deepens. One night the dance club they are attending is raided by immigration police. Roberto is deported but quickly returns to the US, this time as a scab hired to break a strike of melon pickers in Colorado. *La migra* launches another raid, after which a migrant worker is found dead. By coincidence, the dead man turns out to be Roberto's father. Roberto discovers that his long-absent father had remarried and had lived in a small corner of an abandoned bus, and that his bag of possessions contained only a few medications and photographs. Roberto realizes that despite decades of labor in the US, his father had lived and died a pauper.

A mournful *corrido* on the soundtrack reflects Roberto's state of mind:

"You leave behind your people
To come earn to eat [*sic*]
. . . I prefer returning to my land
Where I have friendship and warmth."[9]

Returning to Mexico, Roberto gets picked up by *la migra*, accelerating his transfer to the border. As he is crossing into Mexico he sees a woman giving birth to a child. She clings to a pole marking the international boundary, desperate to ensure that her baby will be born on US soil and hence qualify as a US citizen. Exhausted from her labor, she cries out ecstatically, "He'll never need papers!"

One of the principal legacies of the Chicano civil rights movement of the late 1960s and early 1970s was the growth of vibrant cultural and political practices among Chicano communities.[10] In keeping with the times, the political goals of the movement were front and center; at least one prominent scholar and activist preferred using the term *Chicano* to refer specifically to political identity and practice and to reserve the term *Mexican American* for referring to creative and critical practices.[11] The subsequent history of Chicanos in film has been described in many ways, and the details often overlap.[12] The present-day Chicanx film enterprise occupies a special space between the two nations; even if some films do not address the border directly, they are often regarded as border film because of the in-between awareness that powers many films.

In the late 1970s, the influential Chicano promoter and producer Moctesuma Esparza offered the role of Gregorio Cortez to Edward James Olmos, who accepted and suggested Robert Young as director (they had worked together on *¡Alambrista!*). The filmmakers set out to create a revisionist Western that took the side of the noble brown fugitive rather than an avenging white lawman. The filmmakers also decided that Spanish-speaking characters would speak Spanish on-screen without English subtitles. And if that was not sufficiently innovative, the film's chronology unfolded in reverse. Full clarity comes only later in the film as each episode is reassembled in chronological order.[13]

*The Ballad of Gregorio Cortez* (1982) is a retelling of a tragic injustice. Set in south Texas during the early twentieth century, the film is based on a 1958 book and popular *corrido* of the time. The facts about the Cortez incident are well-known. Two Mexican American farmers, Gregorio and his brother Romaldo, were questioned one day about a stolen horse. In the ensuing confusion, Romaldo was shot by the sheriff, who then turned his gun on Gregorio, who shot the sheriff in self-defense. Not expecting a fair trial, Gregorio fled, pursued by local lawmen and Texas Rangers for hundreds of miles through south Texas. Cortez's flight captured the public imagination at the time, though he surrendered to authorities after his wife and children were imprisoned as ransom. He was tried and sentenced to life imprisonment, but after many appeals was pardoned sixteen years later.

The "first wave" of Chicano film in the late 1960s was mainly about consciousness raising and consisted mainly of short documentaries such as Luis Valdez's *Yo soy Joaquín* (1969). It expressed a kind of *Aquí estamos y no nos vamos* ("We're here and we're not going away") sentiment felt by documentary filmmakers who were locked out of mainstream filmmaking. The second wave, beginning in 1977, is usually traced to the appearance of the pathbreaking *¡Alambrista!*, which involved independent filmmakers who were making commercial features aimed at wider audiences. The films included *Zoot Suit* (Luis Valdez, 1981), Young's *Ballad of Gregorio Cortez* (1982), and Gregory Nava's *El Norte* (1983). Beginning around 1987, a third wave of Chicano films was made inside Hollywood, involving a tight network of Chicano filmmakers and consumers. Films included *La Bamba* (Luis Valdez, 1987), *Born in East L.A.* (Cheech Marin, 1987), and *Stand and Deliver* (Ramón Menéndez, 1988; made for PBS). Robert Young continued his participation in Chicano filmmaking by coproducing *American Me* (1992), with Edward James Olmos directing.[14] Gregory Nava returned with *Mi Familia* (1995) and later, Jennifer López as the Tejana music star *Selena* (1997), coproduced by Moctesuma Esparza. Robert Rodríguez brought his own brand of filmmaking to the party with *El Mariachi* (1993) and has stayed ever since.

## THROUGH A MEXICAN LENS: *BABEL, 7 SOLES, DESIERTO*

As the number of border films grew after 2000, filmmakers were offered opportunities to experiment in different genres, and their choices of topic and content diversified and underwent complication. The story of Amelia (played by the Mexican star Adriana Barraza) is one of three connected threads that comprise the film *Babel* (Alejandro González Iñárritu, 2006).[15] In this large-budget, star-studded Mexican-US production, Amelia is a devoted nanny for the two children of an Anglo couple in San Diego, California, who also happens to be undocumented. While she is caring for the children at home, their parents are abroad (their story is told in another of the film's episodes). Amelia is invited to attend her son's wedding just outside Tijuana, but she lacks the parents' permission. Fatefully, she decides to take the two children with her, enlisting the help of her nephew Santiago (Gael García Bernal) to drive them to the wedding.

Upon returning they are questioned at the border crossing.[16] Amelia is unable to provide evidence of parental consent for taking the children out of the US, and the car is pulled over for secondary inspection. But Santiago has reasons for wanting to avoid questioning by *la migra*, so he spontaneously crashes the car through a barrier and drives off at high speed into the US. Veering off-road to avoid his pursuers, the panicked Santiago eventually stops the car, abandons Amelia and the two children in the desert, and disappears into the night.

Waking the following morning, Amelia realizes that Santiago is not coming back. She leaves the children in the shade while she seeks rescuers. She hails a border patrol officer; but when they return to the place where she left the children, they are no longer there. Panicked and incoherent, Amelia is taken into custody. She is later informed that the children have been found, and that the parents will not be pressing charges against her. Any relief she feels is short-lived because the authorities discover that she has been working illegally in the US for the past sixteen years and declare that she will be deported immediately.

*Babel* is especially interesting as a blockbuster by a star Mexican director mainstreaming the plight of undocumented migrants employed as domestic workers in the US. This situation is, needless to say, characteristic of migrant domestic workers throughout the world.[17] Also, it bears repeating that separation and deportation are experienced by males, too.[18]

The dangers confronting Mexican migrants in Mexico before they cross over are the subject of *7 Soles* (Pedro Ulteras, 2008; Seven suns). The film is set around the notorious Devil's Highway near the southern Arizona border, well known as a place where many die because of the extreme heat and absence of water. One of the characters vocalizes migrant fears by warning, "The desert is a huge graveyard." A small group consisting of young and old men, women, and children sets out to cross the sere Arizona landscape, aiming to cross into the US under the guidance of a belligerent, cokehead coyote/smuggler. The group is forced to diverge from its route to avoid vigilantes, as its members run out of water and food and one man breaks his ankle. As the journey unfolds, some broken-down travelers are left behind, and another is stabbed. The migrants just keep on dying. It is a small consolation when the remaining child in the group is eventually reunited with family members in Chicago.

The most degenerate Mexican example of the cinematic species of migrant slaughter is *Desierto* (Jonás Cuarón, 2016). A group of border crossers from Mexico enter the US and are immediately spotted by a determined Anglo vigilante, who uses a high-powered rifle (and a vicious dog) to execute the entire column. One by one they die, until only two remain alive: a wounded woman and a courageous, capable man. After he shoots the dog, the male survivor (played by Gael García Bernal, no less) manages to wound the killer, whom he abandons to die in the desert. The two survivors stumble toward the border, visible in the far distance. We never learn if they make it. Mexican government policy at the time was to discourage border crossers, and perhaps *Desierto* served as a warning to deter some would-be migrants. I simply tucked it into my filmography under the category "Mexicans: Execution by Dog and Rifle."[19]

## THOSE WHO REMAIN: *IXCANUL*

Border films have paid only scant attention to what happens to those who remain behind after migrants have departed. One exception is *Ixcanul* (2015), Guatemala's entry in the Academy Awards competition of that year. A debut feature directed by Jayro Bustamente, *Ixcanul* is set in a Guatemalan coffee-growing region similar to that of *El Norte*. In the shadow of an enormous active volcano, Pepe (Marvin Coroy) plans to escape from his servitude to the region's oppressive landowners. In a voice filled with wonder, he describes his vision: "Behind the volcano, it's the United States. There are big houses with gardens. People have cars." María is desperate to join Pepe in his flight and becomes pregnant with his child. There's only one problem: María is already promised in marriage to another man. The volcano acts as a constant beacon beckoning migrants toward opportunities beyond, but it also casts a shadow symbolizing entrapment by wealthy landholders and enforcers who exploit the workers. In the film's finale, her mother prepares María for marriage to the long-promised suitor. She is prisoner of a social tradition that is another form of slavery echoing that imposed by plantation owners. María's mother was held in such bondage, as will be María's unborn child should it be a girl. The generational legacy seems inescapable for those who remain behind.

Migration by undocumented persons remains a powerful theme in border films. The earlier films in this category (see chapter 6) retain their vitality and relevance in the present: the perils of crossing, challenges of adaptation, and enduring longing for the homeland. In the films of the current era migrant motivations are not that much different, yet the scale of migration these days is larger, more global in its extent, and increasingly dangerous. In addition, the films' intense portrayals of border fences, walls, and other security devices are manifestations of a continuing war on migrants, binational failure to deal with migration issues, and indifference toward the problems being created for communities on either side of the line.

Film representations of the migration experience in the early twenty-first century are tending to fall into two categories: (1) accounts of the violence and dangers awaiting migrants as they travel through Mexico and after they arrive in the US; and (2) deeply felt, searing portraits of the courage and suffering endured by migrants who are forced to depart their homelands by life-threatening events and repression. The first category is by now scarred by an almost fetishistic obsession with ingenious ways of bloodletting (the trademark of slasher movies worldwide). Migrants are preyed on by thieves in Mexico or slaughtered by avenging vigilantes in the US. Nothing on the screen is allowed to distract from gruesome killings. Simply seeing the trailer for *Juárez, Mexico* (James Cahill, 2007; a film about femicides) elevated my heartbeat, and by the time I caught up with *Juárez 2045* (Chris Le, 2015), self-medication seemed the only relief.

In the second category of migrant biographies, *El Norte*'s director, Gregory Nava, spoke of how he imagined that undocumented migrants were like "shadows" in the US, where punitive laws and hostile public attitudes combined to criminalize and marginalize the lives of courageous, hard-working people.[20] The migrant episode in *Babel* ends with the deportation of a nanny after sixteen years of service in the US. Yet we never see the consequences of her deportation, a topic that border films have been regrettably slow to address.[21] Thousands upon thousands of deportees are dumped in Mexico every year without money, family contacts, the ability to speak Spanish, or copies of their original birth certificates (the principal proof of ID in Mexico). Their difficulties are aggravated because Mexican border towns lack sufficient accommodation and services to assist them. I used to know the temporary encampments of homeless deportees that were established along the concrete channel of the Tijuana River, surviving only until Mexican authorities saw fit to dismantle them. Does anyone care what happens to these people?

# 12 Moral Tales, Border Law

For most of the early nineteenth century, Tejas (as it was then named) was ground zero for volatile shifts in populations and interracial attitudes. When the Mexican government granted colonization rights in the province to entrepreneur Moses Austin, waves of Anglo settlers streamed into the territory after 1821. The newcomers regarded Mexicans as primitive beings who were "religious pagans, purposelessly indolent and carefree, sexually remiss, degenerate, depraved, and questionably human."[1] Stephen F. Austin followed his father Moses into the settler business, expressing an almost predatory desire to populate Texas by "whitening" or Americanizing Texas.[2] The Anglo newcomers quickly extended their blanket disdain to descendants of colonial Spain, whom they considered the embodiment of impurity as a consequence of long-ago racial mixing on the Iberian peninsula.

Not surprisingly, Mexicans in Tejas were none too happy with their new Anglo neighbors. José María Sánchez was a Mexican military man sent in 1828 to investigate the troubles in that province. Like other educated Mexicans living on the frontier, Sánchez deplored the backwardness of frontier people as a whole. He wrote a two-faced assessment of the Tejanos in east Texas: "The character of the people is care-free, they are enthusiastic dancers, very fond of luxury, and the worst punishment that can be inflicted upon them is work."[3] But Sánchez reserved his most cutting remarks for the upstart Anglos, accusing them of immigrating constantly and building homes wherever it suited them. The Tejanos themselves were longtime residents who took a more pragmatic view of the Anglo newcomers. They complained about the neglect of Tejas by Mexican authorities and argued that Anglo immigration would promote the import of goods, develop roads and commerce, encourage good government, and protect them from Indian attacks. Theirs turned out to be the most prescient vision of the future borderlands.

Meantime, on the Pacific coast, a turbulent Alta California was also adjusting to newcomers. Settlers from colonial Mexico who arrived on the California frontier before the 1846–48 war formed a prosperous ranching class, calling themselves *gente de razón* (people of reason) as distinct from *gente sin razón* (people without reason, meaning pretty much everybody else). These were the Californios, who for the most part enjoyed congenial relations with Anglo newcomers.

On the eve of war in 1846, anti-Mexican sentiments boiled over. In a dyspeptic frame of mind, former US newspaperman Rufus B. Sage reported on his visits to Taos and nearby Nuevo México: "There are no people on the continent of America, whether civilized or uncivilized . . . more miserable in condition or despicable in morals than the mongrel race inhabiting New Mexico."[4] Bitter in defeat, Mexico developed an enduring mistrust of its northern neighbor. Writing from Stanford University in 1912, Samuel Bryan conceded that Mexican immigration was a necessary evil but also offered this contemptuous litany of Anglo complaints against Mexican migrants: "Their low standards of living and of morals, their illiteracy, their utter lack of proper political interest, the retarding effect of their employment upon the wage scale of the more progressive races, and finally their tendency to colonize in urban centers, with evil results, combine to stamp them as a rather undesirable class of residents."[5]

## HONOR: *VALDEZ IS COMING, ALL THE PRETTY HORSES*

Beginning in the 1970s, a spate of otherwise conventional Western films featured more complicated moral worlds than was typical of earlier releases. I think of these ethical Westerns as "moral tales."[6] They presented a more nuanced perspective on the Old West, usually by incorporating a greater variety of viewpoints (Lakota Indians in *Dances with Wolves* [1990], for instance). In so doing the films inevitably focused on the consequences of the mixing of races, identities, and cultures in the historically violent borderlands. Avoiding stories on an epic scale, they favored plots assembled in close-up from minor lives, nuance, and intimacy.

One prominent film in the shifting moral landscapes of the later twentieth century is *Valdez Is Coming* (Edwin Sherin, 1970), from a novel by Elmore Leonard.[7] The plot is straightforward. Valdez is an aging Mexican American lawman who fought against Apaches in earlier times. He takes up arms once more to combat Frank Tanner (Jon Cypher), a murderous Anglo gunrunner. Their dispute hinges on Valdez's insistence that $100 in compensation be paid to a pregnant indigenous woman who has been widowed as a consequence of the actions of Tanner's gang.

Set during the Mexican Revolution, *Valdez* is a glorious hodgepodge. All the protagonists have blood on their hands, and their moral codes are fluid. Valdez is played by Burt Lancaster, who had previously played an Indian warrior in *Apache* (1954). The pregnant Apache woman, who is portrayed as implacably courageous under gunfire, cohabited with a Black man who is shot during the film's first scene. The film uses explicit racial language. Many outlaws in Tanner's gang are Mexican, and they speak Spanish without subtitles in the film. The only prominent female in *Valdez* is Gay (Susan Clark), the woman whom Tanner intends to marry. At first she seems an atypical frontier lady, snooty, white, well-dressed, and entirely out of place. However, she tumbles from this pedestal after we learn that she murdered her previous husband (Tanner's brother) so that she could be with Tanner, whose bed she now shares. When Valdez takes Gay hostage, he treats her with an old-world courtesy, except when he leaves her tied up on the desert floor to run an errand.

For much of the film, Tanner is haunted by a message that Valdez sends via gang members he has vanquished: "Tell him Valdez is coming." When he finally confronts Tanner and his gang, things do not go as Tanner planned. First, the fallen Lady Gay has learned of Tanner's true nastiness and refuses to take her place at his side. Then Tanner's second in command, El Segundo (Number 2; Barton Heymen) rejects Tanner's command to shoot

Valdez and also releases his Mexican bandidos from any obligation to kill Valdez. So Tanner must face Valdez alone, though he quickly backs down after issuing the customary threat of the defeated: "Next time." Valdez responds that there will be no next time and again asks for the $100 for the widow to bury the father of her child. The film ends at this point, without resolution.

*Valdez Is Coming* is a compact account of the moral reckoning occurring before and after the Mexican Revolution. With the exception of the white man Tanner, the film assembles a cast of tainted characters representative of white, Black, brown, and indigenous origins, all of whom exit the narrative with honor. The key exchange in the film occurs between Valdez and Tanner's enforcer, El Segundo, who respects Valdez as a worthy warrior from the Apache wars, when they fought on the same side. (Such alliances are historically correct.)[8] Their dialogue is classically terse yet dense with meaning:

SEGUNDO: Hunt?
VALDEZ: Apache.
SEGUNDO: When?
VALDEZ: Before I knew better.

In Elmore Leonard's novel, this response is given as: "When they were here."[9] I prefer the book version, which universalizes the erasure of Apache from their lands, instead of the film's rejoinder emphasizing something that Valdez has learned about himself, albeit important. The code of honor shared by both men is born out of shared experience in battle and mutual respect; the fact that they both survived the Indian wars is sufficient evidence of courage and endurance. For them, it represents a superior calling embracing a sense of fairness and justice that ultimately supersedes other moral codes.

The weight of two separate moral universes almost takes the lives of the protagonists in *All the Pretty Horses* (Billy Bob Thornton, 2000), a thematically rich film with origins in a Cormac McCarthy novel.[10] The film version is more exclusively focused on the romance between a US cowboy and a beautiful señorita from a rich family in Mexico. It is Texas in 1949 when two young ranch hands, John Grady Cole (Matt Damon) and his friend Lacey Rawlins (Henry Thomas), head out in search of adventure and fortune in Mexico. You feel the exhilaration as they splash and whoop their way across the Rio Grande. Horses have a place of reverence in the plot, as a symbol of freedom, wealth, and abiding loyalty; but ultimately as a source of tragedy.

John and Lacey find work at the prosperous stud ranch of Don Héctor de la Rocha (Rubén Blades). John's skills with horses finds favor with the Don, but John jeopardizes this connection by romancing Don Héctor's daughter, Alejandra (Penélope Cruz). Alejandra's brittle aunt Doña Alfonsa (Miriam Colón) is determined to extinguish any traces of budding affection between this white Yankee ranch hand and her beautiful aristocratic niece. Yet despite opposition, the two become lovers. When they are discovered, their world crumbles.

As punishment, Alejandra is sent away. Much worse, John and Lacey are imprisoned in Mexico on the basis of concocted charges linking them to an impetuous young American, Jimmy Blevins (Lucas Black), whom they had met on entering Mexico. The three Americans are subsequently transported to a dangerous prison in Saltillo, but before they arrive Blevins is taken off and summarily executed by a vengeful police captain. Once in prison, John and Lacey must fight every day for their lives. They are rescued only when Doña Alfonsa extracts a promise from Alejandra that she will never again see John.

Freed now, Lacey returns to his parents' ranch in Texas, but John Grady Cole begins a self-defined search for atonement and redemption. First, he engineers one more meeting with Alejandra. She still loves him but honors her promise. They see each other one last time, but never again thereafter. John next seeks out and detains the police captain who brutally mistreated and executed Blevins. He intends to bring the captain to justice but is weakened by the hardship of the desert journey. He is rescued by a small group of indigenous people, which coincidentally includes the man with whom they shared a cell in the Saltillo prison and who suffered greatly under the captain's heel. Without discussion, the man and his friends carry off the captain to a place of their own justice. Then John risks his life to recover the three horses that were stolen from him, Lacey, and Blevins. Back in the US, John is arrested as a thief because he has three horses with different brands in his possession. After confessing his troubles to a sympathetic judge (Bruce Dern), the guilt-ridden John is released, with the judge's admonition not to be so hard on himself. John rides on to Lacey's ranch and returns his partner's horse, refusing Lacey's invitation to stay. "This is still a good country," Lacey reminds him. But John, alienated from the world, declares: "Yeah. I know it is. But it ain't my country."

Such declarations about land, place, and homeland are woven throughout the fabric of *All the Pretty Horses*. When the two adventurers optimistically ride out, they giddily fantasize about what Mexico could hold for them. Only later does John discover that crossing over the borderline into Mexico was much simpler than breaching the racial and class lines separating him from his Mexican sweetheart. The erratic loner Blevins justifies all his actions in Mexico by insisting pathetically: "I'm an American," which is no protection against the cruel suffering and death that he endures. Upon his return to the US, John slumps heavily onto the earth in an ecstatic, exhausted communion. A judge tries to absolve him, and his old friend Lacey offers a hand. But something is broken beyond repair in John Grady Cole's heart and mind. This was the enduring legacy that was left to him after crossing over the border.

REMEMBERING: *LONE STAR, THE THREE
BURIALS OF MELQUIADES ESTRADA*

A pivotal film in the shift to post-Western moral tales is *Lone Star* (1995), written, directed, and edited by John Sayles. It is a richly complicated film relating the lives of several closely linked characters in a saga of three generations of white, Black, and brown people in a Texas border town. *Lone Star*'s subjects include racism, incest and miscegenation, corruption and murder, perilous crossings by undocumented migrants, and guilt and memory; it also reveals the many borders (both literal and metaphorical) that configure borderlanders' lives. In short, the film is as complicated as life. *Lone Star* can also be confusing, as the narrative slides without warning into many flashbacks pertaining to different generations. For simplicity, I focus only on two threads in the story.[11]

The hulking monolith at the core of this film is Sheriff Charlie Wade (Kris Kristofferson), a corrupt lawman feared by all townspeople and justifiably regarded as a race-baiting killer by brown and Black residents. (He may not match Hank Quinlan in *Touch of Evil*, but it's a close call.) Charlie Wade's memory still wafts across the town years after he apparently absconded with a large sum of money from the county's coffers. The film opens just as Wade's skeleton, surprisingly, is uncovered in the desert near the town, the victim of a shooting death.

The murder of Charlie Wade ends up on the desk of present-day sheriff Sam Deeds (Chris Cooper), the son of Buddy Deeds (Matthew McConaughey), who had been a trusted deputy of Charlie Wade. Buddy was an overly-strict father to Sam; he also favored a mistress in town, Mercedes Cruz (Míriam Colón), who had crossed into the US without papers many years before. Mercedes had borne Buddy a daughter named Pilar (Elisabeth Peña). Both Sam Deeds and Pilar Cruz shared their childhoods without knowing they also shared a father. Once signs of affection developed between the pair, they were rigorously kept apart by their parents, Buddy and Mercedes. Disconsolate, Sam Deeds moved away but returned much later to take up the job of town sheriff. When he meets Pilar again, they warily rediscover warm feelings for each other.

Sheriff Sam Deeds makes progress in discovering the fate of his predecessor, the tyrannical Charlie Wade. Wade's murder had taken place at a local saloon in Darktown owned by Otis Payne (Ron Canada), a stalwart member of the local Black community. In flashback, Wade is readying to shoot the young Otis in his saloon when a deputy enters and shouts his name: "Charlie Wade!" Shots ring out, and Wade slumps to the ground, dead. The assailant is actually a prominent local businessman who had wearied of Wade's killing ways.

Beyond its violence, racial tensions, and hidden memories, *Lone Star* is a complex suite of minor-key movements that testify to evolving hybridity and diversity in the borderlands, including the invisible personal borders that exist in *Lone Star*'s small town. One day Sheriff Sam Deeds is sitting alongside a white manager of a local bar, who nods in the direction of a Black woman and white man affectionately sharing a booth. He tells Sam that twenty years ago Sheriff Charlie Wade would never have allowed such socializing. The bar owner makes clear that he is happy that Black and

*Figure 12.1. Lone Star* (1995). A successful civilization requires lines of demarcation.

white can sit together in public nowadays, but that he still respects limits. Referring to the present-day racial/ethnic diversity of the town, he insists: "To run a successful civilization, you've got to have your lines of demarcation." He tells Sam that his father, the popular Sheriff Buddy Deeds, understood that "most people don't want their salt and sugar in the same jar," and then ruefully predicts: "You're the last white sheriff, Sam." He offers his bar as a place for the last stand, ironically proclaiming, "Se habla American" (American spoken here).

A Mexican perspective on such social changes is provided when Sheriff Sam crosses over into Mexico on police business. The tone and rhythms in this episode echo those of the bar scene: quiet and flush with bitterness. On the other side, Sam meets the local tire repair guy (El rey de las llanteras, or The Tire King). After pleasantries are exchanged, Sam begins asking some awkward questions. Smiling wryly, the King grabs a soda bottle and draws a line in the dirt, inviting Sam to cross over to his side of the line. When Sam does so, the man cries: "¡Ay qué milagro! [Such a miracle!] You're not the sheriff of nothing no more ... just some Tejano with a lot of questions I don't have to answer." Such quiet assertiveness by a Mexican to an Anglo sheriff lands like a sledgehammer in the film script when compared with contemporary real life on the Texas side of

MORAL TALES, BORDER LAW

the divide, where non-white people are expected to act respectfully in the presence of white people.

In its final movement, *Lone Star* returns to the border that divides Sam and Pilar. Sam explains their shared family history (same father, different mother), and Pilar murmurs that she always felt they were connected. They affirm their intention to stay together. Pilar removes the obvious hurdle blocking their union by revealing that she is no longer able to have children. Seeking further assurance of Sam's willingness to face the stigma connected with the "big sin" of incest, Pilar is defiant: "All that other stuff, all that history. To hell with it, right? Forget the Alamo."

*The Three Burials of Melquiades Estrada* (Tommy Lee Jones, 2005) unfolds episodically in the manner of a biblical tale or epic poem, building cumulatively to a surreal climax that involves the protagonists in crossing the Mexican border in search of a transcendental redemption. Mike Norton (Barry Pepper) is a volatile US Border Patrol officer in a West Texas border town, where he lives in modest circumstances with his bored wife Lou Ann (January Jones). Norton has notably poor judgment; he smashed the nose of a young woman named Mariana (Vanessa Bauche) whom he intercepted while she was crossing illegally into the US. One day, Norton hears rifle shots in the hills and mistakenly thinks he is under attack. He returns fire, killing a local ranch hand, Melquiades Estrada (Julio Cedillo). He hurriedly buries the corpse. His supervisor is not interested in opening up an inquiry, but Estrada is quietly reburied in a local cemetery.

Estrada was a Mexican cowboy who worked at the ranch of Spanish-speaking Pete Perkins (Tommy Lee Jones). Perkins cared little about Melquiades's undocumented status and more about his skill with horses. Pete learns from his watchful married lover, Rachel (Melissa Leo), that Melquiades was shot by Mike Norton. Following a promise he'd made to Melquiades early in their friendship, Pete embarks on an odyssey to bury Melquiades's corpse in his hometown somewhere near Jiménez, Mexico. Pete decides that Norton should atone for his deed and forces him to exhume the body, after which the two men and one corpse set out to search for Jiménez. The journey across the Big Bend Mountains of Texas is long and arduous. (In real life, as I mentioned, Big Bend is an almost impassable jumble of boulders and canyons where the gods reputedly dumped the leftovers once the labor of creating the earth was completed.)

*Figure 12.2.  The Three Burials of Melquiades Estrada* (2005). Two pilgrims and Four Wise Men.

In the first of a series of surreal episodes during their odyssey, Pete and Norton encounter a blind old man living alone in an isolated shack. His son used to bring food, he says, but has not visited in a long while. He shares scraps of food with the visitors, then asks Pete to shoot him, because he fears offending God by taking his own life. Pete declines because then *he* would be the person causing celestial offense by agreeing to the old man's plea. Moving on, Norton is bitten by a rattlesnake, and the pair cross the Rio Grande in search of a woman who can heal Norton. Coincidentally, the *curandera* (folk healer) is Mariana, whose nose Norton had broken when she tried crossing into the US. Once Norton recovers from the snakebite, Mariana exacts her own revenge by smashing his nose with a coffee pot.

The search for Jiménez continues. In a mountain pass, the pilgrims encounter four cowboys with a truck, watching television and eating. Pete asks to buy some food, but the men offer food and provisions as a gift. The television program reminds Norton of his wife, and when he reacts tearfully one of the cowboys offers hard liquor in consolation for "his troubles." These Four Wise Men came bearing gifts of food, alcohol, consolation, and television soap operas for the two weary travelers and a corpse.

Pete is certain they are close to Jiménez. When they come to a ruined house, Pete declares it's the place. They dig a third grave for the corpse of Melquiades Estrada. Pete insists that Norton seek forgiveness from the corpse of Melquiades, firing his gun into the ground as an incentive. Terrified and weeping, Norton begs forgiveness from the corpse. The following morning Pete wakes Norton with a curt: "You can go now." He then adds more softly: "You can keep the horse [pause] . . . son." When Pete rides off alone, Norton calls out: "You gonna be alright?"

*The Three Burials of Melquiades Estrada* has evident foundations in director Tommy Lee Jones's deep affection for West Texas. The film is also unmistakably Christian in its recourse to trial, guilt, and atonement. The epic nature of the pilgrimage is evidenced by clearly marked stations along the way, including the last one, where the travelers receive succor from the wise men. The final call-and-response between Pete and Norton ("You can keep the horse" / "Will you be alright?") represents forgiveness and reconciliation between two warring souls. Their journey is a voyage through purgatory, preparatory to entering heaven somewhere near Jiménez, Mexico.

In an audio commentary on the DVD version of *Three Burials* the director's spiritual intentions are confirmed. On-screen, Norton is unconvinced that they have arrived at Jiménez, but he desperately needs this journey to end. So he acquires a hazy commitment to Pete's pilgrimage, ultimately declaring its success by repeatedly asserting: "You found it, Pete!" At this point in the audio commentary, director Tommy Lee Jones (who earlier had asserted: "Believing is seeing") now confirms his perspective on the point of the pilgrimage: "The kid [Norton] is starting to grow up." January Jones (who plays Lou Ann in the film) adds that Norton finally "gets it."

## LAW AND ORDER: *THE BORDER, TRANSPECOS*

One of the earliest films devoted to the US Border Patrol was *The Border* (1982), directed by Tony Richardson, a highly regarded English filmmaker best known for his Academy Award for Best Director for *Tom Jones* (1963). The film tells of a rookie border patrol officer, Charlie Smith (Jack

Nicholson), who arrives in El Paso with his materialistic wife Marcy (Valerie Perrine). Charlie is a morally upright lawman who gets drawn unwillingly into a human smuggling racket operated by his corrupt superior (Harvey Keitel) in cooperation with crooks on the Mexican side.

*The Border* was ahead of its time in representing depravity and corruption on the US side and including cruelty inside migrant detention centers. The film also made good use of El Paso environments (even though the Rio Grande/Río Bravo appeared to be only a few steps wide and ankle deep). The visually compelling desert landscapes convey the threatening aridity and alienation of border life and forefront the border as a place capable of *generating* alienation, violence, and lawlessness among border dwellers.

Other parts of *The Border* have not aged so well. The wives of border patrol officers come across as one-dimensional cutouts. Regarding his wife Marcy, Charlie tells a friend: "I married a banana." I am not sure if he means that she's squishy, sweet, and nutritious, but it's probably not meant as a compliment. Lost in dreams about financial security and acquiring more stuff, the women come across as witless, braying consumers. Not so Maria (Elpidia Carillo). She is a dark-skinned angel, with flawless beauty and the capacity to bring out the best in Charlie. They are drawn together after Charlie devotes himself to finding Maria's kidnapped child after she had recovered hubcaps stolen off his vehicle by her kid brother. (Seems like a fair exchange, no?) Like the best of white knights, Charlie finds the baby and slays his corrupt boss.

The lives of border patrol officers are brought into much sharper focus in *Transpecos* (Greg Kwedar, 2016). The story covers a day and night in the lives of three US Border Patrol officers who are confronted by moral choices. The film's tone is prefigured in a brief prologue in which a man stops his car in a desolate desert spot, drags a captive out of the trunk, and bludgeons him to death with a shovel. This border is serious business.

Three US Border Patrol agents gather one morning at a remote highway checkpoint. They are Lance Flores (Gabriel Luna), the officer in charge; Lou Hobbs (Clifton Collins Jr.), a cynical veteran with a sixth sense for spotting smugglers; and Davis (Johnny Simmons), a rookie agent with a secret. There is almost no traffic along this two-lane highway, so the trio passes the day idly playing games and telling tall tales. When it's the rookie Davis's turn to motion a car through the checkpoint, Hobbs is suspicious and motions the driver to pull over. Instead the driver attempts to burst through the roadblock; Hobbs shoots him before falling to the ground with a broken arm. Flores then discovers drugs in the trunk of the car and instructs Davis to report the matter to headquarters. Davis refuses the order and instead draws a gun, explaining that he is under cartel orders to allow this vehicle and its cargo of drugs to pass through the checkpoint unhindered. If he does not do this, his entire family will be eliminated.

Hobbs is disgusted by this dereliction of duty. Flores wants to help Davis, so together they hide the contraband car and its dead driver, load the drugs into their patrol vehicle, and set off to deliver the drugs to the cartel. The reluctant Hobbs lies handcuffed in the back of the vehicle. They find the drop-off point, but when Davis opens the back door of the truck, Hobbs unexpectedly jumps out, and in the ensuing tussle Davis shoots Hobbs. At this point, cartel members passively observing the scuffle from afar decide to leave without their delivery. Davis refuses to take Hobbs to a hospital, so Flores drives to a village where he knows a Quiche Maya *curandera* who can help. She predicts that Hobbs will die. Hobbs asks to be taken to a hilltop where he can "hear the wind." Rambling incoherently about Apache and Comanche who fought over this land before borders existed, Hobbes dies. Flores weeps, but he and Davis again resolve to deliver the drugs to the cartel in order to save Davis's family.

Arriving at night at a small-plane hangar, the duo encounter a belligerent old white man who works for Tío (uncle), the ruthless local cartel chief. Flores insists on meeting Tío, but the old man warns: "If you see him, make sure he doesn't come out alive, for all our sakes." Back on the road again, Flores is forced to make an emergency stop. Cartel members shoot Davis and Flores, leaving them for dead. As dawn breaks, Flores regains consciousness, but Davis is dead. A weakened Flores takes his turn to climb a low hill and await death. He is discovered there by a group of cocaine-toting migrants crossing the desert. Their guide offers to stay with Flores until help arrives. At a later debriefing, his commanding officer recommends that Flores should keep silent about the entire incident and offers him reassignment to some distant location. Flores declines, preferring to remain at the Mexican border serving his own community.

Despite flashes of violence and tension, *Transpecos* proceeds in a ru-minative manner that allows the predicament of each protagonist to emerge. As a consequence, the shocking deaths of Hobbs and Davis and the anticipated demise of Flores are keenly felt. Each man has a different sense of honor and loyalty: Davis to his family and Flores to his border patrol brothers and the craft; underneath his practiced cynicism, Hobbes remains devoted to his malleable code of law enforcement and justice. We last encounter Flores instructing a rookie agent in the art of "sign-cutting" (i.e., tracking). The stark desert landscape and the infinite sky reflect the enormity of the border's moral universes (cinematography by Jeffrey Waldron). When the neophyte agent casually brushes a scorpion from his pants leg, Flores warns him to pay attention: "This is the desert. This thing will kill you."[12]

In popular usage, the terms *hybrid* and *hybridization* apply to any pro-cess of mixing or fusion that alters structure and relationships among groups of people, things, plants, animals, and so forth. Nowadays the terms are applied in so many circumstances that mixing appears to be happening everywhere at all times, essentially turning the history and geography of peoples into a forensic exercise in deciphering changing cul-tural practices. Outcomes of hybridization are rarely uniform, usually pro-ceeding in different places and epochs at variable speeds. Certain kinds of geography (especially frontiers and cities) and social process (war, migra-tion, pandemics) are regarded as being especially conducive to rapid change and innovation.

The films chosen for this chapter reveal the small-scale cultural colli-sions and fusions among individuals that arise from modes of interper-sonal communication such as trade, marriage, and beliefs. They outline a diverse litany of everyday behaviors that combine to represent social change and stagnation.

The codes of honor linking Valdez to his rivals are founded in enduring connections born from shared wartime suffering and survival. They have no direct experience of friendship or collaboration, yet assumptions about bravery and valor are sufficient to provide a common reference point that creates trust and respect among them. In *Pretty Horses*, the protagonists share suffering at every stage of their journey in a land (Mexico) with gaping cultural and class differences that are alien to them. The consequent conflicts find expression in alienation from and attachments to land and territory, in which horses take on symbolic moral force and the measure of a man and his future.

The powers of remembering, memory, traditions, and difference are distilled into pure essences in *Lone Star* and *Melquiades Estrada*. In the former, a small border town is riven by often unseen structures of tradition and prejudice, but a series of collisions among the characters' pasts cause revolutions in the foundations of racial attitudes and behaviors and challenges at the intimate level of incest. The latter film addresses the manner of death, grieving, and redemption, again at the personal level. Misunderstandings (and worse) occur when conventions differ across space and time, between countries and generations.

The last group of films in this chapter considers law and morality along the border as represented through agents of the US Border Patrol. In *The Border* and *Transpecos*, agents in the field are always conscious of their code of honor. This pertains to a cherished set of skills and a dedication to service, both of which are almost religiously revered. The narrative in each film is set in motion when adherence to the rules is breached. Crises are typically provoked by violent acts or betrayals. An officer is forced to commit a crime when his family is threatened by narcos; another is repulsed by the levels of corruption that he discovers in his fellow officers. The consequence of breaking the rules is often severe: death or the erasure of self worth. Throughout all this, the land prevails: it warrants respect and nurturing; it provides a place of solitude for dying; and it has agency, it kills.

# 13 Border Walls

When I first began gathering comedy border film titles I was struck by how many of them seemed anchored in satires about true life. This impression was vindicated in the case of Cheech Marin's *Born in East LA* when a friend's father who lived in Tijuana during the 1980s swore that the border life in the film was a very accurate representation of Tijuana at that time. (Coincidentally, both he and Cheech's character in the film were named Rudy.) Further vindication of border film as comic verité arose one evening when my friend Héctor and I drove into a small border town whose name is best forgotten. There was a choice of two motels, and we chose the nicer-looking option. The desk clerk was reluctant to have us as guests, but we persisted. After a while he said bluntly that we'd be better off in another hotel where they did not charge by the hour. Not exactly *Touch of Evil* material, I concede, but we laughingly retold the story later as our narrow escape from borderland vice.

## ABSENT FENCES: *UP IN SMOKE, BORN IN EAST LA*

It seems inevitable that a security-obsessed, post-terrorist Washington, D.C., intent on foisting upon the borderlands an aggressive architectural

191

folly called a "Border Wall" should inspire fantasy-prone border filmmakers. Sometimes these imaginary worlds could be outrageously funny, bitingly satirical, even surreal. These exuberant new films did a genre-busting number on the world of border film.

An early precursor of what was to come is *Cheech and Chong's Up in Smoke* (Lou Adler, 1978), which was totally preoccupied with how the eponymous pair could ensure a steady supply of quality marijuana from Mexico. A key moment establishing the film's untethered mood occurs when an undocumented Mexican in Los Angeles telephones *la migra* to arrange for immigration enforcement agents to raid his home. The family is anxious to visit Tijuana for a wedding party, and they know that *la migra* will deport them for free, "plus you get lunch!" The film maintains this blissed-out aura to its final frames, with an earnest US lawman on camera with a local television news crew at a border crossing point. He is ranting on about how shocked, shocked he is to see the volume of drugs crossing the border. Meanwhile in the background, we observe a van slowly weaving its way through the official port of entry into the US. The vehicle is entirely constructed of marijuana (surely a precursor of contemporary 3-D printing?).

*Up in Smoke* refers to a more innocent, optimistic time before fences and walls became part of the border landscape. By the mid-1990s, the era of Operation Gatekeeper, the first walls and fences had just begun appearing in cities (principally San Diego, Nogales, and El Paso), and border films were taking a sharper, more satirical gaze along the borderline. The most memorable comedy of this period was *Born in East LA* (1987), starring Cheech Marin as Rudy, US born but of Mexican origin, who is living with his crazy-happy family in the East Los Angeles barrio. The film begins with a slapstick scene in the tradition of early silent films and Mexican *sexy-comedias*. Rudy is just starting his day when he spots a voluptuous red-haired woman descending from a bus. She is light-skinned, wears a green dress, and moves like a goddess down the sidewalk. Utterly undone, Rudy jumps in his VW bug and follows her around the neighborhood, sometimes murmuring his admiration. Other men in the neighborhood are comically felled by a glimpse of the goddess, probably because her red-white-green combination is reminiscent of the tricolor Mexican national flag.

One day Rudy is accidentally swept up during an immigration raid at a friend's workplace. He is promptly deported (without money or ID), and

*Figure 13.1. Born in East LA* (1987). Rudy the Chicano in Tijuana teaches the nuances of being Mexican to Asian border crossers.

the rest of the film is the story of his struggle to return to the US. Once in Tijuana, Rudy is evidently a stranger in a strange land. He finds himself in jail, where his protestations "Don't touch me! I'm an American citizen!" are met with scorn from a demented jailer named Feo (translates as ugly). After release, Rudy accepts any job that comes his way in order to survive, including touting for patrons outside a local bar, hawking oranges on a street corner, and selling fake green cards in the "Pollo Lounge," where undocumented migrants (known as *pollos*, or chickens) prepare for illegal crossing into the US. He teaches classes to Asian immigrants on how to walk and talk like Mexicans. (Two basic rules: 1. Keep repeating: "Whaaa Sappenin?," and 2. cuss a lot.)

Time passes, and Rudy's efforts to cross back into the US are unsuccessful. He settles into steady work, grows fond of a woman from El Salvador, and starts a band called The New Huevos Rancheros.[1] He proves to be a resourceful survivor in Tijuana's informal economy. He is also generous, impulsively giving away all his oranges to a hungry woman and child and handing over his ticket for a border-crossing van to an elderly couple (who could afford only one ticket), enabling them to cross together. The pressure of waiting to return to the US intensifies until Rudy is joined by what appears to be the entire cast of the film, who together rush the borderline, intent on reaching *el norte*. On the film soundtrack, Neil Diamond's anthem "[Coming to] America" swells up in support of their dash for freedom. Two hapless border patrol agents guarding the fenceless crossing are overrun by joyful pilgrims.

The film ends at a rambunctious Cinco de Mayo celebration in East LA. An anonymous manhole cover opens, and out pops Rudy, followed by his gang of Asian students of Mexican culture, each vigorously mimicking Mexicans. They strut and smile at the cops, wearing bandannas and exclaiming: "Go Raiders!" and "Ay te watcho!" Nobody bothers them, and everyone joins the party. This time the high-volume soundtrack plays the triumphant "Born in East LA," a revised version of Bruce Springsteen's famous "Born in the USA," sung by The Boss himself.

The farcical humor in *Born in East LA* is way over the top and stuffed with stereotypes: heartless immigration bullies, inept border patrol buffoons, a visiting country bumpkin, and so on. Just like *Up in Smoke*, *Born in East LA* has its origins in simpler (unfenced) times. Nevertheless, the films are acutely self-aware in their representation of migrant lives, including both the trials awaiting new arrivals in the US and the fate of deportees returned to Mexico. They also draw attention to the physical landscapes of the border: the infrastructure of official ports of entry and the sites of informal crossings, which for the most part still lacked walls and fences.[2]

## ELECTRIFYING FENCES: *A DAY WITHOUT A MEXICAN*

*A Day without a Mexican* (2004) highlights the significance of the border by closing it. This was a debut feature film for director Sergio Arau, son of Alfonso Arau, famous for *Como agua para chocolate*. It focuses on the vital contributions made by Mexicans and people of Mexican origin in California. Referring to the ubiquitous but often unacknowledged presence of Mexicans in the US, a character poses the question that lies at the heart of the film: "How do you make the invisible visible? You take it away."

*A Day without* begins as a thick fog descends over the California-Mexico border, cutting off all communications beyond the state line.

The following morning, all Mexicans except one have disappeared from California. Thirteen million people have simply vanished. Crops remain unharvested, streets are empty, gardens and homes are unkempt, and stores are closed. A forlorn leaf blower rests abandoned on a sidewalk. As the state grinds to a halt, a black market in fresh fruits and vegetables swiftly emerges. Later, martial law is proclaimed. The remaining Latina, Lila Rodríguez (Yareli Arizmendi), is believed to hold the secret to the "L-factor," a vaccine to counter the disappearance of Latinos.

The film's humor favors wordplay and sight gags. The credits solemnly declare: "No Mexicans were harmed during the making of this film." As the crisis deepens, Anglo Californians begin organizing "Come Back Amigos" events to entice Mexicans to return. When a migrant is asked "Tiene papeles?" (Do you have papers?), he replies, "No, tengo hambre." (No, I'm hungry. The joke works better in Spanish.) The film's sharp satire is interrupted by captions announcing the facts about the Mexican presence in California: the numbers of Mexican farmworkers and domestic workers in the state, how many of the LA Dodgers baseball team are of Mexican origin, and the like. This quasi-documentary approach to fact checking demonstrates the dependence of California's economy on imported labor as well as the fact that undocumented migrants in the US are not only from Mexico. In the jargon of *la migra*, these people are OTMs, that is, Other Than Mexicans.

Suddenly the fog disperses, as mysteriously as it arrived. Mexicans begin reappearing. Border patrol officers, who had quickly realized that their jobs were jeopardized by the absence of border crossers to chase, celebrate the return of their clientele. Newscasts show street signs proclaiming: "Welcome border crossers." California slowly returns to normal. Media pundits intone that the fog was nature's way of reminding the two countries that "our destinies are irrevocably intertwined."

The central conceit in *A Day without a Mexican* is its metaphysical gesture of closing the border with an impenetrable and inexplicable fog bank. Its cause is never explained, but the effects of the closure are immediate and disastrous, causing all aspects of life and work in California to come to a halt. The film may be fantasy, but its prediction is entirely true: take away the Mexicans and California collapses, and the US too. When the US-Mexico border was sealed after 2016 by anti-immigrant legislation and punitive policing, the absence of imported labor brought many sectors of the US economy to the point of collapse (especially agriculture).

WALLS: *MACHETE*

*Machete* (Robert Rodríguez and Ethan Maniquís, 2010) conjures up the moment when exploited immigrants from Mexico rise up in revolt. *Machete* is a typical Rodríguez smorgasbord of sex and violence laced with plentiful heapings of warped humor. The film's prologue introduces Machete Cortez, a Mexican federal police officer played by the immortal Danny Trejo. After a raid goes horribly wrong, Machete is left for dead by drug lord Rogelio Torrez (Steven Seagal, a laugh-out-loud miscasting), who had previously murdered Machete's wife.

Recovered and exiled in the US, Machete ekes out an existence at day-labor sites in Texas. One hungry day, he is offered credit at a taco truck operated by Luz (Michelle Rodríguez), who, under the name Shé, secretly leads a multiracial resistance group known as The Network. Machete is recognized as a former Mexican cop by a glamorous ICE agent, Sartana Rivera (Jessica Alba). He is also being targeted by a crooked Anglo businessman, Michael Booth (Jeff Fahey), who is on the payroll of drug lord Torrez. Booth coerces Machete into assassinating State Senator John McLaughlin (Robert de Niro), who is rabidly anti-immigrant and an advocate of electrifying the border fence to stop the "infestation" by Mexican laborers. In reality, Booth intends to shoot Machete and blame him for attacking McLaughlin, thereby boosting McLaughlin's chances of reelection. The Mexican drug lord, Torrez, also backs McLaughlin's plan since it would make things easier for his cartel to manage its exports through the border ports of entry (precisely the situation that operates in real life).

Machete escapes Booth's trap at the assassination but is badly injured. Luz shelters him, and we are introduced to The Network in the form of two nurses who care for Machete. A group of border vigilantes led by the evil Von Jackson (Don Johnson) declare war on Machete and all who harbor him. One of his first victims is Luz, whom he cruelly shoots in the eye. The Network and vigilantes prepare for war and intense sloganeering. Agent Sartana switches her allegiance from ICE to The Network, telling her boss: "There's the law, and there's what's right. I'm going to do what's right." She recruits others to the cause, chanting a favorite slogan of Mexican and Chicano demonstrators: "We didn't cross the border. The border crossed us!" As the conflict escalates, Machete's priest brother (Cheech Marin) is crucified in his own church by the Anglo enforcer Booth. In response Machete kidnaps Booth's wife and daughter, June and April (Alicia Marek and Lindsay Lohan). Before they leave, Machete records a video of himself partying with the two naked women in the family pool, leaving the video for Booth to find.

Now the revolution flares up, and director Rodríguez's anarchy is the first thing to be liberated. A fleet of low riders moves to attack the vigilante compound, called the new Alamo by Von Jackson. An entire universe of undocumented workers storms the compound: nurses, domestic workers, farm laborers, dishwashers, supermarket shelf stockers, gardeners, mechanics, janitors, and students. Even Shé/Luz—not dead after all!—joins in, wearing a fetching eye patch accessorized by copious military-grade weaponry. Machete engages in swordplay; Torrez demonstrates a deep knowledge of truly absurd samurai poses before toppling ignominiously to defeat. Later that night, with the revolutionaries' victory secured, the corrupt Senator McLaughlin is fleeing along the border fence disguised as a Mexican farmhand. Ironically, he is intercepted by a vengeful rump of Von Jackson vigilantes, who see him as just one more illegal. They open fire, leaving McLaughlin's corpse draped over the electrified border fence he had labored so mightily to authorize.

In the film's calm climax, a solitary Machete is seen leaving town (as all heroes must do once they have fought the good fight). His motorcycle is pulled over by the flashing lights of a police vehicle. It is driven by Sartana, the former ICE agent, now a Woman Warrior for The Network. She offers Machete a green card, promising that he can now be a "real person." Machete growls: "Why should I be a real person, when I'm already a myth?" Sartana considers this for a moment, then changes tack: "Where will you go?" "Everywhere," is Machete's iconoclastic reply. Sartana fetchingly hoists herself onto the chopper's passenger seat, and they drive off together into the night. (It's a perfect ending.)

*Machete*'s violence, sex, nudity, outrageous stereotyping, foul language, crude humor, and driving music are all basic ingredients in Robert

Rodríguez's scrambled filmmaking.[3] In *Machete*, they combine to produce a rapid-fire film offering electrified fences, corrupt politicians who mistreat migrants for personal gain, racist vigilantes who freely assassinate migrants, cartels that profit from migrant miseries, the exploitation of undocumented migrants working in the US, and revolution in pursuit of justice and equality. Rodríguez even reprises the Battle of the Alamo, recapitulating the significance of the land ceded to the US after the 1846–48 war. Today efforts to reassert Mexican and Chicano presences in these long-ago conquered territories is sometimes referred to as a peaceful *reconquista* (reconquest).

## VIRTUAL WALLS: *SLEEP DEALER*

In the expanding worlds of border film, Alex Rivera's *Sleep Dealer* (2008) is an astonishing departure into the realm of science fiction. A low-budget US-Mexico production, the film was a decade in the making and won two awards when it opened at the Sundance Film Festival. It adopted the conventions of sci-fi to offer a penetrating critique of emerging technologies, globalization, giant corporations, ubiquitous surveillance, the widening chasm between rich and poor, and privatization of life's essentials. Rivera wrote the screenplay with David Riker, and they invented a vivid new imaginary and vocabulary for their border dystopia.

On his father's farm in rural Oaxaca, Memo (Luis Fernando Peña) longs to move to Tijuana. The family farm once had access to plentiful water, but now water is contained in a nearby fenced-off dam, and people are obliged to pay a private US-based corporation for their daily water needs. Distressed because their traditional way of life is no longer possible, Memo's father asks his son: "Is our future a thing of the past?" Ironically, whenever he has free time Memo disappears into the tech world, hacking into communications on the other side. His virtual presence attracts the attention of security forces in the US, and Memo's farm is identified as the location of hackers, labeled "aqua-terrorists." A drone missile piloted remotely from the US by Rudy (Jacob Vargas) is dispatched to destroy the farm, but in so doing it also kills Memo's father. A distraught Memo seeks refuge in Tijuana, where the border is completely sealed except to authorized personnel. Signs on the US side warn: "Enter Mexico at your own risk." But the word on the streets is "The border is closed, but people still come."

*Figure 13.2. Sleep Dealer* (2008). Cybracero bodies perform in Mexico, but their labor is executed in the US.

Migrants arrive in Tijuana without any expectation of crossing the border to find work. Instead Memo seeks employment as a "node worker" in the new global economy. A "coyotek" can get you across the line or introduce you to "teki" (for tequila) in a bar that features nude female dancers referred to as "live node girls." Older people are nostalgic about the days when migrant workers crossed the border on foot, but Memo yearns to be implanted with nodes connecting him to robots that execute tasks in the US while his body remains in Tijuana. It's a perfect solution for US employers who want "all the work . . . without the workers." A beautiful, mysterious young woman named Luz (Leonor Varela) helps Memo to get his node implants on the black market. In true noir tradition, she has her own reasons for helping him, which involve poaching his memories for use in her creative work.

Memo gets a job in a factory called Cybracero S.A de C.V. (the suffix is equivalent to "Inc." in the US). Its name is an ingenious play on two words: *cyber*, meaning the virtual world, and *bracero*, referring to the mid-twentieth-century Bracero Program, which permitted contract workers from Mexico to enter the US legally during and after World War II. Memo is ecstatic: "Finally, I could connect my nervous system to the other system—the global economy." We catch glimpses of the factories, known as "sleep dealers," where workers fueled by teki are arrayed in lines hooked into machines like exhausted marionettes. Later, we encounter groups of discarded node workers, blind and dying, living rough at the abandoned urban edge. Memo's future is grim, but he knows that.

Then Rudy arrives in Tijuana. He is the now guilt-ridden drone pilot who played a part in the death of Memo's father. Together they conspire successfully to destroy the dam in Oaxaca, after which Rudy heads south deep into Mexico, as far as possible from the border and the US military and corporations. Memo quits his node job and is last seen carrying water jugs and tending to his own *milpa* (a small vegetable patch) adjacent to the border wall. The *milpa* represents a sentimental link to his father's farm, but it is also indicative of Memo's radical move off the grid, a personal Declaration of Independence. The border remains a place of potential and resistance, even if crossing into the US is no longer an option. A screen caption announces that the border wall is "on the edge of everything."

The harsh yet seductive world imagined in *Sleep Dealer* is littered with bisected bodies. The days when people crossed through Tijuana to *el norte* are long gone. The new world splits people in two: Memo's body (his corporeal self) resides in Mexico, powering robotic labor in the US; his mind (or virtual self) is subordinated to the controllers of the global metaverse. If capitalists are said to control the *modes* of production, in *Sleep Dealer*'s imagination the digital elites control the future's global *nodes* of production. The vast reserve of humanity exists as unconnected slaves confined in digital deserts, passive consumers at best. International boundary lines may still mark the territorial limits of former nation-states, but their primary purpose in the metaverse is to quarantine and control the have-nots in countries such as Mexico. Yet despite the extreme concentrations of wealth and power, authoritarianism, and sundering of mind and body, *Sleep Dealer* still imagines borders as the edge of everything, existing as liminal, in-between places where autonomy and resistance remain possibilities.

Comedy is good. Provoked by the harsh realities of turn-of-the-century political economies, new border films broke conventions and embarked on inventive explorations. The comedy-fantasy films of the early twenty-first century conveyed an urgent topicality (walls and fences), novel themes (deportations and social unrest), and diversification into hitherto neglected genres (comedy, political satire, and fantasy science fiction). An overarching theme linking all these films is the diversity of human connectedness across the borderline.

In *Born in East LA*, connectivity is expressed through family; in *A Day without a Mexican*, it's a matter of economic integration and interdependence. In a short feature describing the making of *A Day without*, scriptwriters Sergio Guerrero and Yareli Arizmendi remembered the first time they crossed over into Mexico to begin filming. They were amazed by the degree of connectedness between the two sides. It was impossible to pinpoint where the US stopped and Mexico began. According to Sergio: "We were already in Mexico before we realized it." And Yareli: "There was only the wall, and in parts no wall. The space between was a no-man's land."[4]

Over the years, the relevance and impudence of Robert Rodríguez's cinematic imagination have thankfully remained undiminished. But mistakes sometimes happen. Rodríguez followed *Machete* with *Machete Kills* in 2013. It was a weak mish-mash featuring Danny Trejo in outer space. *Machete Kills* had only one line worth recalling: "You want world peace? Tear down that wall!" But it's worth recalling that Rodríguez has helped tear down many other walls during his film career. According to Danny Trejo, Rodríguez has "done more for Latinos in film than any other director."[5]

*Sleep Dealer* offers a chilling vision in which Mexico and the US are physically separated, but individuals remain linked through nodal connections, and nations favor digital authoritarianism, surveillance, and violence. Yet in its final scene, *Sleep Dealer* imagines active resistance alive on the Mexican side, on the edge of everything. The film deserves a place of honor in any catalog of border films for its clever contemplation of the borderlands' future.[6]

Incidentally, I want to bookmark a short note about that future (the subject of chapter 17). The neglected topic of the cross-border consequences of environmental and climatic change was raised unforgettably in a short scene from *The Day after Tomorrow* (Roland Emmerich, 2004). Since their country is being transformed by intense cold, panicked US citizens are shown storming the border with Mexico, seeking refuge in its warmer territories. It's a delightful irony. *Sleep Dealer* reminded us about water wars, but there is plenty of room for much more attention to these topics.

# 14 The Mexican Dream/ El Sueño Mexicano

## MEXICAN DREAM/AMERICAN DREAM

Asked to define the "Mexican Dream" of a typical family, a prominent public figure in Mexico, Jorge Castañeda, suggested it was to "find a well-paying job, improve their income level slightly over time, eventually obtain papers, bring their family or create a family . . . in the United States. And then later on in life . . . maybe go home to Mexico to retire."[1] One Mexican couple, preparing to cross over at Tijuana, expressed their wish succinctly: "Our dream is to cross the border. To work and earn money to be able to live well with the family that we will have."[2] Such aspirations toward self-improvement obviously apply to Mexicans who have no desire to leave their homeland.

Mexican Dreams are also held by non-Mexicans. I used to spend a lot of time at Estero Beach south of Ensenada, where my in-laws had a small oceanside trailer home, just like a hundred or so other US citizens. The accommodations were conversions of small trailer homes, since in those days Mexican law prevented foreigners from owning coastal properties. The expats were mostly retirees or military veterans interested in stretching their pensions and savings in a Baja locale where the cost of living was lower than in the US. These exiles possessed a variety of skills that they often traded, offering help with boat and car maintenance in return for legal advice, or metalworking for fresh vegetables.

Some migrants make longer, hazardous journeys to Mexico in search of refuge and opportunity. One such Haitian migrant, Ustin Pascal Dubouisson, described how he traveled across ten countries by bus, by boat, and on foot to get from Brazil to the US-MX border, initially with the intention of crossing into the US: "When I first got to Tijuana, I couldn't wait to leave. The city seemed loud and chaotic, and I didn't speak a word of Spanish. . . . I got a job washing dishes at a restaurant, and then a different job at a tire factory. I applied to Mexican authorities for a humanitarian visa, and then was able to get a four-year work visa."

Two years later, Dubouisson was making a life for himself in Tijuana: "I know most people migrating to the U.S. have their minds set on the 'American Dream,' but I have come to realize there's a 'Mexican Dream,' too."[3] He was among several thousand Haitians who came to Tijuana hoping to cross over from Mexico before the US abruptly sealed the border crossing in 2017. The Mexican government offered visas that helped many find work in Tijuana. "It's the Mexican dream for many of them," said one local man who employed Haitians at his car wash. "Mexico has given them an opportunity. Mexico has opened up and let them achieve their dreams."[4]

There are also intergenerational effects of migration that are often overlooked. In a poignant essay, Ecuadorian Karla Cornejo Villavicencio recalled her parents' sacrifices to provide her with their version of the American Dream, which involved "an education, a New York accent, a life that can better itself." But *her* version of the dream is "seeing [her parents] age with dignity, being able to help them retire, and keeping them from being pushed onto train tracks in a random hate crime."[5] Parents too feel a sense of alienation as their offspring become more distant as time passes and later generations become unrecognizable to the first.

The "American Dream" is a phrase with many shades of meaning. In its original formulation, the American Dream referred to a set of ideals pertaining to the nation's founding principles: liberty, justice, equality, and all that. By the end of the nineteenth century, the term had absorbed a more collective sense of the national values presumably shared by most Americans. The dream also became associated with a call for "America

First," echoing contemporary isolationist sentiments that rejected US involvement in World War I. During the Great Depression of the 1930s and the years preceding World War II, the American Dream as it referred to the common good figured prominently in public consciousness.[6] As time passed, the American Dream began acquiring a more specific reference to immigrants and immigration. The US gained a reputation as a haven of freedom and opportunity for certain categories of newcomers from around the world, who were offered the chance to merge into the great American melting pot. Many other manifestations of the dream have emerged over time to muddy interpretations of the term, including Dr. Martin Luther King Jr.'s famous oration "I have a dream," as well as regional variations such as "California Dream."

## FIRST CUT: *THE MEXICAN DREAM*

*The Mexican Dream* (2003) is a US production of twenty-eight minutes written and directed by Gustavo Hernández Pérez. It's the story of Ajileo Barajas (Jesús Chuy Pérez), who dreams of becoming a Hollywood actor in order to give his family a better life. He leaves Mexico to cross the border disguised as a woman, in the belief that if he is captured, he will be treated like a lady by the border patrol. The film interweaves the telling of Ajileo's border crossing and his subsequent career in Hollywood.

His journey begins easily; crossing the line involves no more than pulling aside a few strands of wire fencing. But after his coyote abandons him, Ajileo runs into two border patrol officers. Recalling the most important English words taught to him by the coyote, Ajileo approaches them and announces: "Thank god. Excuse me." Still wearing a long dress that resembles a wedding gown, he then turns and walks away. From a distance, his elongated figure resembles a dust devil or a spirit floating on the waves of heat rising from the desert. As Ajileo floats away, the words of his planned Academy Award acceptance speech echo plaintively on the soundtrack.

The border agents are puzzled. The more senior of them, an Anglo guy, slowly voices the facts of the matter: "That's a man, dressed as a woman, crossing the desert, at nine o'clock in the morning." The younger agent, a Latino, replies gravely: "No, sir. That's *La Llorona*." (He refers to a famous

Mexican legend of a crying woman who drowned her children when she discovered that her husband had been unfaithful. In anguish, she then drowned herself but was destined to spend eternity searching for the children.) Not understanding the reference, the Anglo officer asks: "Is there any way we can stop her?" The young Latino replies with finality: "It's impossible." The peak of Ajileo's film career is when he dresses as a clown for a television commercial and gets a pie thrown in his face.

*The Mexican Dream* is a modest film with outsize importance because mystical notions of the Mexican Dream surface early as part of Ajileo's journey. To be sure, he is driven to cross by ambition to become a Hollywood actor, but his Mexican self and aspirations become folded into deeper psychological gestures. Ajileo dresses quite formally as a woman (in a wedding dress?) to cross the border, trusting in the kindness of strangers. He is greeted with sexual crudities from his coyote but treated courteously by the awed border patrol officers. When he is mistaken for the Crying Woman; his story is elevated to legend and the supernatural. But Ajileo has *two* dreams simultaneously: in his Mexican self, he imagines himself an ethereal woman worthy of respect, even reverence, but his American Dream of Hollywood success is extinguished when that cream pie is thrown in his face. The lesson from *The Mexican Dream* is that even modest Mexican Dreams may incorporate mysticism, legend, and deep spiritual longing, together with ghosts and dilemmas of self-identity, along with a practical desire for material success.

## EL SUEÑO PRIVADO/PRIVATE DREAMING: *MI QUERIDO TOM MIX*

The dreams of older people are not the same as those of the young. *Mi querido Tom Mix* (Carlos García Agraz, 1991; My dear Tom Mix, ) is the story of an aging woman and man who dream of one more adventure in their lives, shared with a special person. Joaquina (Ana Ofelia Murguía) plays the woman who is living out her days in a small Zacatecas town during the 1930s. Never married, she now shares the home of her nephew, the town doctor, Evaristo (Manuel Ojeda), and his chilly, ambitious wife Antonia (Mercedes Olea).

The small household is joined for the summer by Evaristo's young nephew, Felipe (Damián García Vásquez), who has an enduring love for his grandmother, Joaquina, calling her Queri, his childhood name for her. They spend much time together, overseen by the punctilious Antonia. Joaquina escapes from daily drudgery into the world of a silent movie cowboy, Tom Mix, at the local cinema, the Cinematógrafo El Edén. She daydreams about Tom and writes admiring letters often seeking his advice.

Joaquina's life is radically upended by two events. The first is when a handsome drifter, Domingo (Federico Luppi), arrives in town from Yuma, Arizona. We see him practicing his skills with lasso and gun belt; Domingo has a past closer to Tom Mix than to a stable hand. The second disruption occurs when a violent gang arrives in a convertible car (shades of *El automóvil gris*!). The leader, Pancho Largo, dresses like a fastidious fashion plate, but the gang wantonly shoots the cinema's piano player and destroys a local emporium. Hearing the disturbances, Domingo prepares himself for battle, gazing threateningly into a mirror and practicing the immortal threat: "Are *you* looking at me?" Repeated: "Are you looking at *me*?" (Neither version approaches the de Niro performance in *Taxi Driver*.) As Domingo exits, the door handle breaks off in his hand, so he fails to join the fight on time.

Matters deteriorate. The town mayor and guards have disappeared. Dr. Evaristo organizes a civil defense unit. Joaquina writes to Tom Mix asking him to help the town. During the next raid Joaquina, Felipe, and Domingo are hiding in the cinema, planning an Alamo-like defense of El Edén. During a lull in the impending battle, Joaquina listens to Domingo's cowboy philosophy: "I come from far away, [and] I don't know [where I'm going]." Joaquina has no time to respond to such overtures of Western seduction because she is unceremoniously kidnapped by Pancho Largo's gang. With Joaquina aboard, the gang drives out of town, followed by Domingo on horseback, Mr. Fong (the town's Chinese laundryman) on a bicycle, and Dr. Evaristo with a posse. Domingo shoots some of the villains while Joaquina bashes her kidnappers with a purloined film canister containing Tom Mix's next episode. Finally, Domingo brings the car to a halt and squares off, Sergio Leone-style, against the gang leader, Pancho Largo. There is much lethal eyeballing, the guns thunder, and Pancho pitches forward, dead.

*Figure 14.1. Mi querido Tom Mix* (1991). In search of one last adventure.

With adolescent enthusiasm, Joaquina and Domingo agree to share one final adventure. Towing a cow through a foggy dawn, they depart the town unnoticed, except for the boy Felipe, who stands on a small hilltop plaintively calling his grandmother's name, "Queri!" (closely matching Brandon de Wilde's cry to the departing Alan Ladd at the end of *Shane* [1953]).

*Mi querido Tom Mix* is catnip for those old enough to remember or cherish the silent serials. (I mostly read the comics version. I even drew a neat pencil portrait of Tom Mix, though I didn't mail it to him.)[7] At its heart, the film is concerned with everyday dreams that exceed personal boundaries. The aging Domingo and Joaquina are still moved by thoughts of adventure and passion and still have the energy to realize them. Antonia (aka Lady Macbeth, forever in my mind) persists in her dream of moving Dr. Evaristo to a bigger town in search of more wealth and status, even though he is already fulfilling his Mexican Dream as a small-town doctor. The cheerful laundryman Mr. Fong has chosen to remain in Mexico and send his wages back to a wife in China, describing the compact succinctly: "I'm here. She's there. The kids are fine. Everyone's happy." Felipe, the nephew, loves his family and dreams of horses and learning to fly.

## EL SUEÑO PORTÁTIL/PORTABLE DREAM:
### *EL JARDÍN DEL EDÉN*

The dream of a *frontera portátil*, or portable border, involves physical travel or virtual mobility in pursuit of an ambition or goal. It is intimately linked to place, which acts as a condition that activates departure through the appeal of a destination. *El Jardín del Edén* (María Novaro, 1994; The Garden of Eden) is concerned with six individuals who journey to the border city of Tijuana searching for something significant in their lives. The first of three women to arrive is Jane (Renée Coleman) from the US, who is trying to reconnect with her brother but also seeking adventure and experiences that could furnish material for a writing career. Second is Serena (Gabriela Roel), a Mexican widow seeking to start a fresh life with her three children. And last is Elizabeth, or Liz (Rosario Sagrav), a Chicana artist in search of her roots in Mexico.

The three male protagonists also possess ambitions they hope to advance in Tijuana's Garden of Eden. Frank (Joseph Culp) is Jane's American brother, a solitary creature who appears already to have realized a Mexican Dream of refuge and solitude. Julián (Alan Ciangherotti) is Serena's eldest child, an almost-teenager still grieving for his lost father and struggling to find his adolescent place in the world. Third is Felipe (Bruno Bichir), a young Mexican man seeking to cross into the US in search of material success; now in Tijuana, only the border fence lies between him and his dream.

*El Jardín* is set in a time when there were few fences and the border was relatively easy to cross. There's even a small pop-up rest stop where waiting migrants can eat at the Comedor el ilegal (The Illegal Diner, much like the Pollo Lounge in *Born in East LA*). From the US side, border patrol officers watch a kid's baseball game in Mexico, applauding when a little guy hits a home run. Jane is attractive and outgoing, generous with her money and affection. Through her we meet border jumper Felipe on the roadside. He repairs her flat tire for her and gets a lobster lunch in return. He recognizes that Jane is maybe a little crazy, but after all, she's American. He shows her the place where would-be migrants wait for the right moment to cross the line. Jane tries on this notion herself, the feeling that she too is awaiting *her* moment. Felipe's moment arrives when he attempts a nighttime border crossing, but he is robbed and brutally beaten on the Mexican side. The following morning, Julián finds Felipe and brings him to Jane's apartment, where she nurses him through a long period of convalescence.

Meanwhile Liz the artist is lonely and dispirited, especially when she drives past a Tijuana hotel called El Edén. She confesses to Jane that she came to Tijuana to find space to hear her own voice, but it was not easy for her. Liz and Jane become friends, but Jane has less success with her estranged brother Frank. When they meet, Frank refers scornfully to Jane's writerly ambitions, her poor Spanish, and her childish enthusiasms that quickly evaporate.

Felipe is by now living with Jane, and they are joined by Julián most of the time. Felipe offers prayers at a shrine to Juan Soldado (the patron saint of border crossers). That night, Jane drives north across the border with Felipe and Julián hidden in the trunk of her car. On the US side, they check into the Garden of Eden Motel. Julián runs away, jealous of the attention that Jane devotes to Felipe and uncomfortable with their growing intimacy. Searching for Julián, Jane and Felipe discover a community of people of Mixtec origin in the midst of a funeral. Jane adds money for a collection to return the deceased's body to Mexico. Felipe berates her: "We may be poor, but we don't need your charity!" (Which is truly bizarre, coming from someone who has lived off Jane's largesse throughout the film.) Next morning, Felipe leaves without waking Jane. All three are now cast out from the American Garden of Eden.

The film wraps by recapitulating the fates of the six salvation seekers. Back in Tijuana, Serena's search for her missing son Julián has been successful. She was (unexpectedly) helped in this search by Jane's hermit brother Frank. Serena tries calling Frank to thank him, but Frank moves outside to avoid hearing her, turning his attention as usual to the ocean. Jane returns to Tijuana but is moving on to Oaxaca, much farther from the US. At Jane's departure, Liz announces that she has found some roots and intends to stay in Tijuana. Felipe crosses the border on a second attempt but is eventually apprehended and deported back to Mexico. He joins Julián on the beach at Playas de Tijuana, watching a pod of dolphins streak northward. Julián and Felipe plan on going north together in pursuit of a now-shared American Dream.

*Figure 14.2.  El Jardín del Edén* (1994). Felipe at the shrine of Juan Soldado, patron saint of migrants.

## EL SUEÑO PROFUNDO/DEEP DREAMING:
### *BAJO CALIFORNIA*

There is a class of people who engage with Mexico's deep past, the *Mexico profundo*. Among the most mystical of deep-dreaming border films is *Bajo California: El límite del tiempo* (Carlos Bolado Muñoz, 1998; Below California: The edge of time).[8] The film's poster described it as "Un alegoría del renacimiento físico y espiritual" (an allegory of physical and spiritual rebirth). The film concerns a pilgrimage made by Damián (Damián Alcázar), a Chicano artist living in Los Angeles with his pregnant wife. He has been racked with uncertainty and guilt since he collided with a woman while driving his car. Unable to locate the body and haunted by not knowing her fate, Damián decides to cross the San Ysidro border and drive south from Tijuana into central Baja California. A recorded message from his wife is supportive of his mysterious decision to undertake this pilgrimage.

Damián drives south along Baja California's coastal highway. He encounters a lone traveler wearing a red cloak and mentions that he is heading for San Francisco de la Sierra, a mountainous region in central Baja formerly occupied by ancient tribes. The man asks if he's going to *las pin-turas* (the cave paintings in the region).[9] Symbolically, they exchange hats, and henceforward Damián starts seeing things differently. He burns his truck and possessions and continues his pilgrimage on foot, creating art-works along his route (such as reconstructing a shattered whale skeleton and building his own "spiral jetty" formation out of found shells). On a dusty ranch, he meets Arce (Jesús Ochoa), who will act as his guide and eventually become his savior.

Arce first helps Damián find the ruined house of his grandmother, where he prays and leaves flowers in her memory. Then the two men begin the taxing ascent into the Sierras, Arce on horseback but Damián on foot. They confront enormous vertical cliffs that were the homes of the ancients, where the first group of paintings is etched in caves on the cliff face. Damián leaves his own handprint on a rock face, and at night they witness an auspicious sign: a large, slow-moving meteor. Damián voices his guilt associated with the car accident.

The stresses of the long walk, both physical and mental, take a toll on Damián. One day he blunders into a cactus patch and gets bitten by a rattlesnake. They hurriedly return to the ranch, where Damián succumbs to dreams and hallucinations featuring whales, his pregnant wife, *las pinturas*, the car accident, and fractured border crossings. After Damián recovers, the two men offer thanks to the mountains for having spared them. He gratefully embraces Arce and begins his return journey north-ward. Once again he meets the red-cloaked stranger, and they re-exchange hats. Later in Santa Rosalía, Damián picks up a letter from his wife that includes a photograph of his new daughter. He begins walking homeward with revitalized energy and determination.

Damián the searcher is an unsympathetic witness. We encounter him at a low point in his life, fleeing LA and abandoning his pregnant wife after a mysterious car accident. He decides to atone and revive himself at the secret domain of the cave paintings in central Baja. He gives up his worldly possessions and exchanges hats with another pilgrim, both actions involving altered perceptions. Many early scenes are without di-alogue, heightening the intensity of Damián's experiences. He indulges in the magic of dreams, maps, meteor, and stars, and creates art as a ritual of expression and self-discovery (the whale skeleton, the spiral jetty, and his handprint). Ultimately, he prostrates himself before the soaring cliffs and ancestral murals, seemingly the only physical and spiritual landscapes capable of accommodating the scale of his existential conundrum. And he dreams of the sea, home to the iconographic whale and its analog, Damián's pregnant wife. He thanks the mountains for sparing him during his trials. We never witness Damián's homecoming and remain ignorant of his future. This uncertainty seems appropriate; *Bajo California* is about a man's journey across the frontiers of time in order to discover his place and how to live his days.

## EXCAVATING THE CORE MEXICAN DREAM

The young Werner Herzog went filming in Africa during 1968 and 1969 and came away with long tracking shots of the Sahara and Sahel Deserts taken from the roof of a VW van. Later he decided to incorporate the Maya creation myth, *Popul Vuh*, into the first section of his film *Fata Morgana* (1971), preferring its primordial and chaotic sentiments to Christian concepts of harmony, equilibrium, and beauty. Fragments are quoted (and subtitled) over a succession of images of desert mirages and landscapes. The effect is hypnotic, fresh, and cleansing.[10]

> This is an account of how all was in suspense, all calm, in silence; all motionless, still, and the expanse of sky was empty.
>
> This is the first account, the first narrative. There was neither man, nor animal, birds, fishes, crabs, trees, stones, caves, ravines, grasses, nor forests; there was only the sky.
>
> The surface of the earth had not appeared. There was only the calm sea and the great expanse of sky.... Nothing existed.
>
> There was only immobility and silence in the darkness of the night. Only the Creator, the Maker, Tepeu, Gucumatz, the Forefathers, were in the water surrounded with light....
>
> Then while they meditated, it became clear to them that when dawn would break, man must appear. Then they planned the creation, and the growth of trees and the thickets and the birth of life and the creation of man.[11]

A Nobel Prize–winning French author traced the deep origins of the Mexican Dream to the interruption of Amerindian civilizations by the Spanish conquest. J. M. G. le Clezio described the confrontation between indigenous peoples and conquerors as the meeting of two dreams: respectively one of magic, the other of gold. The catastrophe of the ensuing collision led him to this judgment: "The silencing of the Indian world [by the Spanish] is without doubt one of the greatest tragedies of humanity."[12]

The indigenous worlds of Mesoamerica were infused with the idea of time, which moved in a cyclical/circular manner such that dreams and legends returned, sometimes with magical restorative powers. This awareness is at the heart of the Florentine Codex, written and assembled after the Spanish conquest by Franciscan cleric Bernardino de Sahagún and today the most fertile of the ancient texts that survived the Spanish onslaught: "Another time, it shall be thus, another time things shall be thus, in another time, in another place. What happened long ago and which is now no longer done, another time it shall be done, another time it shall be thus, as it was in very distant times. Those who live today shall live another time, they shall live once again."[13]

In this universe, there was no separation between people and gods or between natural and supernatural; each domain freely interacted with the others. Spiritual beliefs were not connected to a monotheistic religion mediated and authorized by clerics (as was the Catholic Church of Spain); instead they were supernatural powers of revelation and fusion (syncretism) that were accessible to all. Festivals, human sacrifice, and hallucinations were means of communicating with the divine world, and dreams had special significance as "voyages of the soul outside the body, during which men could know the future and receive divine warnings."[14]

Far from the centers of power, along the splintered northern edges of Mesoamerica (including today's borderlands), small-scale family and tribal cults gained prominence during and after the Spanish conquest. Once the intense cruelty of the conquistadors became widely known, and religious clerics recognized as accomplices of a genocidal invader, most rebellions in the north were orchestrated by visionaries. Shamans organized resistance. And in battle, dreamers would stand alongside great warriors and sometimes take their place.[15]

Using Sahagún's *History*, le Clezio reconstructed a rich canvas of pre-Columbian Mesoamerican society using categories such as gods, devils, rulers, astrology, festivals, and commoners. He concluded by offering a vision of Mexico as a land of dreams made from a different truth, an alternate reality. It was the recovery of these pulverized indigenous traditions that would foreshadow the content of the present-day Mexican Dream: "It was the discovery of the ancient magic of the conquered peoples that gave new value to the contemporary indigenous world and which has enabled the Mexican dream to be perpetuated. The dream of a new land where everything is possible; where everything is at the same time very ancient and very new."[16] In *La otra conquista* (see chapter 8), the task of preserving the old ways fell to Topiltzin; in *Bajo California*, Damián's pilgrimage took him so close to the ancients that he almost perished.

Many Mesoamerican traditions and beliefs persist into the Mexican present. The most famous may be the Legend of the Plumed Serpent, known in human incarnation as Quetzalcóatl and usually depicted as part man, snake, and bird. Before the conquest, confederations of royal families in Southern Mexico called themselves Children of the Plumed Serpent; they were successful in resisting Spanish subjugation and were responsible for elevating Quetzalcóatl to the status of deity. The legacy of the Plumed Serpent continued permeating Mexican life during the twentieth century, enhancing spiritual and cultural life most notably through the art of Mexico's great muralists.[17] Current debates about *Mexico profundo* and *Mexico imaginario* also echo the immovable opposition between traditional indigenous cultures and those imported from Spain and Europe. Indeed, several films in this book reflect legacies of Quetzalcóatl, the Plumed Serpent.

PART 3  Witness

But it was not an unpleasant sensation, this unsteady
trembling of the borderline.

—Robert Musil, *Agathe*, 113

## 15 A Golden Age for Border Film

BORDER FILM GENRE

The term *genre* refers to films that share common characteristics relating to themes and styles of filmmaking.[1] For example, referring to a film as a Western is instantly recognizable shorthand for describing a film's topic and storytelling conventions. Such typologies are useful in categorizing films for potential audiences, deciding production and marketing strategies, and enabling comparisons and judgments made by film critics. Genre analysis also helps identify distinct historical periods in filmmaking, ranging from "experimental" through a "classical" era (sometimes referred to as a golden age), followed by the proliferation of subgenres and bowdlerization. Enterprising filmmakers can sometimes revive a sliding toward self-parody and terminal decline, which is how we get *neo*-noir, for instance.

Genre definition is a subjective exercise, but that's not a bad thing; it's a starting point and simply means that someday, somewhere, someone will start suggesting alternatives. My task of genre identification began indirectly from the moment I arranged film titles into chapters and continues now by synthesizing the evidence accumulated in parts 1 and 2 of this book.

I chose to focus on 72 films as the principal evidence defining a border film genre (see appendix 1). Three-quarters of these films were released after 1990, even though in total I examined more than 130 films from the period between 1914 and the present (see appendix 2). The 72 films were classified according to theme and stylistic approach into eight subgenres, counting each film once only and ignoring possible overlap with other categories:

| Genre | Number of films | Percent |
| --- | --- | --- |
| Drama | 17 | 24 |
| Migration | 13 | 18 |
| Mystery/crime | 13 | 18 |
| Western | 11 | 15 |
| Fantasy | 6 | 8 |
| Revolution | 5 | 7 |
| Comedy | 4 | 6 |
| Historical drama | 3 | 4 |
| **Totals** | 72 | 100 |

The concentration of border films in a small number of thematic categories may be surprising. The drama, migration, and mystery/crime subgenres constituted over half the films. If Westerns are added, three-quarters of all film selections are accounted for.

Resisting the temptation to rank my favorite border films, I chose twenty-five canonical films that constitute the foundational films in my border film genre. These are border film classics of particular quality and distinction, as judged by originality, visuals, screenplay, music, performances, and overall impact and significance. Women directors are indicated with an asterisk.

Half the films originated in Mexico, the rest in the US (although as mentioned, coproductions confound efforts to identify a single country of origin). Listed by chronology, the films suggest three stages in the evolution of border film: emergence, consolidation of the theme, and the rise of a golden age in the early twenty-first century connected with an explosion of interest in narco-related themes. (The final title on the list is new and is introduced in the next section.)

| Title and year of release | Director | Subgenre | Era |
|---|---|---|---|
| *Vámonos con Pancho Villa!*, 1936 | Fernando de Fuentes | Revolution | **Emergence** |
| *Border Incident*, 1949 | Anthony Mann | Migration | |
| *Espaldas mojadas*, 1955 | Alejandro Galindo | Migration | |
| *Touch of Evil*, 1958 | Orson Welles | Crime | |
| *The Wild Bunch*, 1969 | Sam Peckinpah | Western | |
| *El Norte*, 1983 | Gregory Nava | Migration | **Consolidation** |
| *Born in East LA*, 1987 | Cheech Marin | Comedy | |
| *Como agua para chocolate*, 1991 | Alfonso Arau | Revolution | |
| *Cabeza de Vaca*, 1991 | Nicolás Echeverría | History | |
| *El Jardín del Edén*, 1994 | María Novaro* | Migration | |
| *Lone Star*, 1995 | John Sayles | Western | |
| *La otra conquista*, 1998 | Salvador Carrasco | History | |
| *Bajo California*, 1998 | Carlos Bolado Muño | Fantasy | |
| *Traffic*, 2000 | Stephen Soderburgh | Crime | **Golden age** |
| *Yo la peor de todas*, 2003 | María Luisa Bemberg* | History | |
| *And Starring Pancho Villa as Himself*, 2004 | Bruce Beresford | Western | |
| *Sleep Dealer*, 2008 | Alex Rivera | Fantasy | |
| *Purgatorio*, 2008 | Roberto Rochín | Migration | |
| *Sin nombre*, 2009 | Cary Joji Fukunaga | Crime | |
| *Machete*, 2010 | Robert Rodríguez | Fantasy | |
| *Sicario*, 2015 | Denis Villeneuve | Crime | |
| *600 Millas*, 2015 | Gabriel Ripstein | Crime | |
| *Transpecos*, 2016 | Greg Kwedar | Western | |
| *Ya no estoy aquí*, 2019 | Frías de la Parra | Migration | |
| *Sin señas particulares*, 2021 | Fernanda Valadez* | Disappeared | |

## NEW THEMES IN A GOLDEN AGE

As a genre becomes established or matures, experiments in filmmaking tend to proliferate. Around 2020, in association with a growing number of women in film (in front of and behind the camera), a wavelet of new films began examining the consequences once drug cartels had taken over the "protection" and "administration" of smaller rural communities. In real life, such occupied zones were often terrorized into submission through the murder of community leaders, while other people were "disappeared" or conscripted into forced labor. Ultimately many families fled for their lives, leaving behind an abandoned husk of a town or village. In an imaginative Brasilian film, *Bacurau* (Kleber Mendonca Fihlo and Juliano Dornelles, 2019), local townspeople are duped into serving as target practice for white supremacist shooters primed to annihilate the residents. They begin to resist and in so doing discover the true villains behind their victimization.[2]

An especially prominent film focused on cartel occupation is *Sin señas particulares* (2021; Identifying features), directed, produced, and written by two women, Fernanda Valadez and Astrid Rondero, and using an almost all-women crew and mostly nonprofessional actors. The film is a striking tale of how migration to the US is entrained into what is happening in the cartel-infested rural hinterlands of Mexico. A young man named Jesús decides to leave his family home and cross over into the US. Time passes without a word from him, so his mother Magdalena decides to search. She discovers that he had traveled on a bus that was attacked by cartel *sicarios* (killers). The sole survivor of the attack, Alberto, lives in a dangerous territory not far away. Magdalena determines to find Alberto and the truth about what happened to her son. She travels into a deserted, distressed landscape now under cartel control. After the occupation, former residents now live in remote caves or holes in the ground, leading marginal lives in seclusion.

Magdalena finds Alberto, who recounts that all the travelers had been dragged from the bus and executed. One of the killers had offered to spare the life of any traveler who would kill Rigo, a young man from the same town as Jesús. Surprisingly, Jesús had accepted the offer and murdered Rigo with a machete; although his own life was spared, he was obliged to become a gang member. Alberto survived by hiding under the heap of corpses. Magdalena now sets out for home, but she is run to ground by one of the killers, who turns out to be none other than her son, Jesús. Magdalena is spared, but thereafter she is haunted by what her son has become.

Film audiences in Mexico were tired of violence, but they loved *Sin señas* for its portrait of people with courage enough to keep alive the memory of the *desaparecidos*.

Another example of cartel-induced apocalypse is *Noche de Fuego* (Tatiana Huezo, 2021; Night flight), a harrowing story of life in a small rural township near Acapulco where drug cartels force local people into working in the local poppy harvest. The sound of approaching SUVs is the signal for mothers to hide their daughters, since the *sicarios* kidnap young girls into slavery. Mothers disguise daughters by dressing them as boys, cropping their hair, and making them ugly; the girls are also hidden underground. Yet many daughters are discovered and taken. Ultimately the terrified mother in the film, Rita, gathers her daughter and they flee.

*Noche de Fuego*'s portrait of the lives of girls is presented as a coming-of-age fable, albeit under horrific circumstances. The film is based on the first half of a powerful novel entitled *Prayers for the Stolen*, by Jennifer Clement. The film does not address border issues, but the novel's climax is the flight by Rita and Ana to the US border. Ana's name in the novel is Ladydi García Martínez, after Princess Diana, who is characterized as the patron saint of betrayed women—a spark of irony that universalizes Ana's story. In the novel Ladydi ends up pregnant in a Mexico City prison. Her Warrior Woman mother Rita—who never gave up on finding her daughter—triumphs by springing Ladydi from prison, and together they begin a determined march toward the US border.

Issa López is the director of *Vuelven* (2019; renamed *Tigers Are Not Afraid* in an English-language version). She has revealed in an interview that she wanted to tell the truth about what was happening to children in Mexico. The "orphans of violence" in *Vuelven* are direct descendants of the dispossessed children of Mexico City who featured in Luis Buñuel's *Los Olvidados* (1950; The forgotten ones). Kids are captured by gangs and forced into criminality. After one struggle an older street kid picks up a gun and cell phone dropped by a gangster. Naturally enough the gang leader, Chino, wants them returned, so the kids' lives are jeopardized. One of the street girls, Estrella, has been granted three wishes that she uses to help the children. Estrella returns the phone to Chino but subsequently delivers Chino to vengeful ghosts. In this act, she is helped by a fantasy tiger because tigers are not afraid.[3]

These different kinds of reckoning find echoes in current explorations by other filmmakers. A film entitled *499* (Rodrigo Reyes, 2021) offers a present-day reflection on the occasion of the five hundredth anniversary of the conquest of Mexico. It brings the conqueror Hernán Cortés back to life in order to witness the effects of the invasion he led. A voice-over asks his opinions of the present. Cortés quickly concludes that "savages" are once again in charge of the Indies; only much later does he concede his own complicity in creating a Mexico where there is so much hatred and death. Despairing, Cortés abandons himself to the mercy of his Holy Mother. The film closes with a plea to avoid evil repetitions of history, offering as evidence the traces of conquest that continue to infect the Mexican present. The theme of poisonous colonial legacies is taken up in *También la lluvia* (Icíar Bollaín, 2010; Even the rain), which connects the depravities of the Spanish conquest with the Cochabamba (Bolivia) water wars of 2000. In a more creative reckoning, Nicolás Pereda's *Fauna* (2021) is a serious imaginative comedy of cartel occupation of the hinterlands that doubles as a commentary on the effects of narco culture in film narrative.

Recent border subjects by US filmmakers lack the edginess of their Mexican counterparts, seemingly content to pursue well-worn tracks of death and mayhem in the desert. As an example, *The Boatman* (Greg Morgan, 2015) is a dreamlike film concerning a man who has devoted his life to getting *mojados* safely over the line into the US, at which task he has a 100 percent success record. When a cartel muscles into his territory and life, the local way of life is upended. Another example, *The Hollow Point* (Gonzalo López-Gallego, 2016), falls firmly into the slasher category of border anguish, in which locals once again battle an occupying cartel.

*No Man's Land* (Conor Allyn, 2021) offers something more promising. Jackson and his father live on a Texas ranch that is tucked into the U-shaped curve of a meander in the Rio Grande. The novelty is that the ranch is hemmed in on three sides by the river, but across the narrow neck of the meander a government border wall has been newly constructed. (This kind of closure happens in real life, but this was the first time I'd seen it used as the mainspring of a film plot.) The entire ranch is now south of a border fence. Every time Jackson wants to leave his ranch he has to pass through a border checkpoint. He posts a frustrated sign at the crossing gate declaring: "We're part of America." (Texas people who live in this ambiguous no-man's land once asked me, "Do we live in Mexico now?") So Jackson and his father run their own "border patrol" across the property, and one night Jackson accidentally kills an immigrant boy. He flees to Mexico in order to escape local law enforcement and to seek forgiveness from the dead boy's father. The rest of the film recounts Jackson's search for redemption. Eventually he makes his peace with the bereaved parent. Back in Texas, Jackson's father has taken to setting out water-filled jugs for migrants passing through his ranch.

## WORLDS OF BORDER FILM

Walls and border fences are present across the world; everywhere they are testaments to failed diplomacy among nations. But even though they may look alike, each wall is unique, born of different circumstances and built to separate entirely different kinds of peoples and disputes. It is impossible to convey the full depth of differences in all such circumstances, but it would be helpful to demonstrate these complexities by considering one of the world's most contentious border zones, the Israeli-Palestine border.

Perhaps the most prolific border filmmaker on the international scene is Amos Gitai.[4] His films focus on borders of many types, including geopolitical edges and concrete walls, as well as the internalized confinements and exclusions of religious persuasions. I talked with Gitai on several occasions about his "border trilogy," *Promised Land*, *Free Zone*, and *Disengagement*.[5] *Promised Land* (2004) is about the global trafficking of women. In the early 2000s, Israel was dramatically reducing the number of Palestinian workers coming into Israel, instead importing workers from Thailand, the Philippines, and China. Criminal networks started supplying women for the sex trade from Eastern Europe and elsewhere. They were flown to Egypt, then brought to an Israeli club called Promised Land and then sold in Israeli cities and Palestinian zones. National borders in *Promised Land* are open and easily crossed, yet women are trapped, isolated, and unprotected.

*Free Zone* (2005) followed one year later. This time, Gitai was motivated to counter the Israeli government's official pronouncement that borders in the Middle East were secure. Instead, he revealed the porosity of the region's borders in everyday personal and commercial lives, as well as the inconveniences and indignities that border crossers daily endure. At the core of *Free Zone* is a car trip by two women from Israel into a "free zone" in Jordan where commercial transactions from multiple origins take place without official regulation. There, the Israeli driver and her American passenger meet a Palestinian woman who owes the driver money. By film's end, the Israeli and Palestinian women are locked in bitter argument; the American woman deserts them, crossing the nearby border back into Israel. The symbolism is obvious, but the film's focus lies elsewhere, in its portrait of "orphaned" in-between spaces and the pragmatism required for border people to survive.

The last of the trilogy, *Disengagement* (2009), was inspired by a novel, Robert Musil's *The Man without Qualities* (1943), but sparked by the forcible ejection of Israeli settlers from Gaza by Israeli authorities. Gitai told me that he disagreed with the settlers' politics, but on a personal level he empathized with their devotion to faith and territory. Given the intensity and political uproar surrounding the real evacuations occurring during the filming, Gitai made extra efforts to create space for voices and viewpoints from all sides. (The screenplay went through seventeen versions.)[6]

Many themes in Gitai's border trilogy are universal, easily adaptable to borders around the world: human trafficking, illicit commerce, forced resettlement, and (more inwardly) religious differences. But the specifics of Israel and Palestine produce original and (to outsiders) sometimes opaque commentaries on borders. For instance, Gitai's well-known "House" trilogy—consisting of *House* (1980); *A House in Jerusalem* (1998); and *News from Home, News from House* (2006)—involves themes of *internal* occupation, displacement, and migration. These documentary-style films trace the fate of a single house over twenty-five years of occupation, first by Palestinians and later by Israelis. The original film, *House*, featured a group of Palestinian stonecutters preparing quarry stone for a house that will soon be occupied by Israelis. Their heavy, rhythmic labor employs hand and hammer, since they are forbidden to use explosives or mechanized power tools. The camera dwells on the scene, inviting us to taste the dust from an architecture of occupation and to feel the weight of change imposed by the Israeli authorities. Upon its release, *House* was banned in

Israel. In the third film, *News from Home, News from House*, Gitai crosses West Bank borders to where the exiled stonecutters now live. Decades older, still fiery and embittered, they voice powerful anti-Israeli sentiments pertaining to their dispossession and forced diaspora. All three films take time to reveal the guilt felt by Israelis who occupy homes in the former Palestinian community.

Beyond Gitai a rich crop of Israeli films congeals around other border issues. One of the best is *The Lemon Tree* (Eran Riklis, 2008), set in the West Bank, where an Arab widow (an unforgettable Hiam Abass) tends her lemon grove. When the Israeli defense minister moves into a house adjacent to her property, for security reasons the grove is destroyed and a high wall is built between the properties. The widow decides to appeal her cause to the Israeli Supreme Court. She loses, but so does the Israeli defense minister, deserted by his wife, who has grown sympathetic to the widow's cause. As the film ends, all protagonists are grieving, and the lemon grove is desolate

Perhaps surprisingly, some of the best comedy in border films originates in the Middle East. *Tel Aviv on Fire* (Sameh Zoabi, 2019) is an Israel-Luxembourg-Belgium-France coproduction advertised as "the comedy that crosses borders and breaks boundaries." It features a young Palestinian man living in Israel who works as a writer on a popular Palestinian soap opera entitled *Tel Aviv on Fire*. Most days, he crosses the border to a studio in Ramallah, and one day he chances to meet the Israeli commander in charge of the crossing. The commander's wife is a huge fan of the show, and he begins offering tips on dialogue, accents, and plot twists to the Palestinian scriptwriter. The show's ratings spiral upward as the scriptwriter incorporates the commander's suggestions as his own, but tensions rise when the commander demands plot changes that he has promised his wife.

Another cross-cultural border comedy is *The Band's Visit* (Eran Kolirin, 2007), an Israel-France-US coproduction. The band in question comprises a handful of mismatched Egyptian police officers who arrive in a remote Israeli settlement to play at the inauguration of a new Arab arts center. They quickly realize they have arrived at the wrong destination. The musicians are obliged to spend the night in the town while they await the next day's bus, thus allowing minor dramas to unfold. By morning new empathies have emerged between Israeli residents and Arab musicians.

A common theme in this film and many others is that left to themselves, different people find ways to accommodate their differences, thus enabling daily life to proceed peaceably.

Any self-respecting inventory of international border film cannot overlook the Canadian masterpiece *Canadian Bacon* (Michael Moore, 1995), in which the US decides to invade its northern neighbor. Another Canadian standout, *Frozen River* (Courtney Hunt, 2008), dwells on the illicit smuggling of humans from Canada into the US across the St. Lawrence River.[7] And from Sweden, there is the totally original *Border*, a fantasy concerning an immigration officer whose acute powers of smell enable her to detect contraband and identify suspicious immigrants (Ali Abbasi, 2018). Other noteworthy international films already mentioned in this book are *Pájaros de verano*, *Ixcanul*, and *Bacurau*.

## STRUCTURES OF STORYTELLING IN BORDER FILM

How are the narrative themes of border film conveyed by filmmakers? What kinds of plots and linguistic devices are engaged? The answers to these questions are foreshadowed by the three epigraphs that introduce the parts of this book. Part 1 began with an outlaw wanting to know how far away the Mexican border is, thus establishing a geography and place in the borderlands; Part 2 concerned witnessing the collision of two border cities and the convergence of different cultures; and part 3 focused on the aftershocks of fusion, those not unpleasant, unsteady tremblings along the border edge. Now, by redirecting attention from individual films toward the genre as a whole, I reveal the general structures and language used by border. Think of them as building blocks for border film.

### Contact and Conquest

Contact and conquest have always been part of border film narratives and vocabularies. The contemplations of history usually possess martial, material, and spiritual dimensions. Conquest involves crossing territorial edges (i.e., borders), occupying territories, and subjugating the conquered. Opportunities for peaceful convergence or syncretism are occasionally offered, but more often conquest is imposed, then reinforced by laws and institutions such as the Inquisition. In one heavily ironic moment of contact during *La otra conquista*, for example, Spanish soldiers interrupt an Aztec ceremony that involves human sacrifice; shocked by the barbarism they are witnessing, the soldiers immediately slaughter the ceremony's participants. At the climax of *Cabeza de Vaca*, a gigantic silver cross is shouldered laboriously on the backs of indigenous people by vigilant conquerors who claim to rule heaven and earth.

### Rupture and Transition

In other eras, contact and conquest may take the forms of war and revolution or historical changes of great vigor and momentum such as industrialization and urbanization. The enormity of social and generational ruptures during and after the Mexican Revolution is an enduring and popular theme in Mexican film. The themes are epitomized by the four women of *Como agua para chocolate*: a dying matriarch whose time has passed; her eldest daughter, steeped in wealth and privilege, who will not survive the transition; a middle daughter who impulsively grabs her freedom by serving the Revolution; and the youngest, who rejects traditional family obligations and instead surrenders to her heart. Appropriately the family home explodes in flames just as the social order crumbles.

The earliest films traded in thematic stereotypes that foregrounded the frontier's mixing of racial and ethnic types, the subordinate status of women, and intergenerational conflict. Later, dramatic inventions including trains, automobiles, and diverse lethal weaponry were adopted to symbolize the rapid overtaking of the old order. Most striking was Pancho Villa's farsighted embrace of the medium of film in support of his revolutionary victories. Film narratives of transition and rupture often commingled revolution and modernization.

### Displacement and Migration

For a century after World War I (1914–18), the content of border films was dominated by migration stories. These narratives portrayed domestic displacement from impoverished rural areas to cities, as well as international

migrations linking poverty-stricken hinterlands in Mexico with affluent destinations in the US. The US welcomed foreign low-wage labor,
although the nation's films tended to dwell on criminal aspects of migration and law enforcement. In contrast, Mexican films told of the courage
and decency of heroic migrants seeking work, their stoicism in the face of
hardship and victimization, and the lingering ties that led many migrants
to return to Mexico.

In the last quarter of the twentieth century a second generation of migration films was triggered by the enormous rise in undocumented migration across the southern border of the US. These films offered more
diverse accounts of the migrant experience, including persecutions and
oppressions at home that forced citizens from Central American countries
to flee. The hazards of border crossing and the suffering and determination needed to succeed on the other side were common plot elements. The
films also highlighted the violence and corruption that existed on both
sides of the border line, and the plotlines in Mexican films sometimes contained direct and indirect warnings discouraging Mexicans from attempting to cross over.

## Space and Place

The worlds of crime, corruption, and contraband have long been a main-
stay of border filmmakers, contributing mightily to an inflated mythology of border places as dystopias. With the border crossing at its heart,
urban-focused film noir conjured up exaggerated visions of ubiquitous
vice and corruption, romance and lust, and universal violence. Today the
dominant borderland dystopia takes the form of narcolandia, in which
the people, culture, and economy of organized crime trade in narcotics,
human beings, and guns. It's worth emphasizing that these dangerous
liaisons occur on both sides of the US-Mexico border, promoting cross-
border ties just as surely as those advanced by legitimate operations.

The storytelling in later narco films shifted attention to the expansion
of drug cartels and trafficking on a global scale, It also probed the war
against drugs in Mexico and the US (which law enforcement agencies in
both countries lost) and the ensuing anarchy of inter-cartel war among
competing *plazas*. In a bold innovation, recent Mexican narco films have

followed the penetration of organized crime into every level of society, with special attention to the devastation cartel interventions have caused.

Another trend in recent border film was the reconstruction of spaces for women. In society at large the status of women was undergoing significant transformation on a global scale. In film the basic stereotypes (saint, whore, mother) persisted, but over time, women emerged in emancipated roles that portrayed strength, courage, and power—plus a familiarity with advanced weaponry and assassination. They smashed through glass ceilings to become warriors and unassailable drug lords, although male actors still took up most of the leading roles in the violent cinema of narcolandia.

## Politics and Morals

In the mid-twentieth century, official collaborations between law enforcement agencies on both sides were successful and celebrated in film. There is no equivalent for this in contemporary border film. Instead there is frank confession of defeat, or at best a standoff expressed as a form of continuous, unresolved warfare between cartels and law. Police forces on either side of the line arrange informal alliances to manage their cross-border incursions against cartels. Their victories tend to be small-scale and short-lived. Violence has seeped into everyday life, at roadside security checks and in narco family kitchens. Rural communities have been depopulated and hollowed out by a suffocating blanket of cartel impositions, despite scattered vigilante uprisings. In extremis, filmmakers reimagine rural places as theme parks where rich tourists with high-powered weaponry pay to assassinate local residents.

More recent dramatic plots concerning the collision of identities and the subsequent alienation, integration, and hybridization are prominent in the genre. They include a spate of "neo-Westerns" in which US Border Patrol agents have displaced the roles formerly devoted to sheriffs and marshals. They are mining a rich vein of moral tales pertaining to the rhythms of small-town life in border communities affecting families, ranchers, generations, and changing notions of honor. The poisonous legacies of racism, incest, and miscegenation are never far beneath the surface. However, buried pasts, twisted legacies, and deep hatreds are being shoved aside by matters relating to altered identities, belonging and alienation, second- and third-generation adjustments, social justice, language, and status.

## Dreams and Fantasies

Since the early days of silent film, the border was a convenient place of refuge or escape. Later themes became more explicitly aspirational, giving prominence to varying configurations of the American dream and the Mexican dream (not always the same). The border itself was actively adopted as a place of pilgrimage where different human emotions, beliefs, and motivations converged. People journeyed to the border edges (*límites*) in search of deliverance, redemption, or something distinct from material concerns. They were motivated by existential doubts, or a longing for solitude, or the pursuit of spiritual and secular pilgrimage. Their odysseys were fraught with uncertainty and danger. A troubled man riven by guilt and doubt seeks physical and spiritual rebirth among the ancient cave paintings in remote mountains. Another seeks a peaceful hilltop in readiness for death.

Mexican and Chicano films in these categories often reached toward more fantastical aspirations tinged with mysticism, legend, spirits, and devils—all wrapped up with ghosts, tigers, guilt, and grief. Comedy and fantasy films unfortunately seem rarer these days.

## Walls and Resistance

A new benchmark for filmmakers was established after the attacks of 9/11 and the creation of the US Department of Homeland Security. Border walls and drug wars came to dominate the language of border film. Some filmmakers responded to the grim reality with hyperbole and humor, partly as acts of resistance. Trucks made of marijuana were waved across the line by oblivious US customs and immigration officials, who had perhaps sampled the product before waving it through. A vacationing family was diverted to a remote Mexican saloon infested by vampires, gangsters, bikers, and snake-toting strippers. A Mexican-Chicano revolution erupted near a taco stand on the US side of the border.

*Sleep Dealer* stood out from the pack for its vision of an emerging, brave new world even though many of its inventions were but minor exaggerations of what was already happening in the world. In *Sleep Dealer*'s imaginary world, the US has sealed and fortified its southern border. Remote surveillance and mechanized law enforcement have removed the necessity for on-the-ground border patrol and border crossings. National security and social order are maintained through dense networks of drone-driven bombings and assassinations. Large-scale cross-border migration is no more. The labor formerly performed by migrant labor (called braceros) is now performed by *cybraceros*, residing in Mexico but connected virtually to robots at job sites within the US. Smaller Mexican settlements are abandoned as food and jobs become scarce, and privatized water monopolies charge exorbitant fees (something like this is already happening on both sides of the border). And yet resistance survives in the face of suppression, exploitation, racism, and poverty. Joy and optimism are nurtured in networks of dissenters hidden in the shadows of border walls. In film (as in real life) the will to revolution endures.

# 16 Ways of Seeing the Border (Beyond Film)

Using border films as evidence has revealed many remarkably faithful representations of parts of real borderland history. Not surprisingly, the cinematic catalog is incomplete and falls short of a comprehensive explanation of borderland evolution. (Perhaps we can say that it misses the "big picture"?) So what other evidence lies beyond film?

## VOICES FROM THE IN-BETWEEN

Over many decades, I have witnessed a vast array of encounters that testify to cross-border linkages, private and public, legal and illegal. One of the most moving was a gathering on the banks of the Río Bravo when the bishops of Ciudad Juárez and El Paso brought together separated families from Mexico and the US for a few minutes' closeness across the line. Flooding from the previous day had caused a change of venue to a place where the riverbank was concretized and secure, and large crowds gathered under still-stormy skies as prayers were offered and honored guests were introduced. They included refugees from Africa, a reminder of the global connections involved in migration and separation. Drones overhead disturbed the intimacy of the reunions. It was almost festive, but on the television news later that day, the event somehow seemed fragile and vulnerable. On other occasions I attended the Hands Across the Border celebration at Brownsville-Matamoros in observance of their centuries-old alliance. And books have been written about how Arizonans and Sonorans invest money and sentiments in their joint future, and how residents of Laredo and Nuevo Laredo have gathered (since 1898) to celebrate George Washington's birthday.[1] The variety and longevity of such connections is testimony to so many special relationships across the boundary line.

Behind every public event is a personal story. A US-born artist friend of mine retains early memories of the border fence from the mid-1980s . As a child living in Tijuana she was dropped off every day at a local school by her parents, who were en route to their jobs in San Diego. Seeing the fence as it sped by, she said, was like having a screen constantly in her peripheral vision. The family lived in oceanside Playas de Tijuana, where there was no border fence at that time. When fences were added in the mid-1990s, she developed a personal sense of "feeling unwanted . . . that I'm a problem." From her bedroom she could not avoid seeing the newly-installed stadium lighting blazing over the line. By the time she began driving herself to school in the US, dead bodies were visible on the roadside where migrants had attempted to outrun traffic or *la migra*. As time passed, she became accustomed to the sight. But after 9/11, she felt a "door slam" as the border was transformed into a fortified military zone. Today this young woman lives mostly in the US but often returns to her childhood neighborhood in Playas, where a glowering border wall has been erected. Expensive houses are built right up against the fence. Rumor has it that the properties with swimming pools are owned by cartels.

Other young people who live on both sides of the border describe how they relate to the current borderline:

"The question in my life is to cross or not to cross. . . . For many people like me . . . crossing is part of our daily routine. . . . I live in Tijuana but my daily life is spent in San Diego. I am what they call a 'transborder' person. . . . I live and socialize in one country, and I work and study in the other."

"I live and dream in Spanish, in English and Spanglish, I am part of here and there. . . . I don't know any more what it means to live in a single country or a single language. . . . In the US I function as an American, and in Mexico I speak Spanish and function as a Mexican."[2]

Borderlanders of all ages adopt diverse vocabularies to describe a sense of shared space, referring to themselves as "transborder" persons and to their twin cities as *ciudades hermanas* (sister cities) or *ciudades amistosas* (friendly cities). Many are so accustomed to living their lives on both sides of the border that they forget which side of the line they're on. Perhaps the best indicator that people are comfortable about their in-between status is when they claim to have more in common with other borderlanders than with citizens of their respective nation-states. For them the border is not an edge but an integrated economic and bicultural society, where nationalities, languages, and cultures converge.

In an altogether different conversation, a young college student in her late teens revealed what is at stake in building a wall. I was south of Nogales (Sonora) talking with a group of students about why the walls eventually will come down. She asked me what it would be like when there was no wall; I responded that things would be as they were before. She seemed puzzled and tentatively asked what life was like before walls were built. I realized then that she had lived most of her life in the shadow of border walls.[3] So had every single person her age or younger. There was an *entire generation* in *every place* along the border (from big city to small farm) with no direct knowledge or experience of the cross-border freedoms that their parents had taken for granted. I am still shocked when I recollect this moment, feeling again the acute sense of displacement and disassociation from the border landscape affecting the new generations of borderlanders.

Mexicali friends, accustomed to crossing the line every day to ferry their kids to school in Calexico, have always regarded the fences as ugly, inconvenient, and a daily reminder of US disrespect for Mexico and its people.[4] Adding injury to insult, the Wall simply does not work.[5] Ironically, it actually promotes an intensification of cross-border connections as residents from both sides make special efforts to maintain contacts. Borderlanders on both sides want their lives back. For them, this means ending the occupation, removing the border wall and substituting more effective and less intrusive methods of border control, repairing the damage caused by wall construction and security operations (with governments and contractors footing the bill for the mess they have created), and diverting the billions earmarked for closing the border to *increasing* the number and capacity of border crossings.[6]

## IS THERE A BORDERLAND THIRD NATION?

Writers, scholars, journalists, and other professionals have long pondered the most fruitful ways to describe the Mexico-US borderlands—the land and its peoples, their relationship with the home nations, even how best to name the area. In 1987, a prominent Chicana cultural scholar named Gloria Anzaldúa referred to *la frontera* as a "third country" between two nations: "The U.S.-Mexican border *es una herida abierta* [is an open wound] where the Third World grates against the first and bleeds. And before a scab forms it hemorrhages again, the lifeblood of the two worlds merging to form a third country—a border culture."[7] This vivid expression has become something of a watershed in borderland studies, making clear that cultural forms cannot be contained within the boundaries of empire, state, tribe, or peoples. Human interventions such as political boundaries may pose temporary barriers and limits, but organic borderlands easily exceed anticipations of cultural homogeneity.

A decade later, Mexican-born artist and border philosopher Guillermo Gómez-Peña took an axe to notions of demographic and cultural divisions in the US: "It is time to face facts: Anglos won't go back to Europe, and Mexicans and Latinos (legal or illegal) won't go back to Latin America. We are all here to stay. For better or worse, our destinies and aspirations are in one another's hands."[8] Instead of a comfortable apartheid, Gómez-Peña envisaged a "new world border" emerging in the gap between the two nations, because the whole world is filled with in-between peoples and hybrid cultures (*culturas híbridas*) who are emblematic of the universal human condition.[9]

By century's end there was no turning away from recalibrations of borderland viewpoints: urbanist Larry Herzog in 1990 characterized it as an *ecosistema urbano transfronterizo* (transborder urban system).[10] Others spoke of "postborder" or "postnational" cross-border spaces.[11] In the early 2000s Norma Iglesias Prieto pointed out that Mexican lives were indelibly marked by the presence of the US whether or not people crossed the real borderline.[12] She referred to the cultural spaces of Tijuana as *un tercer espacio social*, a social third space, and referred to cross-border connections as *la doble ciudadanía*, or joint citizenship.[13]

In contemplating what to call these in-between people, I opened with the conventional term *nation*—referring to a group of people whose members voluntarily identify with others on the basis of shared experiences connected to their history, geography, ethnicity, traditions, language, and (occasionally) alliances against external threat. The actual sentiment of belonging and unity is commonly referred to as *nationalism*. When a nation acquires the sovereign right to govern a territory (and that right is recognized by others), the territory is deemed to be a *nation-state*.

A *third nation* may be regarded as a community of identity and affiliation carved from the territories of two or more existing nation-states. It occupies an interstitial space that transcends the formal boundaries of the host nation-states, creating from them an overlapping hybrid space. Third-nation sentiments and spaces have many historical precedents, commonly in situations where indigenous peoples have had borderlines imposed on them by rapacious settlers. One of the most prominent cases along the US-Mexico border is the Tohono O'odham Nation between Arizona and Sonora, sliced in two by the 1848 Treaty of Guadalupe Hidalgo. The Nation still possesses an enduring sense of identity along with autonomous tribal institutions and laws and a formal territorial organization (albeit subject to respective federal governments).[14]

In Canada, too, not far from the capital city of Ottawa, the Akwesasne Mohawk Nation has an identity that has survived being dissected into five separate political geographies by Anglo and French newcomers. For centuries the Nation inhabited Cornwall Island and adjacent riverbanks of the St. Lawrence River. When the international boundary between Canada and the US was created in 1783, their land was split among those two nation-states, plus the state of New York and the provinces of Ontario and Québec (that's five jurisdictions!). The outcomes of such overlapping sovereignties are often comical. On land, there are no walls and fences to mark the international boundary line, except around official ports of entry; the boundary is sometimes recorded only by occasional changes in the materials used to surface roads. The community radio station building is cut in two by the international boundary, and the front and back parts of the building have different area codes. Parking on the wrong side of a street may invalidate your car insurance. Along the river boundary, people I met were terribly vague about where Canada ended and the US began, which explained why customs and immigration officials hereabouts prefer to avoid water-based apprehensions. In winter when the river is frozen, people drive over the frozen river into the other country. The ice is plowed for safer travel.[15]

The idea of integrated political spaces with mixed sovereignties between Mexico and the US is not new. In the late 1980s, commentators on both sides acknowledged the emergence of new cultures and attitudes along the border, even to the extent that people there were "more like each other than either is like its nation."[16] Mexican voices mentioned that ideas of a "third state" or a "new border nation" were consistent with what they were observing on the ground.[17] After NAFTA was signed in 1994, expectations of borderland integration intensified, and US enthusiasts characterized transborder areas as "testing grounds of socio-economic integration in North America."[18] (You can understand why Mexicans with long memories of historic US land grabs might regard this suggestion as threatening.)

In the present century the term *MexAmerica* surfaced in Mexico to describe a border region where interchangeable cultures, ethnicities, and languages are distinct from those of the host nations.[19] Unsurprisingly, the order of naming was reversed in the US to *Amexica* in Ed Vulliamy's account of the border as "a country in its own right, which belongs to both the United States and Mexico, yet neither."[20] In 2011 American political scientist Robert Pastor captured the essence of different ways of seeing the border: "The closer you live to the borders, the more you see them connecting the people on both sides. The further you live from the borders, the more you see them as separating the countries."[21] I call this a "first law of geographical proximity" that influences the formation of distinctive borderland identities.

I am comfortable using the term third nation to identify the in-between spaces aligned along the Mexico-US border, although I concede that it might raise hackles among Mexicans suspicious of any whiff of incursions on their national sovereignty from *el norte*. Yet the US-Mexico borderland is a place that is better understood by going beyond conventional histories of nations and their boundaries. Exceptional insights may lie in viewpoints that run parallel or even counter to the narratives of "grand history." It's not that conventional history should be abandoned, but that third-nation perspectives could usefully exist alongside the conventional narratives.

And what do we gain by choosing this name? Calling an interstitial space a third nation raises the stakes above a narrow focus on the (in)conveniences of daily life to a level of subhemispheric awareness concerning how two nations intersect and collide at subnational levels of political geography. In addition, it may better explain what is happening on the ground, such as the intensity of resentment toward occupying police and national guards. Most importantly, a third-nation consciousness shifts understanding of the border, not as an edge where two countries grind together, nor as an open wound causing injury, and still less as a periphery or hinterland of little consequence. By my reckoning, a third nation matters as an agent for social change on its own terms. The spaces it occupies function as an active connector, not as a passive container. The third nation is categorically not some peripheral appendage where residents have a taste for cat food.

And there is more to recommend the term. In an era of climate change, geoeconomic and geopolitical realignment, global pandemics, and massive displacements of population on domestic and international scales, I am certain that fractured sovereignties and third nations are likely to attract increasing attention as targets for superpower incursions. Countries such as Ukraine become pawns in global geopolitics, paradoxically a status that only incites more urgent movement toward regional autonomy.[22] In such circumstances border walls are reduced to the status of tokens commemorating failed diplomacy. It is all the more distressing, then, that so many countries nowadays rush to build walls as a first (and sometimes only) response to external threat.[23]

## HOW THE THIRD NATION BECAME A WAR ZONE

The twin towns and military installations that were established immediately following the 1848 Treaty of Guadalupe Hidalgo were defensive in purpose. When one nation established a settlement or military presence at

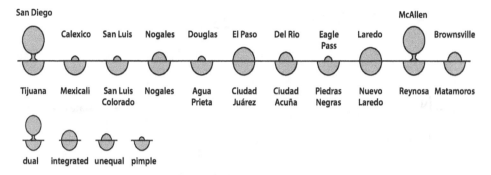

*Figure 16.1.* The borderland twin cities.

the border, the other side would quickly follow suit. Over time the border-line came to resemble a two-thousand-mile "necklace" hung by a cluster of twin-town "pearls."

The border twin cities were often dissimilar in form and historical gen-esis. The eleven principal twins (*cuates*) extend from San Diego–Tijuana in the west to Brownsville-Matamoros in the east. The oldest pair is El Paso–Ciudad Juárez, which developed as a single settlement (called Paso del Norte) during the era of Spanish exploration. After the 1848 treaty split the town in two, El Paso and Ciudad Juárez continued to grow as a strongly *integrated* urban community. By and large, the post-treaty towns on the Mexican side grew larger than their US twins, producing asym-metric urban forms. Some US settlements were much smaller than their Mexican twin; Calexico for instance is little more than a suburban expan-sion of Mexicali, from the air resembling a small pimple on the face of its larger neighbor. Some larger twins have grown separately into distinct yet related *dual* cities, with one settlement geographically removed from the borderline. The most prominent examples are San Diego and Tijuana and McAllen and Reynosa. Both sets of twins have strong connections to nearby metropolitan areas (respectively Los Angeles and Monterrey).

Beyond the international boundary itself there exists a dense hierarchy of government and nongovernmental territories and agencies that regu-late lives and behaviors throughout the wide-reaching borderlands. Analo-gous overlays exist on both sides of the line even though the functions and practices of government in the two countries differ. Closest to the line are

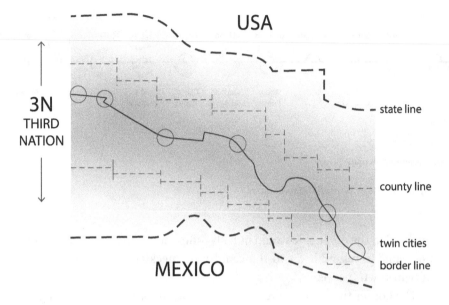

*Figure 16.2.* The borderland third nation.

municipal governments associated with the twin cities and other smaller settlements; these districts are combined into counties, which are then aggregated into states, which ultimately constitute the territories of the federal government at the national level. Sprinkled throughout the hierarchies are joint institutions and special districts such as the International Boundary and Water Commission (IBWC) and its Mexican equivalent, the Comisión de Límites y Aguas (CILA), a long-established alliance that was created to manage the two nations' shared water resources. In addition, at the state and local levels networks of voluntary and nonprofit institutions serve myriad constituencies, such as cross-border chambers of commerce or sporting alliances.

The net consequence of these divisions into separate but overlapping political geographies and bureaucratic hierarchies is that daily life in border towns and cities is impacted by a mish-mash of overlapping agencies with different responsibilities and objectives. Typically, municipalities are responsible for local services such as schools, while government agencies at county, state, and federal levels have alternative mandates, such as public utilities and supervision of elections; national defense is principally a federal responsibility. The segmentation of responsibilities and accountability across and among many levels of government often has the effect of confounding effective service provision and accountability. Confusion and ambiguity are intensified when governments engage private contractors to provide "public" services such as health care or water and power. Lack of transparency at every level of government inhibits effective local autonomy and self-determination in what becomes a plethora of opaque bureaucratic mandates. Privatization is not the answer since private agencies are notably less transparent and accountable in their operations putting profits before people and frequently condoning substandard services and other forms of malfeasance.

A divergence between national and local interests lies at the heart of current borderland tensions because the US federal government has designated border communities as the locus where the wars on terrorism, drugs, and undocumented immigration will take place. All three national priorities are being contested at the US-Mexico border, irrespective of borderlanders' culpability in these problems. (I was living in Britain when President Richard Nixon announced that Europe would be the designated theater of war if and when the US confronted the Cold War threat from the Soviet Union. Europeans were not pleased. Different era and different situation, I understand, but I can attest that the feeling of being dumped on is similar.)

Fundamentally, the responsibilities foisted on the borderlands have their origin in complications pertaining to territory, identity, and authority. From the federal perspective in both countries the border is a nation's *edge* and its integrity must be secured, but for people who live there, the border is their *center*, the source of livelihood and community, worthy of self-defense. In legal terms the nation and borderland have different standing in debates over national security, and it is solely the federal government that has authority to impose on the borderlands the burden of executing federal policies. Borderland municipalities have no choice but to comply.

At the same time, the border region is a fulcrum for binational and global trade and home for millions of cross-border residents. It serves also as the base of operations for agricultural and manufacturing industries of global importance. The enormity of the socioeconomic imperative to keep the border open for international trade cannot be exaggerated. But it is also the front line of US immigration policy and home (by now) to an enormous national security apparatus. The simultaneous demands from all these interested groups (they are not partners) for closed *and* open borders cannot be satisfied. Building walls and fences addresses the needs of none of the interested parties, except perhaps the traffickers in narcotics and human beings.

In essence, the US federal government has devised a territorial scheme based on *distributed benefits and concentrated costs*. That is, the nation as a whole benefits when the costs of national security are confined to a geographically limited territory and borne by a small subset of its citizens. For the communities and people directly obliged to shoulder the responsibilities and consequences of defending the nation's borders, this scheme lacks appeal: the delegated tasks are dangerous and life-threatening; they undermine the integrity and well-being of the impacted communities; and the federal aid offered to beleaguered communities tends to arrive in the form of funds for law enforcement personnel, equipment, and detention centers (the armature of the federal "army of occupation"). Complicating matters, the infusion of cash that accompanies this "border industrial complex" doubles as an engine of local economic development, and by now great numbers of people, industries, and communities have become accustomed to the jobs and paychecks they have received from the government. Needless to say, not all residents share equally in either the burden or the bounty.

The situation is similar in Mexico, although the particulars differ. The country has its own problems relating to inequality, poverty, migration, and the spreading influence of drug cartels. Fearful of doing anything that would upset trade and commerce with the US, President Lopez Obrador (AMLO) concentrated on not antagonizing the volatile Trump by agreeing (among other things) to regulate the flow of migrants passing through Mexico en route to the US. As a consequence, the border in Mexico became a gigantic enterprise devoted to managing enormous waves of people in transit: those who arrived at the Mexican border from the south seeking to cross, and those deported from the US who were unable or unwilling to move on without assistance.

## A BORDERLANDS' DEMOCRACY PROJECT

A persistent theme throughout this book has been that the territories and peoples on either side of the US-Mexico border are a closely integrated single ecology, each side identifying with the other and codependent in advancing its interests in the past, present, and future. So what is to be done?[24] Democracy in the third nation starts from the ground up. Borderlanders require freedom to determine their own future; by this I mean that local self-determination and autonomy must be part of the foundation of a renewed democracy in the borderlands. Political scientists describe this condition as "popular rule" or "open democracy."[25] Following is a sketch of how to think of such a project, using the example of California and Baja California Norte.

"The largest integrated economic zone along the U.S.-Mexico border" is how the border states of California and Baja California Norte were described in a 2022 study by the Ahlers Center for International Business at the University of San Diego. The study refers to this 160-mile border corridor as "CaliBaja." (This sounds like a stomach virus. My preferred name for the border spaces between California and Baja California has long been "Bajalta," a historically accurate and sweet-sounding combination of Spanish names for Alta [or Upper] and Baja [Lower] California.) CaliBaja comprises eight border counties: Imperial and San Diego Counties in California; and Ensenada, Mexicali, Rosarito, San Quintín, Tecate, and Tijuana Counties in Mexico. The region has a population of seven million, an annual regional GDP of $250 billion, and an estimated $70 billion each year in cross-border trade flows. Economically diverse, its largest manufacturing sectors are audio and video equipment, medical equipment and supplies, and semiconductors, mostly located on the Mexican side. An estimated fifty-four thousand people cross the border each day from Baja into San Diego and Imperial Counties for work, largely in health and health-related occupations. Almost five thousand workers live in San Diego and Imperial Counties and cross over to work in Baja. The Ahlers report calls for investment in reskilling the labor force (through training and education), infrastructure development, and promoting cross-border integration.[26]

There can be little doubt about the significance of the Bajalta region in local, national, and even global economies. Apart from its economic prowess, Bajalta also possesses a solid institutional infrastructure accustomed to cross-border dealings. Many private and public institutions are devoted to promoting and maintaining transborder ties. They include the state-level Border Governors' Conference, the Border City Mayors' association, private business councils, joint economic development alliances, nonprofit humanitarian aid agencies, law enforcement, cultural organizations, and tertiary education establishments. Local business leaders in San Diego and Tijuana already work toward similar ends but through different organizational structures such as the Smart Border Coalition.[27] And border scholar Christophe Sohn has reported on the CaliBaja region's "place-branding" initiative that seeks to promote the binational megaregion focused on Tijuana and San Diego.[28]

Journalist Joe Mathews coincidentally published an open letter to the governors of Baja California Norte and California and the mayors of Tijuana and San Diego, dated November 4, 2021, in which he proposed letting border residents in those two states govern themselves by creating a "citizens' assembly." Citing evidence from experiments in Ireland, France, Finland, and Belgium, Mathews touted the value of bringing together people who have no need to win elections and as a result have greater freedom to work together and advance new agendas and innovative solutions *for their own nation*. He was emphatic that the sufferings of US-Mexico border residents were the consequence of national politicians' having mismanaged the region. Recognizing the widespread indifference to and ignorance of border issues in Mexico City and Washington, D.C., he called on state and local politicians to empower a citizens' assembly with direct legislative and oversight powers. Such assemblies, he asserted, could be effective in addressing issues that governments have failed to solve or even take up, such as intrusive surveillance and protecting sanctuary cities. He ended with a challenge: "So, why not cross one more border—and give both sides a shot at self-government?"[29]

# 17  Border Witness of the Future

As I began purposeful contemplation of border film over a decade ago, I noticed that many authoritative film histories ended their surveys around the year 2000. This meant that the post-2000 boom in border film was largely unrecorded in the history books (although it was not unnoticed elsewhere). Fragments of the legacy of a Mexican new wave in the 1990s got a mention in some books, but coverage of emerging Hollywood narco blockbusters or of Mexican independents and coproductions was absent. Yet the tally of border films from both countries was accumulating at such a rate that it seemed to me that some kind of revolution in border filmmaking was underway. This book is an original account of the latest innovations in border film, unique in its focus on over one hundred years of border film production and in affording equal attention to films from Mexico and the US.

I was drawn by the idea of describing the cross-border region between the US and Mexico as a place where people shared powerful senses of shared identity and affiliation together with a clear-eyed understanding of the benefits they derived from cross-border cooperation. Identifying as a cross-border resident was something many embraced. I recognized that a focus on Mexico-US border film presented a rich opportunity to

245

examine the idea of a third nation through the eyes of filmmakers who had been actively representing borderland lives and places on-screen for over a century. My personal experience and knowledge of the border provided a foundation for judging the cultural knowledge that was accumulating in films. As it turned out the border film genre I outlined revealed a surprising degree of fidelity between real life and screen life; most of the time, the filmmakers of Hollywood and Churubusco *did* get the border right in the stories they told.

In his later works, James Baldwin considered the "after times" that followed the collapse of the US civil rights movement. While white America rebuilt its defenses, Black Power organizations crumbled under the dual pressures of internal ideological conflict and government harassment.[1] Out of his despair at that time, Baldwin recognized a calling as witness, "to tell the story. . . . Make it real. To force it on the world's attention."[2] His assessment of race in American film (in *The Devil Finds Work*) compared film fiction with what he knew from his own life. Adopting an equivalent approach, I turned to what I knew in order to corroborate what was on the screen. Recognizing the limits of direct experience, I also adapted knowledge from other sources, especially historical accounts, art, literature, geopolitics, and interviews, as well as films from other global borders. The combination of border cinema with direct and acquired witness offered the opportunity to approximate the Baldwin standard.

The premium placed on witness goes some way toward explaining why so many film stills in this book involve faces and encounters—pairings that juxtapose dynamic situations of fusion and change: killer with victim, hunter with prey, powerful with peon, brown with white and Black. Such encounters usually involved unequals. The standard of witness also accounts for the inclusion in the text of many nonfilm borderland photographs and literal evocations representing landscapes and people. The photographs, for instance, can be enjoyed simply as representations of (say) a desert's beauty or humanity's quirky hand, but they also serve as tacit benchmarks through which film evidence may be judged.

Now I turn my attention to the future. What do film and real-world evidences suggest about the borderlands' future? I suggest ways to begin thinking about this question by taking three broad perspectives, on border film, real life, and personal experience.

If I had to choose three recent films that most accurately represent the current aftertimes of the borderlands, they would be *Sicario*, *Sin señas particulares* (Identifying features), and *Sleep Dealer*.

*Sicario* is a devastating account of the endless struggle between drug cartels and law enforcement agencies along the borderline. The film represents a state of inertia or social stasis, in which the endless routine of war offers gains and losses that are small and temporary, and which governments are powerless to prevent. *Sicario* is steeped in the noir moods and vocabularies of narcolandia and failed states.

*Sin señas particulares* portrays the aftermath of cartel conquests. Small towns in Mexico's hinterlands are abandoned by fleeing residents once narcos have displaced community, order, and government, substituting instead their own logic of compliance backed by terror. The film is about the gulag, where nations are held hostage and sentimental notions of patria and "who we are" are pulverized by the propaganda of the kleptocrats.

*Sleep Dealer*—though lighter in mood—foresees a high-tech world of robot labor, intrusive surveillance, and social control managed by the military at the behest of the richest civilians. Its logic is that of the plutocrat and the military junta, where a peripheral nation (Mexico) is confined behind walls and policed by death-dealing drones (operated by the US military from inside the US). The onset of digital and technological revolutions has rendered total control a possibility, although pockets of resistance linger along border edges.

These three films are deeply pessimistic dystopias. To compensate, here is a selection of more positive scenarios from among my genre list: *Como agua para chocolate*, for its optimism about progressive change associated with younger generations; *Mi querido Tom Mix*, for the undying passions and courage of the older generations; *Machete*, a rousing anthem rallying domestic and service workers to revolution; and *The Mexican Dream*, a short ode to one man's Hollywood ambition and his accidental transformation into a legendary woman spirit, La llorona. It is insightful to put the films together in conversation with one another.

The real world of the Mexico-US border has been described in many digressions throughout these chapters. Instead of recapping this history, at this stage I simply offer a choice between two images. Each symbolizes a different prospect for the future of the third nation's borderlands: unification or separation.

Boundary monument number 1 was erected soon after the 1848 Treaty of Guadalupe Hidalgo ended the war with the United States, at the point where the land boundary met the Rio Grande/Río Bravo del Norte. The monument sits in the background on the right side of a photograph behind the bust of revolutionary leader Francisco Madera (foreground in the first photograph), who headquartered part of his revolutionary campaign at this very location. The monument is on the US side of the line; Madero rests in Mexico. This section of the boundary line remained without fences or other forms of physical fortification until 2020. Even though electronic surveillance was put in place before that date, and a low earthen berm constructed to mark the line more clearly, the absence of any fences or other obstructions made it possible to have unimpeded conversations with people on the other side. For this reason, it was always one of my favorite places along the line.

Friendly encounters across the line at monument 1 are no longer possible. In 2020 a local landowner gave permission for an immense wall to be built on his land, thereby obliterating any opportunity for cross-border exchange. The new fortification extends from the riverbank (foreground in the second photograph) and stops at the top of a hill on the right side of the second photograph. The monument itself is no longer visible from the US side. The future of this once active place is silence, alienation, surveillance, and nothingness.

How will future generations understand the border and its peoples? Current film offers versions of dystopia and utopia, while the real borderlands are poised between favoring unification and suffering an imposed apartheid. Are there alternative ways of seeing and knowing the border?

I am unlikely to get closer to the actual experience of illicit border crossing than I experienced in *Carne y Arena* (2017; Flesh and sand), an immersive, film-based virtual reality installation by the prominent Mexican film director Alejandro Gonzalez Iñárritu. It ran for one year at the

*Figure 17.1.* Before the wall, monument 1 in 2011, Ciudad Juárez and El Paso border.

*Figure 17.2.* After the wall, monument 1 in 2020, Ciudad Juárez and El Paso border.

Los Angeles County Museum of Art (LACMA) starting in the summer of 2017. I want to recollect the impact it had on me because this may be the way we will know life from screens yet to come.

Three separate spaces were involved: a small waiting room, a large tent-like arena, and finally a narrow photo gallery. The freezing cold waiting room resembled the holding area of a detention center. Shoes and socks had to be removed and stored with personal belongings in a small locker. The only sound was the very loud blaring of an air conditioner. I waited nervously. After I was buzzed into the tent, two aides strapped a pack on my back and placed a VR headset over my eyes and ears.

From that moment, I found myself walking in a desert at night, in the company of a small group of migrants, hearing their agitated voices. Suddenly a helicopter arrived in a deafening roar, panicking the migrants. Bullhorn commands were barked out in Spanish and English. Border patrol agents began forcing migrants onto the ground, separating men from women and children. I moved freely in the VR space, but carefully avoided the migrant bodies now strewn across the ground. When I bumped into one, the body faded away, leaving only a beating heart that glowed red in the darkness.

After everyone was rounded up a calm descended, and it seemed that the raid was over. But the helicopter returned, angrier than ever. This time I was the target. I pushed my cold hands into my pockets in an effort to warm them. But a voice commanded: "Take your hands out of your pockets!" (I obeyed.) Next, the voice ordered: "Get down on your knees!" (I almost did but somehow managed to detach my body from the situation.) A total blackout descended on the arena, and I wanted this experience to end. Finally, streaks of dawn reached across the sky. All that remained of the panic was a pair of children's shoes scattered akimbo in the sand.

Relieved of my backpack, I was ushered alone into the corridor-like gallery: one wall was lined with metal border fencing reminiscent of the 1990s and the other with portraits and biographies of real migrants who had offered their stories for the film and acted in it.

A sliver of light shining through a tiny gap in the gallery's fence attracted my attention. Looking through, I saw a woman in the arena wearing her backpack and headset just as I had done. I heard a loud sob from the arena and saw the woman kneel on the sand, unable to ignore the virtual voice commanding her to do so. Mortified to be observing her misery—which was real!—I moved hurriedly to the exit.

Once I was outside the installation, a passing stranger sensed my distress and asked if I needed help. I was chilled and disoriented, sensing (against all reason) that I was only just arriving in the US. The sunlit museum gallery before me was entirely occupied by the high walls of a circular steel maze by Richard Serra. I crept into its deepest interior and shut my eyes.

The notion that film itself possesses a special power of witness, able to inform and motivate action, was one of Baldwin's main teachings. Currently the ubiquitous agency of screen exists in myriad forms and settings, including conventional theaters, homes, streaming, sidewalks, moving vehicles, pocketbooks, phones, social media, and more. Every film explored in this book, from Chaplin to Gonzalez Iñárritu, is an invitation to bear witness. More than ever, screen images have the potential to guide every audience to witness and then to act.

# Acknowledgments

It is a pleasure to acknowledge the assistance of many friends and colleagues in Mexico, the US, and farther afield who contributed to the completion of this book.

I begin with special thanks to those who introduced me to the border several decades ago, especially Norma Iglesias Prieto and Larry Herzog in San Diego/Tijuana, and Tony Payan in Ciudad Juárez/El Paso. Also my endless gratitude to Gustavo Leclerc, Héctor Lucero, and Bob Steward, who accompanied me at different stages of my border explorations.

I want to acknowledge the amazing collection of film scholars at the University of Southern California whose collaborations and friendships provided me with an unparalleled education in film in Los Angeles for more than two decades. Most of my interaction back then was through Todd Boyd, Elizabeth Daley, David James, Marsha Kinder, Dana Polan, and Michael Renov. Beyond film, I encountered Dana Cuff, Edward Dimendberg, Robbert Flick, Norman Klein, Josh Kun, and Sofía Ruiz-Alfaro. Selma Holo, the director of USC's Fisher Museum, was generous in developing my curatorial skills and understanding. For many years Dallas Dishman and Andrew Burridge were vital collaborators on many projects.

After moving to Northern California I fell in with another group of fine film folks at UC Berkeley, most especially Weihong Bao and Mark Sandberg. A graduate class I taught with Weihong on film and urbanism brought prominent personalities from the film world to campus, such as J. P. Sniadecki and Francesco Casetti. Berkeley's Pacific Film Archive was a valuable source of archival materials and helpful assistance from Jason Saunders and Steve Seid. At Berkeley's

Center for Latin American Studies, Harley Shaiken and Beatrice Manz invited a rich stream of films, filmmakers, and actors from Latin America, including Demián Bichir and Diego Luna from Mexico. UC Berkeley's College of Environmental Design was a congenial workplace where I began a long collaboration with border architect and artist Ronald Rael. It's also where I first met filmmaker Amos Gitai, beginning many years of conversation about film.

Such interactions exposed me to a remarkable range of creative minds and critical outlooks on the cultures of art and the practice of filmmaking. I crossed paths and engaged with artists, activists, curators, and filmmakers from the San Francisco Bay area, Southern California, and Baja California; from New Mexico and Texas; from Chihuahua and Tamaulipas and Veracruz; and from Mexico City, New York City, Poland, France, and South America. These included Judy Baca, Amalia Mesa-Bains, Lowery Stokes Sims, Katie Doyle, Kate Bonansinga, Einar and Jamex de la Torre, Marcos Ramirez ERRE, Coco Gonzales, David Taylor, Joe Lewis, Jesse Lerner, Rita Gonzalez, René Peralta, Teddy Cruz, Fonna Forman, Rafal Milach, Ana Teresa Fernández, Guillermo Galindo, Richard Misrach, and Stephanie Syjuco. At the Los Angeles County Museum of Art, Stephanie Barron and Ilona Katzew expanded my historical and geographical horizons in art, as did diverse projects at the Getty Research Institute and the Craft & Folk Art Museum of Los Angeles (now known as the Craft Contemporary).

In academic circles I was welcomed into the Association for Borderlands Studies and the Borders in Globalization group in Ottawa. Thanks to Victor Konrad, Randy Widdis, Tony Payan, and Kathleen Staudt, I received early invitations to present my border film outlook in public settings. In geography, Stuart Aiken, Daniel Arreola, Larry Herzog, Reece Jones, and Christophe Sohn (among many others) produced pioneering works that helped me get oriented. In Mexico, various colleagues at El Colegio de la Frontera Norte (COLEF) in Tijuana, Juárez, and Matamoros produced an invaluable flow of knowledge and insight from *el otro lado*.

Border studies worldwide involve a collection of convivial, multidisciplinary researchers whose published works provided firm foundations for my own investigation. The extent of my indebtedness to these many experts is evident from the list of references that accompanies the text, although even this long list does not exhaust my indebtedness.

At the University of California Press in Oakland, California, I am indebted to Kim Robinson, the press's editorial director and my editor, whose support and gentle "nudges" turned a sometimes flailing manuscript into a coherent book. Thanks also to the entire team involved in the book's production: Summer Farah, Teresa Iafolla, Katryce Lassle, and Julie Van Pelt; and beyond the Bay Area, Jon Dertien and Sharon Langworthy.

Early drafts of the manuscript were read by David James and Edward Dimendberg, who offered direction and encouragement. Norma Iglesias Prieto and Jesse

Lerner provided invaluable formal reviews of the completed manuscript. Marc Treib was always available with tea and conversations about books. And long ago, Denise Klarquist and Jennifer Wolch endured my first stilted conversations about the possibility of a book on border film. They read everything up to and including the final draft and helped to assemble the final manuscript. Their faith in the project and readiness to assist never faltered.

I offer special thanks for permission to use the spectacular image on the front cover from the Project Archive of *El otro lado de la línea/The Other Side of the Line.*

*Mil gracias a todos.* Thank you everyone. None but I shall be blamed for the opinions and errors that adorn this book.

Michael Dear
Berkeley, California, and the United Borderland States

Chronological Filmography

Border Film Genre, 1914–2021 (N = 72)

| Year of Release | Title | Director |
| --- | --- | --- |
| 1914 | *Shorty's Trip to Mexico* | Francis Ford |
| 1923 | *The Pilgrim* | Charles Chaplin |
| 1935 | *Bordertown* | Archie Mayo |
| 1936 | *Vámonos con Pancho Villa* | Fernando de Fuentes |
| 1949 | *Border Incident* | Anthony Mann |
| 1952 | *Aventurera* | Alberto Gout |
| 1952 | *Viva Zapata!* | Elia Kazan |
| 1953 | *The Hitch-Hiker* | Ida Lupino* |
| 1953 | *Jeopardy* | John Sturges |
| 1953 | *Espaldas mojadas* | Alejandro Galindo |
| 1958 | *Touch of Evil* | Orson Welles |
| 1960 | The Magnificent Seven | John Sturges |
| 1961 | One-Eyed Jacks | Marlon Brando |
| 1966 | The Professionals | Richard Brooks |
| 1969 | *The Wild Bunch* | Sam Peckinpah |
| 1970 | Valdez Is Coming | Edwin Sherin |
| 1973 | The Long Goodbye | Robert Altman |

| Year of Release | Title | Director |
| --- | --- | --- |
| 1977, 2004 | ¡Alambrista! | Robert M. Young |
| 1978 | Cheech & Chong's Up in Smoke | Lou Adler |
| 1982 | The Border | Tony Richardson |
| 1982 | The Ballad of Gregorio Cortes | Roberto Young |
| 1983 | El Norte | Gregory Nava |
| 1987 | Born in East LA | Cheech Marin |
| 1992 | Como agua para chocolate | Alfonso Arau |
| 1991 | Mi querido Tom Mix | Carlos Garcia Agraz |
| 1991 | Cabeza de Vaca | Nicolás Echeverría |
| 1994 | El Jardín del Edén | María Novaro* |
| 1995 | Lone Star | John Sayles |
| 1995 | Mi Familia | Gregory Nava |
| 1996 | From Dusk til Dawn | Robert Rodríguez |
| 1998 | La otra conquista | Salvador Carrasco |
| 1998 | Bajo California: El límite del tiempo | Carlos Bolado Muño |
| 2000 | All the Pretty Horses | Billy Bob Thornton |
| 2000 | Traffic | Stephen Soderburgh |
| 2003 | Yo la peor de todas | María Luisa Bemberg* |
| 2003 | The Mexican Dream | Gustavo Hernández Pérez |
| 2004 | A Day without a Mexican | Sergio Arau |
| 2004 | *And Starring Pancho Villa as Himself* | Bruce Beresford |
| 2004 | Maria Full of Grace | Joshua Marston |
| 2005 | How the Garcia Girls Spent Their Summer | Georgina García Reidel* |
| 2005 | Three Burials of Melquiades Estrada | Tommy Lee Jones |
| 2006 | Babel | Alejandro González Iñárritu |
| 2006 | Bordertown | Gregory Nava |
| 2007 | No Country for Old Men | Coen Brothers |
| 2007 | La misma luna/Under the same moon | Patricia Riggen* |
| 2008 | Julia | Erick Zonca |
| 2008 | Sleep Dealer | Alex Rivera |
| 2008 | *Purgatorio* | Roberto Rochín |
| 2008 | 7 Soles | Pedro Ulteras |
| 2009 | Sin nombre | Cary Joji Fukunaga |
| 2010 | Machete | Robert Rodríguez/ Ethan Manaquis |
| 2011 | Miss Bala | Gerardo Naranjo |

| Year of Release | Title | Director |
|---|---|---|
| 2012 | Savages | Oliver Stone |
| 2013 | The Last Stand | Kim Jee-Woon |
| 2013 | Go for Sisters | John Sayles |
| 2014 | Frontera | Michael Berry |
| 2015 | Sicario | Denis Villeneuve |
| 2015 | 600 Millas | Gabriel Ripstein |
| 2015 | Ixcanul | Jayro Bustamante |
| 2015 | The Boatman | Greg Morgan |
| 2016 | Transpecos | Greg Kwedar |
| 2016 | Desierto | Jonás Cuarón |
| 2016 | The Hollow Point | Gonzalo López-Gallego |
| 2017 | Carne y Arena | Alejandro González Iñárritu |
| 2019 | Miss Bala | Catherine Hardwicke* (remake) |
| 2019 | Pájaros de verano | Kristina Gallego*/Ciro Guerra |
| 2019 | Ya no estoy aquí/I'm no longer here | Fernando Frias de la Parra |
| 2019 | Los Lobos/The Wolves | Samuel Kishi Leopo |
| 2019 | Vuelven/Tigers Are Not Afraid | Issa López* |
| 2021 | Sin señas particulares/ Identifying features | Fernanda Valadez* |
| 2021 | 499 | Rodrigo Reyes |
| 2021 | Noche de Fuego/Prayers for the Stolen | Tatiana Huezo* |

Italicized titles refer to films in part 1 of the book, the remainder to films in part 2 and part 3.
*Woman director.

Alphabetical Filmography

Women directors are indicated with an asterisk.

## COMPLETE BORDER AND
## BORDER-RELATED FILMOGRAPHY

*¡Alambrista!*, Robert M. Young, 1977; 2004

*All the Pretty Horses*, Billy Bob Thornton, 2000

*And Starring Pancho Villa as Himself*, Bruce Beresford, 2004

*Aventurera*, Alberto Gout, 1952

*Babel*, Alejandro González Iñárritu, 2006

*Bacurau*, Kleber Mendonca Fihlo and JulianoDornelles, 2019

*Bajo California*, Carlos Bolado Muñoz, 1998

*The Ballad of Gregorio Cortes*, Roberto Young, 1982

*Bandidas*, Joachim Roenning and Sandberg, 2006

*The Band's Visit*, Eran Kolirin, 2007

*The Boatman*, Greg Morgan, 2015

*Border*, Ali Abbasi, 2018

*The Border*, Tony Richardson, 1982

*Border Incident*, Anthony Mann, 1949

*Bordertown*, Archie Mayo, 1935

*Bordertown*, Gregory Nava, 2006

*Born in East LA*, Cheech Marin, 1987

*Cabeza de Vaca*, Nicolás Echeverría, 1991

*Canadian Bacon*, Michael Moore, 1995

*Carne y Arena*, Alejandro González Iñárritu, 2017

*Cheech & Chong's Up in Smoke*, Lou Adler, 1978

*Como agua para chocolate*, Alfonso Arau, 1991

*Cry Macho*, Clint Eastwood, 2021

*The Day after Tomorrow*, Roland Emmerich, 2004

*A Day without a Mexican*, Sergio Arau, 2004

*Desierto*, Jonás Cuarón, 2016

*Disengagement* Amos Gitai 2009

*Distinto amanecer*, Julio Bracho, 1943

*Don Juan Tenorio*, Salvador Toscano Barragán, 1898

*El automóvil gris*, Enrique Rosas, 1919

*El Jardín del Edén*, María Novaro\*, 1994

*El Norte*, Gregory Nava, 1983

*El puño de hierro*, Gabriel García Moreno, 1927

*El reinado del terror*, Edmundo y Félix Padilla, 1932

*El tren fantasma*, Gabriel García Moreno, 1927

*Espaldas mojadas*, Alejandro Galindo, 1953

*Fata Morgana*, Werner Herzog, 1971

*Fauna*, Nicolás Pereda, 2021

*The Fence: Making of Two Men in Town*, Sacha Wolff,\* 2014

*The Forever Purge*, Everardo Gout, 2021

*499*, Rodrigo Reyes, 2020

*Free Zone*, Amos Gitai 2005

*From Dusk til Dawn*, Robert Rodríguez, 1996

*Frontera*, Michael Berry, 2014

*Frozen River*, Courtney Hunt, 2008

*Go for Sisters*, John Sayles, 2013

*House*, Amos Gitai 1980

*A House in Jerusalem*, Amos Gitai, 1998

*Historia de la Revolución Mexicana*, Julio Lamadrid, 1936

*The Hitch-Hiker*, Ida Lupino, 1953

*Hold Back the Dawn*, Mitchell Leisen, 1941

*The Hollow Point*, Gonzalo López-Gallego, 2016

*How the García Girls Spent Their Summer*, Georgina García Reidel,* 2005

*The Infiltrators*, Alex Rivera, 2020

*Inmate # 1:Rise of Danny Trejo*, Brett Harvey, 2020

*Ixcanul*, Jayro Bustamante, 2015

*Jeopardy*, John Sturges, 1953

*Julia*, Erick Zonca, 2008

*La otra conquista*, Salvador Carrasco, 1998

*La reina del sur*, 2011 (telenovela)

*La venganza del General Villa*, Edmundo Padilla/Félix Padilla, 1937

*La vida de Sabina Rivas*, Luis Mandoki, 2012

*The Last Stand*, Kim Jee-Woon, 2013

*The Lawless*, Joseph Losey, 1950

*The Lemon Tree*, Eran Riklis, 2008

*Liberty*, Jacques Jaccard/Henry MacRae, 1916

*The Life of General Villa*, Raoul Walsh, 1914 (lost)

*The Life of General Villa*, William C. Cabanne, 1914

*Lone Star*, John Sayles, 1995

*The Long Goodbye*, Robert Altman, 1973

*Los Lobos*, Samuel Kishi Leopo, 2019

*Lost Reels of Pancho Villa*, Gregorio Rocha, 2003

*Machete*, Robert Rodríguez/Ethan Manaquis, 2010

*The Magnificent Seven*, John Sturges, 1960

*Maria Full of Grace*, Joshua Marston, 2004

*Mary, Mary, Bloody Mary*, Juan López Moctezuma, 1975

*The Mexican Dream*, Gustavo Hernández Pérez, 2003 .

*Mi Familia*, Gregory Nava, 1995

*Mi querido Tom Mix*, Carlos García Agraz, 1991

*Miss Bala*, Gerardo Naranjo, 2011

*Miss Bala 2*, Catherine Hardwicke,* 2019 (remake)

*My Mexican Shiva*, Alejandro Springhall, 2006

*News from Home, News from House*, Amos Gitai, 2006

*No Country for Old Men*, Coen Brothers, 2007

*No Man's Land*, Conor Allyn, 2021

*Nuevo orden [New Order]*, Michel Franco, 2020

*One-Eyed Jacks*, Marlon Brando, 1961

*Pájaros de verano*, Kristina Gallego/Ciro Guerra, 2019

*Pancho Villa en Columbus*, Edmundo Padilla/Félix Padilla, 1934

*The Pilgrim*, Charles Chaplin, 1923

*Prayers for the Stolen* [*Noche de Fuego*], Tatiana Huezo,* 2021

*The Professionals*, Richard Brooks, 1966

*Promised Land*, Amos Gitai, 2004

*Purgatorio*, Rodrigo Reyes, 2012 (documentary)

*Purgatorio*, Roberto Rochín, 2008

*Que Viva México*, Sergei Eisenstein, 1932

*Savages*, Oliver Stone, 2012

*7 Soles*, Pedro Ulteras, 2008

*Shorty's Trip to Mexico*, Francis Ford, 1914

*Sicario*, Denis Villeneuve, 2015

*Sin nombre*, Cary Joji Fukunaga, 2009

*Sin señas particulares*, Fernanda Valadez,* 2020

*600 Millas*, Gabriel Ripstein, 2015

*Sleep Dealer*, Alex Rivera, 2008

*Solo con tu pareja*, Alfonso Cuarón, 1991

*También la lluvia*, Icíar Bollaín, 2010

*Tel Aviv on Fire*, Sameh Zoabi, 2019

*Tepeyac*, José Manuel Ramos/Carlos E. Gonzales/Fernando Sayago, 1917

*Three Burials of Melquiades Estrada*, Tommy Lee Jones, 2005

*3:10 to Yuma*, Delmer Daves, 1957

*Tigers Are Not Afraid/Vuelven*, Issa López,* 2019

*Touch of Evil*, Orson Welles, 1958

*Traffic*, Stephen Soderburgh, 2000

*Transpecos*, Greg Kwedar, 2016

*Two Men in Town*, Rachid Bouchareb, 2014

*Under the Same Moon*, Patricia Riggen,* 2007

*Valdez Is Coming*, Edwin Sherin, 1970

*Vámonos con Pancho Villa*, Fernando de Fuentes, 1936

*Víctimas del pecado*, Emilio Fernández, 1951

*Viena & The Fantomes*, Gerardo Naranjo, 2020

*Villa Rides*, Buzz Kulik, 1968

*Viva Zapata!*, Elia Kazan, 1952

*Waiting for the Barbarians*, Ciro Guerra, 2020

*The Wild Bunch*, Sam Peckinpah, 1969

*Ya no estoy aquí*, Fernando Frías de la Parra, 2019

*Yo la peor de todas*, María Luisa Bemberg,* 2003


## TELEVISION

*The Bridge*, season 1, Gerardo Naranjo, 2013

*The Day I Met El Chapo: The Kate Del Castillo Story*, Carlos Armella, 2017 (documentary series)

APPENDIX 3   Map of US-Mexico
Borderlands

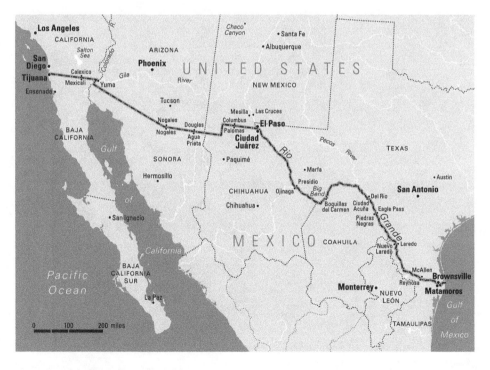

Artwork by Dreamline Cartography

# Notes

1. Glendinning (2000).

2. Griswold del Castillo (1990, 188).

3. The standard history of the boundary surveys is Rebert (2001). See also Dear (2015, ch. 1).

4. The basic cartographic sources used by the first survey were a John Disturnell map published in New York in 1847 and a Spanish map published in 1802 by Don Juan Pantoja. The US boundary survey commissioner, William H. Emory, fulminated against all the cartographers who provided his source maps, including Alexander von Humboldt, who had been rapturously received in 1804 by US president Thomas Jefferson. See Mendoza (2021). Von Humboldt's reception in Washington, D.C., is recounted in Wulf (2015, ch. 8).

5. St. John (2011, ch. 1).

6. Mendoza (2021, 209).

7. Chatfield (1893).

8. For a Mexican perspective on the border fortifications, see Córdova and de la Parra (2012) and Boullosa and Quintero 2020

9. For early records of Biden's presidency, see Pierce and Bolter (2020), Meissner (2020), and Chishti and Bolter (2022).

10. United States Court of Appeals for the Ninth Circuit (2016, 22–23).

## CHAPTER 2. BISECTED BODIES

1. In a book entitled *The Devil Finds Work* (1976), James Baldwin combines personal biography with a critique of the portrayal of Black people in Hollywood films. Its opening sentence instantly grabbed my attention: "Joan Crawford's straight, narrow, and lonely back." Baldwin is referring to his fascination with Crawford's screen image in a film he saw at the age of seven with his mother (or aunt; he's unsure). Baldwin ([1976] 2011, 3).

2. Chaplin as a "mythical figure" is discussed in Bazin (1967, 144–53).

3. Iglesias [Prieto] (1991, 1:17). Since her original conceptualization, the issue of defining border film has provoked much discussion. The extensions typically reflect changing times and emphases, plus a maturing and refinement of border film studies. For instance, the impact of a director's ethnicity on film representation, the significance of "internal borders" such as those brought about by different languages and traditions, and the consequences of migration and circulation in the border region and beyond have been raised.

4. *LA Plays Itself* (2003). In this film, Anderson's three categories are loosely defined and informal in usage. I have adopted a more precise version better suited for my needs.

5. See Berg (2002a) and Maciel (1990) for historical overviews of Mexican and US stereotypes.

6. Sariñara-Lampson (2011).

7. Iglesias [Prieto] (1991, 2015).

8. Morris (2005, ch. 6).

9. Hershfield (1996, chs. 1 and 5).

10. Mora (2005) is a useful compendium of films made in Mexico from the silent era to the early twentieth century, with some reference to border film. It is especially valuable for its collection of film stills from all eras.

11. García Riera (1963, 20).

12. Gates (2019, 74).

13. Racial antipathy and mistrust and fear regarding miscegenation existed for centuries before filmmaking. See Katzew (2004), Martínez (2008), and Katzew and Deans-Smith (2009).

14. Gates (2019, 75).

15. Gates (2019, 151–57) has a concise critique of the much-discussed *Birth of a Nation*.

16. Fregoso (2003, 132). Her chapter 7 discusses miscegenation, including *Shorty's Trip to Mexico*.

17. Haygood (2021). This is an essential source in Black American filmmaking. Chapters 1 and 2 deal respectively with Griffith and Micheaux; chapter 7 covers miscegenation.

18. PCA staff member, reported in Vasey (1997, 139).

19. Klawans (1999, 115).

20. Robinson and Cabral (2003, 1–20).

21. See, respectively, Hershfield (1996, 81–100) and Delgadillo (2006).

22. Berg (2015, 56).

23. The three films discussed in this section were restored by Filmoteca at Mexico's National University, UNAM, in 2017, 2004, and 2016, respectively. Versions are available on YouTube, with intertitles in Spanish and musical accompaniment. (*El puño de hierro* also has English subtitles.) Note that unrestored versions of the films are included on the same site, so take care to identify the UNAM restoration. The fragmentary, battered quality of the unrestored films is testimony to the remarkable success of the UNAM restorations.

24. The surrealist presence in Mexican film is usually connected with Luis Buñuel. The account by Ripley (2017) is relevant to my topic since he adopts a geographical lens to explore the works.

25. Drew and Vasquez Bernal (2003).


CHAPTER 3. MAKING FILMSCAPES

1. Jacobson (2015, 2020) offers a collection of essays (his own and others') that take a wide view of production in places including southern California, Paris, Italy, and Mexico.

2. Bruno (1993, esp. 37–470).

3. For comparison, a fine study of early film culture in Paris is Lehmbeck, Salveson, and Schwartz (2022).

4. Irwin and Castro Ricalde (2013, 1–34).

5. Uribe (2009). Ana and I worked together during her LA-based research for her book.

6. King (2000) provides a valuable survey of cinema in Latin America including Argentina, Bolivia, Brazil, Chile, Colombia, Cuba, Ecuador, Mexico, Paraguay, Peru, Uruguay, and Venezuela.

7. Babitz ([1974] 2016, 8).

8. Babitz ([1974] 2016, 330).

9. Babitz ([1974] 2016, 130). Apart from her appreciation of landscape, Eve was a peerless dissector of human nature, especially her own. She attracted many admirers, yet in the presence of a man she found attractive, her tilt toward self-deprecation could overtake her: "He is dressed in tweeds and tailoring whereas I look as though I've been roused from a bed of bon bons, ostrich feathers, and tuxedo highballs" (38). On another occasion, she contrasted the suffering of a poverty-stricken writer friend in wintertime England with her own LA days of champagne cocktails and diets, arriving at a moment of epiphany: "The world wasn't *all* power struggles between me and pasta" (13).

10. My brief history of Hollywood draws from Scott (2005, 11–34). See also Christopherson and Storper (1986). Thomson (2005) covers the same period, with more emphasis on films and personalities.

11. Black film critic Melvin B. Tolson wrote a scathing review of *Gone with the Wind* (1939), comparing it with *Birth of a Nation* (1915). He concluded that GWTW is a thinly disguised apology for racism and the Ku Klux Klan. Reprinted in Lopate (2006, 140–44).

12. Scott (2005, table 2.1, 26).

13. Marez (2004, 57–82).

14. James (2005).

15. Anker, Geritz, and Seid (2010).

16. Scott (2005, ch. 3).

17. Brownstein (2021) recounts one year of creative intersections among film, music, television, and politics in Los Angeles.

18. Scott (2005, ch.4).

19. Scott (2005, 105).

20. Another sparkling history of the birth of the business, this time in Paris, France, is Lehmbeck, Salveson, and Schwartz (2022).

21. Basic sources on Mexican film are Mora (2005) and Berg (2015). For the recent New Wave in Mexican cinema, see Wood (2006). An updated edition (Wood 2021) appeared as this manuscript was being completed.

22. A concise history of the beginnings of silent film in Mexico is Tomadjoglou (2017).

23. Berg (1992, 26).

24. Berg (2015, ch. 3). Schroeder Rodríguez (2016, 37–40) puts *Automóvil Gris* in historical perspective.

25. Berg (1992, 27).

26. Hershfield and Maciel (1999). Part II recounts the golden age (33–191).

27. Serna, in Jacobson (2020, 85–102). The Estudios Churubusco in Mexico City were opened in 1945 and acquired by the federal government in 1950. They are still operating.

28. Wood (2006, xii).

29. Maciel (1992, 70–85); and King (2000, 140–43).

30. See the account of a pathbreaking 1999 exhibition, in *Mexperimental Cinema*, by Lerner and González (1998). A more recent overview of this history is Lerner and Piazza (2017).

31. Wood (2006, xi–xiii).

32. In these three paragraphs, I draw on Bregent-Heald (2015), esp. 1–90.

33. Iglesias [Prieto] (1991). Since then, she has periodically revised and updated her account. The most comprehensive update in Spanish is Iglesias [Prieto] (2015), and in English, Iglesias [Prieto] (2013, 183–213).

34. Maciel (1990).

35. Mora (2005, 155–64). A churro is a popular snack in Mexico, consisting of a doughnut mixture shaped like a hot dog, deep-fried and dunked in sugar.

36. Avalos (2009).

37. Iglesias [Prieto], in Hershfield and Maciel (1999, 232–48).

38. Irwin and Castro Ricalde (2013, 33).

39. Box office returns are from Mora (2005, 163 and 159).

40. Agrasánchez (2006, 2, 8).

41. Agrasánchez (2006, 43–46).

42. Dell'agnese (2005); and Staudt (2014).

## CHAPTER 4. USING FILM AS EVIDENCE

1. Lane (2020, 80).

2. Von Tunzelmann (2015, 7).

3. James (2016, chs. 8, 9, and 11).

4. Quoted in Nuwer (2020). See also Juhasz and Lerner (2006).

5. David Fincher, quoted in Buchanan (2021b, C2).

6. Thomson (2012, 461–72) offers an idiosyncratic insider's view of the director's world.

7. *Solo con tu pareja* DVD extras.

8. See, for example, Stratton (2019) and Wasson (2020).

9. Neumann (1996) offers many perceptive examples of filmmakers' artfulness, including cuts, edits, camera angles, close-ups, color, and music.

10. Thomson (2017, 85).

11. Serna (2014, especially ch. 6) provides an excellent history of Mexican migrants' filmgoing habits.

12. Cinema practices and audience experiences in Wales that are similar to mine have been described by Richards (2003).

13. Lopate (2006, xx–xxvii).

14. Lopate (2006), respectively, xx and xxiv.

15. Lane (2002, xviii).

16. BFI (2021).

17. James (2008).

18. Kracauer ([1932] 1994, 634–35).

19. Hoberman (2019, 2012).

20. Baldwin ([1976] 2011). A short introduction to Baldwin's life and work is *I Am Not Your Negro* (2017), a film documentary directed by Raoul Peck. A comprehensive source of his writings is Morrison (1998a, 1998b).

21. The four quotes in this paragraph and the next are from Baldwin ([1976] 2011), 9, 26, 112, and 112, respectively.

22. A present-day assessment of Baldwin's writings on race in America is provided by Glaude (2020).

23. Quoted in Dym and Offen (2011, 51).

24. A recent account of this encyclopedia is Peterson and Terraciano (2019).

25. For a compelling investigation of the textual differences, see Terraciano (2019, 45–62).

26. Anderson and Dibble (1978, 87). See also Lockhart ([1993] 2004).


## CHAPTER 5. REVOLUTION AND MODERNIZATION

1. A concise pictorial history of the Mexican Revolution is by Brenner ([1943] 1971). Also see the summary in Dear (2015, chs. 2–3).

2. Knight (2016).

3. Cándida Smith (2017, 33–44).

4. Knight (2016, 64–69).

5. Knight (2016, 52).

6. Escobedo and Gori (1989).

7. Lacey (2011, A16).

8. A history of the making of *The Wild Bunch* is recounted in Stratton (2019), who concludes, "I've never seen a better movie" (305).

9. Thomson (2005, 333).

10. Stratton (2019, 272–73).

11. Stratton (2019, 8).

12. Stratton (2019, 66–67, 76–77).

13. The incredible story of Mutual and Villa is told in de Orellana (2009).

14. Noble (2011, 68, 38–59).

15. Berg (2015, 63–64); Mora (2005, 43–49).

16. Berthier (2011).

17. Morseberger ([1975] 2009, 138 and xxvii).

18. Walsh (1974, 88).

19. Reed ([1914] 1983, 95)

20. Torres ([1931] 1973, xi).

21. Rocha (2006).

22. Lerner (2011, 23); and Rocha (2006, 56–57).

23. Rocha (2006, 57).

24. Stratton (2019, 218).

25. Feldman (1968).

26. The two final quotations are from Stratton (2019, 309, 304).


## CHAPTER 6. THE GREAT MIGRATIONS

1. Dorado Romo (2005, 223–44).

2. Hernández (2010, 88–93).

3. Today the border patrol is part of the Department of Homeland Security and is formally known as Customs and Border Protection. Throughout this book, I retain its original title, US Border Patrol, which was in use for most of the period covered in this account. See also Dear (2015, chs. 4, 7, and 11).

4. Hernández (2010, 93–97, 6–7, and 83–85).

5. Balderrama and Rodríguez (1995).

6. Although the Bracero Program was introduced as a wartime effort, it lasted until 1964 and involved more than two million guest workers. See McWilliams (1990, ch. 14) and Hernández (2010, 109–14).

7. Hernández (2010, 130–32).

8. Hernández (2010, 155–57).

9. Smith (1998, 4th ed., 197).

10. Dana Polan in voice-over commentary, *Border Incident* DVD.

11. Mexicali architecture is discussed in Lucero Velasco (2002) and Burian (2015).

12. Noble (2005, 147).

13. Translation from Noble (2005, 150, also 152).

14. Translation from Fox (1999, 109).

15. Translation from Fox (1999, 113).

16. Translation from Mora (2005, 90–93). In this context, the term *pocho/a* usually refers to a Mexican person living in the United States.

17. Translation from Fox (1999, 112).

18. My translation from "Para una mujer no hay mas mundo que el hombre que uno quiere."

## CHAPTER 7. BORDER FILM NOIR

1. Silver and Ursini (1998).

2. The classic era of US film noir produced several hundred films without a border emphasis, including such unforgettable classics as *The Maltese Falcon* (John Huston, 1941), with a cast including Humphrey Bogart as private eye Sam Spade and Mary Astor as Gladys George, his fidgety client, together with the immortal pair, Peter Lorre and Sidney Greenstreet. Noir films were popular among audiences, and many talented filmmakers and performers were attracted to the genre. Among the still-admired early noir classics are *Double Indemnity* (Billy Wilder, 1944), starring a glorious Barbara Stanwyck, a hapless Fred MacMurray, and a dyspeptic Edward G. Robinson; and *The Big Sleep* (Howard Hawks, 1946), which introduced the legendary pairing of Lauren Bacall and Humphrey Bogart. Later gems were Billy Wilder's *Sunset Boulevard* (1950), pitting operatic diva Gloria Swanson against William Holden; and *Gilda* (Charles Vidor, 1946), with Rita Hayworth in a performance that cedes no screen time to any mortal. Although the classic noir era ended after the late 1950s, the tradition endured

through "neo-noir" films such as *Chinatown* (Roman Polanski, 1974), *Devil in a Blue Dress* (Carl Franklin, 1995), and the "future-noir" *Blade Runner* (Ridley Scott, 1982). A comprehensive history of urban noir is available in Dimenberg (2004).

3. Shiel (2010, 75–103).

4. Christopher (1997, 31). The film referred to is *Once a Thief* (W. Lee Wilder, 1950).

5. Bregent-Heald (2006, 126).

6. James Ursini, commentary on *Out of the Past*, accompanying the DVD version of the film.

7. The homosexual connection between Marlowe and Terry Lennox is more evident in the novel than in the film (Freeman, 2007, esp. 167–68, 285–87).

8. Thomson (2012, 165).

9. Comito (1985, 22–23).

10. Mora (2005, 144).

11. Vega Alfaro (1999, 165–91).

12. Hershfield (1996, ch. 4).

13. Extended critiques of *Distinto amanecer* (also titled Another dawn) may be found in Berg (2015, 188–99) and Hershfield (1996, 84–91). See also Hoberman (2017).

14. King (2000) discusses Agustín Lara's role in film music, particularly *Distinto amanecer*.

15. Ninón Sevilla played many *cabaretera* roles during her very successful film career. See Mora (2005, 86–89).

16. López (1993, 158).

17. Schroeder Rodríguez (2016, 122). Schroeder Rodríguez also quotes Gilberto Pérez on 317n11.

## CHAPTER 8. BORDERLANDS BEFORE BORDERS

1. Dear (2013, 2015 chs. 1–4).

2. Knight (2002a, 2002b).

3. The two quotes in this paragraph are from Elliot (2019, 44–45).

4. Reséndez (2016, 198–99); Weber (1992, ch.8).

5. Hämäläinen (2008, 9).

6. Jacoby (2008).

7. Lerner (2011); and Evans (2004). An imaginative retelling of Mexico's indigenous history and conquest is the film by Lerner and Ortiz, *Fronterilandia* (1995).

8. Pohl and Lyons (2010, x).

9. Evans (2004, 153).

10. Evans (2004, 130–39).

11. Quoted in an audio commentary included in the DVD release. Carrasco discusses his film in Wood (2006, 49–56).

12. For an account of Topiltzin's life see Nicholson (2000).

13. Mundy (2015).

14. Adorno and Pautz (2003).

15. Reséndez (2007, 6).

16. Reséndez (2007, 222).

17. King (2000, 266–67) writes that Luisa Bemberg's "work remains one of the most important and coherent initiatives in Argentinian cinema."

18. A good introduction in English to the work is de la Cruz (1997).

19. Paz (1988). Also Stavans (2018).

20. Paz (1988, 389–502).

21. Cruz (1988, ch. 3).

22. Simmons (1991).

23. de Oñate, (2011, 82).

24. These two terms are used, respectively, by Kessel (2002, 83) and Weber (1992, 86).

25. Romero (2017).

26. Romero (2020, A18).

27. Bonfil Batalla (1996, xv).

28. The translations by Sayers Peden are especially well-crafted and a pleasure to read. For a present-day rendition of selections of the works, see Grossman (2014).

## CHAPTER 9. FROM FINAL GIRL TO WOMAN WARRIOR

1. For a fuller consideration of causes of femicide in Juárez and Chihuahua City, see Guillermoprieto (2003), and Rivera Garza (2020, esp. ch. 14).

2. Vulliamy (2010a, 2010b, 42); and Ainslie (2013).

3. Guillermoprieto (2010). For comparison, the murder rate in Mexico City was eight per one hundred thousand inhabitants, twice the national average in the US at that time.

4. Iglesias [Prieto] ([1985] 1997).

5. An account of evolving housing finance arrangements in Mexico at that time is UN Habitat (2011).

6. Cave (2012). For a more up-to-date account, see Garza (2020, ch. 14).

7. Clover (1992, 35–41).

8. Aldama (2014).

9. *Satánico Pandemonium* was the title of a Mexican "nunsploitation" horror film directed by Gilberto Martínez Solares and released in 1975. It was one of a

series of voluptuous Mexican horror films of this period, including the ground-breaking *Mary, Mary, Bloody Mary* (1975), directed by Juan López Moctezuma, who was also known as the Walter Cronkite of Mexico and had worked on the famous cult film *El Topo* (Alejandro Jodorowsky, 1970). In *From Dusk* the character's name was slightly altered to Santánico Pandemonium.

10. Rodríguez discusses *From Dusk Til Dawn* (and other films of his) in a 2000 interview, in Berg (2002b, 240–61).

11. In 2002, Arturo Pérez-Reverte published a popular novel entitled *La reina del sur* (Queen of the south), about a Mexican woman who becomes the most powerful drug trafficker in southern Spain. It was adapted as a telenovela in 2011. Following strict telenovela conventions, the cast of characters is long enough to resemble a job creation program. The bad men are as large as refrigerators, and the sex involves only beautiful people. In the episodes set in Spain, much is made of Teresa's Mexican origin. She is referred to as la Mexicana; her accent is regarded as cute, weird, or incomprehensible. In low-class settings she is called a "beaner" or "beaner bitch." When one of her Spanish coworkers initiates sex, she urges him to call her a "horny Mexican." Yet in a tender moment, Teresa's first real friendship in Spain is marked by the realization that she is learning to speak Spanish at the same time that her companion is learning Mexican. See also Armella (2017), an account of the star's real-life involvement with the drug lord El Chapo.

12. There's a special irony in this vilification of people of Chinese origin, since Chinese immigrants built the railroads in Baja California before being subjected to the US Chinese Exclusion Act of 1882, prohibiting immigration of all Chinese-origin laborers. Even so, until the 1930s there were still more people of Chinese origin than Mexicans in Mexicali, and the Chinese presence is still evident to this day. See Lucero Velasco (2003).

13. In an audio commentary accompanying the film, director Sayles expressed a particular fondness for this scene, calling it his "$1.98 version of *Blade Runner!*"

## CHAPTER 10. NARCO NATIONS

1. A useful source on the emergence of drug wars is Heinle, Ferreira, and Shirk (2014).

2. On the rise of cartel violence in Mexico see Vulliamy (2010a, 2010b) and Campbell (2009). The best Mexican-origin accounts in English are by Grillo (2012) and Hernández et al. (2013).

3. Ainslie (2013).

4. Payan (2014, 435–47).

5. Tijuana-based writer Heriberto Yépez supported a ban: "*Narcocorridos* are war propaganda," he wrote. "Drug dealers reinforce their role-model status

thanks to the music that portrays them as heroes. With no positive role models around and plenty of misery, cartel music is exactly what we don't need on our streets." Jorge Castañeda, former minister in the administration of Vicente Fox, criticized corrido bans: "You cannot blame *narcocorridos* for drug violence. Drug violence is to blame for *narcocorridos*." See Kun (2010).

6. Finnegan (2010).

7. Finnegan (2010, 65).

8. Archibold (2010, A11).

9. Schladen (2011, 1B).

10. Malkin and Thompson (2010, A6).

11. Martinez-Cabrera (2011a, 1A, 2011b), 1A).

12. For more on the comparison between Tijuana and Juárez, see Shirk (2014, 481–502).

13. Cave (2011, A10).

14. Adams (2015, 164–78).

15. An authoritative account of the Iron River is Grillo (2021). A novelistic treatment of the same issues is Parker (2010).

16. For real-world assessments of the difficulties of containing cartel operations in Mexico and the US, see respectively Aguilar Camín and Castañeda (2009a, 2009b) and Payan (2016).

## CHAPTER 11. LIVES OF THE UNDOCUMENTED

1. An anthology of extracts from (fictional) global migration literature, with emphasis on departures, arrivals, and generational change, is Ahmad (2019), although this collection pays almost no attention to Latin American literature in Spanish or Portuguese.

2. Magaña (2003) has an extensive appendix summarizing the history of US immigration law.

3. Quoted in Hernández (2010, 217).

4. Authoritative accounts of recent Mexico-US migration history are Massey, Durand, and Malone (2003), Durand and Massey (2006), and Zúñiga and Hernández-León (2006). See also Nevins (2000).

5. Good accounts of this era are in Dunn (2010, chs. 3–4), Vila (2000, ch. 5), and Nevins (2002, ch. 6).

6. The number of migrant deaths doubled to 472 per year between 1995 and 2005, mostly occurring in the mountains and deserts of the US Border Patrol's Tucson sector in Arizona. Mexican sources reported 5,607 deaths between 1994 and 2008; the US Border Patrol counted 4,111 deaths since 1998, though US agencies typically undercount because of inconsistent classification practices. The ACLU concluded that the increase in migrant deaths was a predictable outcome of fencing off the border and moving migrants into harsher crossing situations.

The major causes of migrant deaths by crossing (in 2008) were exposure (30%); water related, including drowning (14%); and motor vehicle related (11%). Three-quarters of the dead were males.

7. My preferred translation is Recinos (1950). A more literal translation and commentary is Tedlock (1985).

8. The film aired on public television in 1977, and a revised version was released in 1999 (Cuellar 2004).

9. Corrido translation from Cuellar (2004, 194 and 200).

10. González (2019, 1–10) and Ybarra-Frausto (1999, 23–34).

11. Berg (2002a, 185–88). For a perspective on Chicanas, see Cortés (1983, 94–108).

12. See, for instance, Maciel (1995, 19–24); Berg (2002a), 185–89); and Noriega (1996, 2000).

13. Berg (2018).

14. An early introduction to Chicano cinema is Noriega (1996, 3–21).

15. Hagerman (2006).

16. The decisive influence of the acts of border crossing in *Babel* is emphasized by Ruiz-Alfaro (2020, 209–30).

17. For instance, Hondagneu-Sotelo (2001) has documented cases in Los Angeles, and Pratt (2012) has focused on Filipino women in Canada, especially British Columbia. See also Ahmad (2019).

18. A good example in film is *A Better Life* (Chris Weitz, 2011).

19. For a different response to *Desierto*, see Bebout and Goldsmith (2019, 147–70).

20. Gregory Nava in voice-over commentary, *El Norte* DVD.

21. Caldwell (2019); and Hing (2019).

## CHAPTER 12. MORAL TALES, BORDER LAW

1. De León (1983, 12). See also Dear (2015, pp. 50–62 and 89–91).

2. De León (1983, 3).

3. Quoted in Weber (2003, 79).

4. Quoted in Weber (2003, 72).

5. Weber (2003, 260). A more detailed account of nineteenth-century settlement along the borderlands is available in Dear (2015, chs. 3 and 4).

6. Between 1962 and 1972, as part of French filmmaking's New Wave, Eric Rohmer directed a cycle of films that collectively came to be known as *contes moraux*, or moral tales. They were elegant films concerned with romance and philosophy, desire and jealousy, mathematics and irony. The series included famous titles such as *Ma Nuit Chez Maud* (1969; My night at Maud's), and *Le Genou de Claire* (1970; Claire's knee), the last of which—to exemplify Rohmer's

delicacy—concludes as the male protagonist finally succeeds in touching the discreet object of his desire, her knee.

7. Leonard (2018).

8. Jacoby (2008) and DeLay (2008).

9. Leonard (2018, 415).

10. McCarthy (1992).

11. For a longer treatment of *Lone Star* see Fregoso (2003, 48–70).

12. Nielsen (2020).

## CHAPTER 13. BORDER WALLS

1. Huevos rancheros is a typical Mexican meal consisting mainly of eggs, refried beans, and tortillas.

2. Photographs taken by Jay Dusard are very reminiscent of the Tijuana border portrayed in *Born in East LA* (Weisman and Dusard 1986).

3. Rodríguez's films are discussed in Aldama (2014, 2019a) and Aldama and González (2019).

4. *A Day without a Mexican*, DVD special features.

5. Quoted in the *Machete* DVD special features.

6. Rivera's film has received much critical attention. See chapters by Fojas, Miranda, and Lozano in Aldama (2019b, chs. 12–14); also an interview with Rivera by Aldama (2019a, ch. 9).

## CHAPTER 14. THE MEXICAN DREAM/EL SUEÑO MEXICANO

1. Radke (2009).

2. Weber (2018).

3. Dubouisson (2019).

4. Spagat (2017).

5. Villavicencio (2021, 31).

6. Churchwell's history (2018) reveals how closely the call for "America First" was linked with notions of the American Dream, especially by President Woodrow Wilson, who was echoing contemporary isolationist sentiments that rejected US involvement in World War I. Wilson also advised caution in the face of "falsehoods" spread by contemporaneous news media.

7. Nicholas (1980).

8. Mora (2005) renders *Bajo California: El límite del tiempo*, as Below California: The limitations of time. I prefer the sense of *límite* as an edge, frontier, or boundary, a place of potential, rather than Mora's sense of finitude or constraint.

9. The Great Murals of central Baja California were first described in the records of eighteenth-century Jesuits. In 1894 a French industrial chemist, León Diguet, published descriptions of some sites. A famous US novelist, Earl Stanley Gardner, attracted modern-day attention to the murals in the 1960s. He was followed in 1971 by a Californian photographer named Harry Crosby, who visited and documented more than two hundred cave sites. Harry told me that in those early days, the locals were not terribly impressed by "their paintings," partly because murals were scattered everywhere in the region. But in 1993 the paintings were designated a UNESCO World Heritage site. As a consequence, local residents came to regard the paintings as part of their region's patrimony. The earliest accepted carbon dating at the Cueva Pintada (featured in *Bajo California*) dated the paintings there at over ten thousand years old. Laylander and Moore (2006); Gardner (1962); and Crosby (1997).

10. *Fata Morgana* was never formally released but continues to find an audience. Popul Vuh was the name of a German musical collective that collaborated with Herzog on many of his films, including *Nosferatu*; *Aguirre, the Wrath of God*; and *Fitzcarraldo*. See Cronin (2019, 58–69).

11. Recinos (1950, 81).

12. Le Clézio ([1988] 1993, 179).

13. The quote is from Le Clezio (1993, 208). The original sources are Sahagún (1932 reprint) and Peterson and Terraciano (2019).

14. Le Clezio (1993, 141).

15. Le Clezio (1993, 143–49, 189).

16. Quotes in this paragraph are from Le Clezio (1993, 161 and 164).

17. Baldwin (1998); Fields, Pohl, and Lyall (2012).

## CHAPTER 15. A GOLDEN AGE FOR BORDER FILM

1. Kuhn and Westwell (2012, 194–96).

2. Ikeda (2020).

3. Also notable in the current crop are *Los Lobos* (Samuel Kishi Leopo, 2019; *The Wolves*) and *Fauna* (Nicolás Pereda, 2021).

4. Amos Gitai's filmography extends to over one hundred titles, including feature films, documentaries, and shorts; he also works in other media including music, theater, and opera. A short summary of Gitai's life and filmography is in Toubiana (2005). A more comprehensive account is the sumptuously illustrated *Amos Gitai*, edited by Marie-Jose Sanselme (2016), which includes text in French and English.

5. Munk (2019) discusses the border trilogy, but be warned that she substitutes another of Gitai's films, *Kedma* (2002), for *Disengagement*.

6. Other Gitai films addressing border issues include *Kedma* (2002), which is set in 1948 during the crucial period when the geopolitical structure of the

Middle East was being altered to accommodate the creation of the state of Israel. A different kind of boundary is imagined in *Kadosh* (1999), which portrays the tragic consequences that ensue when a deeply religious Orthodox man is obliged to abandon his wife, who has not produced a child after ten years of marriage. Both films are discussed in Toubiana (2005, 93–103, 171–82, and 192–99).

7. Dodds (2013).

CHAPTER 16. WAYS OF SEEING THE BORDER
(BEYOND FILM)

1. See, respectively, Cádava (2013) and Peña (2020).

2. Both quotes are from Iglesias [Prieto] (2008, 44–45) (my translations).

3. Nogales was one of the towns where in-town fences were set up to stop undocumented migrant crossings in the early 1990s.

4. A selection of Mexican opinions (translated into English) on the Wall and immigration is collected in Boullosa and Quintero (2020).

5. Aguilar Camín and Castañeda (2009a, 79): "The cost of closing the northern border of Mexico is enormous; its efficacy, minimal" (my translation.)

6. Dear (2015, chs. 3 and 11).

7. Anzaldúa (1987, 3).

8. Gómez-Peña (1996, 70).

9. In an influential early work on cultural hybridity, García Canclini defines the term *hybridity* as encompassing "all the processes that combine discrete social structures or practices, which already exist in distinctly separate forms, to create new structures, objects and practices in which the antecedents merge." See García Canclini (2003, 279). For a fuller treatment of his approach, see García Canclini (1990). The universality of the hybrid is emphasized in Burke (2009).

10. Larry Herzog was one of the first US researchers to identify the emergence of a border "transfrontier metropolis." See Herzog (1990).

11. See Dear and Leclerc (2003) for more on postborder and postnational cross-border spaces.

12. My translation and rephrasing of "Una realidad fronteriza . . . y que aunque nunca han cruzado, su vida está marcada por el hecho de vivir en una ciudad vecina a EEUU" (46). See the discussion in Iglesias [Prieto] (2008, 42–47).

13. The phrase "social third space" is drawn from Velasco Ortiz (2004).

14. A history of the Tohono O'odham is told by Erickson (1994). The dynamics of shifting borderland identities among Indians, Mexicans, and Anglos in Arizona are described in Meeks (2007).

15. A film entitled *Frozen River* (Courtney Hunt, 2008) took advantage of this location to portray the lives of two women embroiled in the illicit trafficking of migrants across reservation lands. The film narrative underscores that the

border is never just a static line on a map but always in a state of becoming. See Dodds (2013, 569).

16. Pastor and Castañeda (1988, 298).

17. Pastor and Castañeda (1988, 303–4).

18. Earle and Wirth (1995, 9).

19. Bustamante, in Earle and Wirth (1995, 193).

20. Vulliamy (2010b).

21. Pastor (2011, 69).

22. Brown (2017). Established nation-states are also being pressured to accommodate "multiple nations" within their borders (as was Chile by its indigenous peoples during 2022 negotiations over revising its national constitution).

23. Jones has written widely about a world of walls; for example, see *Border Walls* (2012) and *Violent Borders* (2016). A collection of essays in McAtackney and McGuire (2020) is valuable for its focus on local walls dividing cities as well as conventional geopolitical divisions between nations. See also Miller (2021b, 2019).

24. For those seeking a more detailed grounding in what is at stake in the borderlands democracy project, the best places to start are Córdova and de la Parra (2012), Payan (2016), and Landemore (2020).

25. These ideas are developed in Landemore (2020). A forceful case from the US-Mexico border is made by Payan (2016, ch. 5).

26. Ahlers Center for International Business (2022).

27. Malone (2020). An excellent example of a regional think tank on public policy and development matters on the other side of the continent is the Bajo Bravo-Rio Grande Valley, Sede Matamoros organization (https://newsletterbbrgv.word press.com/).

28. Sohn (2022).

29. Mathews (2021). Local business leaders in San Diego and Tijuana work toward similar ends but through different organizational structures, such as the Smart Border Coalition (Malone 2020).

## CHAPTER 17. BORDER WITNESS OF THE FUTURE

1. Glaude (2020, 148). The example of Los Angeles during this era is powerfully recounted in Davis and Wiener (2020).

2. This characterization is from Glaude (2020, 53).

# References

Adams, Jeffrey. 2015. *The Cinema of the Coen Brothers*. New York: Wallflower Press.

Adelman, Jeremy, and Stephan Aron. 1999. "From Borderlands to Borders: Empires, Nation-States, and the Peoples in between in North American History." *American Historical Review* 104, no. 3: 814–41.

Adorno, Rolena, and Patrick Charles Pautz. 2003. *The Narrative of Cabeza de Vaca*. Lincoln: University of Nebraska Press.

Agrasánchez, Rogeli. 2006. *Mexican Movies in the United States: A History of Film, Theaters and Audiences, 1920–1960*. Jefferson, NC: McFarland.

Aguilar Camín, Héctor, and Jorge G. Castañeda. 2009a. *El Narco: La Guerra Fallida*. México, DF: Punto de Lectura.

——. 2009b. *Un Futuro para México*. México, DF: Punto de Lectura.

Ahlers Center for International Business. 2022. *The CaliBaja Regional Economy*. San Diego: Knauss School of Business, University of San Diego.

Ahmad, Dohra, ed. 2019. *The Penguin Book of Migration Literature*. New York: Penguin Books.

Ainslie, Ricardo C. 2013. *The Fight to Save Juárez: Life in the Heart of Mexico's Drug War*. Austin: University of Texas Press.

Aldama, Frederick Luis. 2019a. "Toward a Transfrontera-Latinx Aesthetics: An Interview with Filmmaker and Artist Alex Rivera." In *Cinema: Reimagining Identity through Aesthetics*, edited by Monica Hanna and Rebecca Sheehan, ch. 9. New Brunswick, NJ: Rutgers University Press.

283

———. 2019b. *Latinx Ciné in the Twenty-First Century*. Tucson: University of Arizona Press.

———. 2014. *The Cinema of Robert Rodríguez*. Austin: University of Texas Press.

Aldama, Frederick Luis, and Christopher González. 2019. *Reel Latinxs: Representation in U.S. Film and TV*. Tucson: University of Arizona Press.

Alton, John. (1949) 1995. *Painting with Light*. With an introduction by Todd McCarthy. Berkeley: University of California Press.

Alvarez, C. J. 2019. *Border Land, Border Water: A History of Construction on the US-Mexico Divide*. Austin: University of Texas Press.

Álvarez, Robert R., Jr. 1995. "The Mexican-U.S. Border: The Making of an Anthropology of Borderlands." *Annual Review of Anthropology* 24: 447–70.

Álvarez de Williams, Anita. 2004. *Primeros Pobladores de la Baja California: Introducción a la Antropología de la Península*. Mexicali: Centro INAH de Baja California.

Anderson, Arthur, J. O., and Charles Dibble. 1978. *The War of Conquest: How It Was Waged Here in Mexico*. Salt Lake City: University of Utah Press.

Anderson, Benedict. 1993. *Imagined Communities: Reflections on the Origin of Nationalism*. Brooklyn, NY: Verso Books.

Anker, Steve, Kathy Geritz, and Steve Seid. 2010. *Radical Light: Alternative Film and Video in the San Francisco Bay Area, 1945–2000*. Berkeley: University of California Press and Berkeley Art Museum/Pacific Film Archive.

Anzaldúa, Gloria. 1987. *Borderlands/La Frontera: The New Mestiza*. San Francisco: Aunt Lute Books.

Archibold, Randal C. 2010. "Tijuana Killings Erode Image of a City Recovering from Past Woes." *New York Times*, October 26, A11.

Armella, Carlos, dir. 2017. *The Day I Met El Chapo: The Kate del Castillo Story*. Netflix.

Avalos, A. 2009. "The Naco in Mexican Film: *La Banda del Carro Rojo*, Border Cinema, and Migrant Audiences." In *Latsploitation, Exploitation Cinemas, and Latin America*, edited by V. Ruétalo and D. Tierney, 185–97. London: Routledge.

Babitz, Eve. (1974) 2016. *Slow Days, Fast Company: The World, the Flesh, and LA*. New York: New York Review Books.

Balderrama, Francisco E., and Raymond Rodríguez. 1995. *Decade of Betrayal: Mexican Repatriation in the 1930s*. Albuquerque: University of New Mexico Press.

Baldwin, James. (1976) 2011. *The Devil Finds Work*. New York: Vintage Books.

Baldwin, Neil. 1998. *Legends of the Plumed Serpent: Biography of a Mexican God*. New York: Public Affairs.

Bazin, André. 1967. *What Is Cinema?* Vol. 1. Berkeley: University of California Press.

Bebout, Lee, and Clarissa Goldsmith. 2019. "On the Border between Migration and Horror: Rendering Border Violence Strange in Jonás Cuarón's Desierto."

In *Latinx Ciné in the Twenty-First Century*, edited by Frederick Luis Aldama, 147. Tucson: University of Arizona Press.

Beebe, Rose M., and Robert M. Senkewicz, eds. 2001. *Lands of Promise and Despair: Chronicles of Early California, 1535–1846*. Berkeley: Heyday Books.

Berg, Charles Ramírez. 2018. "*The Ballad of Gregorio Cortez*: A Cinematic Corrido." The Criterion Channel, August 14. www.criterion.com/current /posts/5821-the-ballad-of-gregorio-cortez-a-cinematic-corrido.

———. 2015. *The Classical Mexican Cinema: The Poetics of the Exceptional Golden Age Films*. Austin: University of Texas Press.

———. 2012. "*¡Alambrista!* Inside the Undocumented Experience." The Criterion Channel, April 17. www.criterion.com/current/posts/2256--alambrista-inside -the-undocumented-experience.

———. 2002a. *Latino Images in Film: Stereotypes, Subversion, Resistance*. Austin: University of Texas Press.

———. 2002b. "The Mariachi Aesthetic Goes to Hollywood: An Interview with Robert Rodríguez." In *Latino Images in Film*, 240–61. Austin: University of Texas Press.

———. 1992. "Figueroa's Skies and Oblique Perspective: Notes on the Development of the Classical Mexican Style." *Spectator* 13, no. 1. 24-41

Berthier, Nancy. 2011. "¡Viva Zapata! (Elia Kazan, 1952): El Caudillo del Sur Visto por Hollywood." *Archivos de la Filmoteca*, October, 190–207.

BFI. 2021. "The 100 Greatest Films of All Time." *Sight and Sound*, June 28. www.bfi.org.uk/greatest-films-all-time.

Bolaño, Roberto. 2008. *2066*. New York: Picador.

Bonfil Batalla, Guillermo. 1996. *México Profundo: Reclaiming a Civilization*. Austin: University of Texas Press.

Boullosa, Carmen, and Alberto Quintero, eds. 2020. *Let's Talk about Your Wall: Mexican Writers Respond to the Immigration Crisis*. New York: New Press.

Boullosa, Carmen, and Mike Wallace. 2016. *A Narco History: How the United States and Mexico Jointly Created the "Mexican Drug War."* La Vergne: OR Books.

Bradshaw Foundation, in association with Harry W. Crosby. 2016. *Baja California: In Search of the Painted Caves*. Documentary.

Bregent-Heald, Dominique. 2015. *Borderland Films: American Cinema, Mexico, and Canada During the Progressive Era*. Lincoln: University of Nebraska Press.

———. 2006. "Dark Limbo: Film Noir and the North American Borders." *Journal of American Culture* 29, no. 2: 125–38.

Brenner, Anita. (1943) 1971. *The Wind That Swept Mexico: The History of the Mexican Revolution*. Austin: University of Texas Press.

Brody, Richard. 2020. "What I Miss Most about Movie Theaters." *The Front Row* (blog). *New Yorker*. April 17. www.newyorker.com/culture/the-front-row /what-i-miss-most-about-movie-theatres.

Brown, Wendy. 2017. *Walled States, Waning Sovereignty.* New York: Zone Books.

Brownstein, Ronald. 2021. *Rock Me on the Water, 1974: The Year Los Angeles Transformed Movies, Music, Television and Politics.* New York: Harper.

Bruno, Giuliana. 1993. *Streetwalking on a Ruined Map.* Princeton, NJ: Princeton University Press.

Buchanan, Kyle. 2021a. "Chloe Zhao Becomes Second Woman to Win Top Directors Guild Award." *New York Times,* April 12, C2.

Buchanan, Kyle. 2021b. "Directors Guild Honors 'Nomadland' Filmmaker." *New York Times,* April 12, C2.

Burian, Edward. 2015. *The Architecture and Cities of Northern Mexico from Independence to the Present.* Austin: University of Texas Press.

Burke, Peter. 2009. *Cultural Hybridity.* Cambridge, UK: Polity Press.

Cádava, Geraldo L. 2013. *Standing on Common Ground: The Making of a Sunbelt Borderland.* Cambridge, MA: Harvard University Press.

Caldwell, Beth C. 2019. *Deported Americans: Life after Deportation to Mexico.* Durham, NC: Duke University Press.

Campbell, Howard. 2009. *Drug War Zone: Frontline Dispatches from the Streets of El Paso and Juárez.* Austin: University of Texas Press.

Cándida Smith, Richard. 2017. *Improvised Continent: Pan-Americanism and Cultural Exchange.* Philadelphia: University of Pennsylvania Press.

Cave, Damien. 2012. "Wave of Violence Swallows More Women in Juárez." *New York Times,* June 24, Y6.

Cave, Damien. 2011. "A Crime Fighter Draws Plaudits, and Scrutiny." *New York Times,* December 24, A10.

Chatfield, W. H. 1893. *The Twin Cities of the Border and the Country of the Lower Rio Grande.* New Orleans, LA: E. P. Brandao.

Chishti, Muzaffar, and Jessica Bolter. 2022. "Biden at the One-Year Mark." Migration Policy Institute Policy Beat, January 19. www.migrationpolicy.org /article/biden-one-year-mark.

Christopher, Nicholas. 1997. *Somewhere in the Night: Film Noir and the American City.* New York: Free Press.

Christopherson, Susan, and Michael Storper. 1986. "The City as Studio, the World as Back-lot." *Environment and Planning D: Society and Space* 4, no. 3: 305–20.

Churchwell, Sarah. 2018. *Behold, America: The History of American First and the American Dream.* London: Bloomsbury Publishing.

Clover, Carol J. 1992. *Men, Women and Chain Saws.* Princeton, NJ: Princeton University Press.

Comito, Terry, ed. 1985. *Touch of Evil, Orson Welles, Director.* New Brunswick, NJ: Rutgers University Press.

Córdova, Ana, and Carlos A. de la Parra. 2012. *El muro fronterizo entre México y Estados Unidos* [The border wall between Mexico and the United States]. Tijuana: El Colegio de la Frontera Norte.

Cortés, Carlos E. 1983. "Chicanas in Film: History of an Image." *Bilingual Review/La Revista Bilingüe* 10: 94–108.

Cronin, Paul. 2019. *Werner Herzog: A Guide for the Perplexed*. London: Faber and Faber.

Crosby, Harry W. 1997. *The Cave Paintings of Baja California: Discovering the Great Murals of an Unknown People*. San Diego, CA: Sunbelt Publications.

Cruz, Gilbert R. 1988. *Let There Be Towns: Spanish Municipal Origins in the American Southwest, 1610–1810*. College Station: Texas A&M Press.

Cuellar, José B. 2004. "Notas en el viento." In *Alambrista and the U.S.-Mexico Border*, edited by Nicholas John Cull and Davíd Carrasco, 173–201. Albuquerque: University of New Mexico Press.

Cull, Nicholas John, and Davíd Carrasco. 2004. *Alambrista and the U.S.-Mexico Border*. Albuquerque: University of New Mexico Press.

Dana, Richard Henry, Jr. 1981. *Two Years before the Mast*. New York: Penguin Books.

Davis, Julie Hirschfeld, and Michael D. Shear. 2019. *Border Walls: Inside Trump's Assault on Immigration*. New York: Simon and Schuster.

Davis, Mike, and Jon Wiener. 2020. *Set the Night on Fire: L.A. in the Sixties*. Brooklyn, NY: Verso.

de la Cruz, Sor Juana Inés. 1997. *Poems, Protest, and a Dream: Selected Writings*. Bilingual ed. Translated by Margaret Sayers Peden. London: Penguin Books.

De León, Arnoldo. 1983. *They Called Them Greasers: Anglo Attitudes toward Mexicans in Texas, 1821–1900*. Austin: University of Texas Press.

de Oñate, Juan. 2011. "Letter Written by Don Juan de Oñate from New Mexico to the Viceroy, the Count of Monterrey, on March 2, 1599." In *The Norton Anthology of Latino Literature*, edited by Ilan Stavans, 77–89. New York: W. W. Norton.

de Orellana, Margarita. 2009. *Filming Pancho Villa: How Hollywood Shaped the Mexican Revolution*. Translated by John King. London: Verso.

Dear, Michael, ed. 2017. "Film, Architecture, Politics: A Conversation between Amos Gitai and Michael Dear, with Marie-José Sanselme." *Frameworks*, October 20. https://frameworks.ced.berkeley.edu/2017/film-architecture-politics/

———. 2015. *Why Walls Won't Work: Repairing the US-Mexico Divide*. Expanded paperback ed. New York: Oxford University Press.

———. 2013. *Why Walls Won't Work: Repairing the US-Mexico Divide*. New York: Oxford University Press.

Dear, Michael, and Gustavo Leclerc, eds. 2003. *Postborder City: Cultural Spaces of Bajalta California*. New York: Routledge.

DeLay, Brian. 2008. *War of a Thousand Deserts: Indian Raids and the U.S.-Mexican War*. New Haven, CT: Yale University Press.

Delgadillo, Theresa. 2006. "Singing 'Angelitos Negros': African Diaspora Meets Mestizaje in the Americas." *American Quarterly* 58, no. 2: 407–30.

Dell'agnese, Elena. 2005. "The US-Mexico Border in American Movies: A Political Geography Perspective." *Geopolitics* 10, no. 2 (July 1): 204–21.

Diguet, León. 1912. *Territorio de la Baja California: Reseña Geográfica y Estadística*. Paris: Librería de la Vda. de C. Bouret.

Dimenberg, Edward. 2004. *Film Noir and the Spaces of Modernity*. Cambridge, MA: Harvard University Press.

Dodds, Klaus. 2013. "'I'm Still Not Crossing That': Borders, Dispossession, and Sovereignty in *Frozen River* (2008)." *Geopolitics* 18, no. 3 (July 1): 560–83.

Dorado Romo, David. 2005. *Ringside Seat to a Revolution: An Underground Cultural History of El Paso and Ciudad Juárez, 1893–1923*. El Paso, TX: Cinco Punto Press.

Drew, William M., and Esperanza Vasquez Bernal. 2003. "*El Puño de Hierro*, a Mexican Silent Film Classic." *Journal of Film Preservation* 10, no. 66 (October 1): 10–22.

Dubouisson, Ustin Pascal. 2019. "Op-Ed: I Traveled across 10 Countries for Asylum in the U.S. I Wound Up Living the 'Mexican Dream' Instead." *Los Angeles Times*, January 13. www.latimes.com/opinion/op-ed/la-oe -dubouisson-mexico-immigration-haiti-20190114-story.html.

Dunn, Timothy. 2010. *Blockading the Border and Human Rights: The El Paso Operation That Remade Immigration Enforcement*. Austin: University of Texas Press.

Durand, Jorge, and Douglas S. Massey, eds. 2006. *Crossing the Border: Research from the Mexican Migration Project*. New York: Russell Sage Foundation.

Dym, Jordanna, and Karl Offen. 2011. *Mapping Latin America: A Cartographic Reader*. Chicago: University of Chicago Press.

Earle, Robert L., and John D. Wirth. 1995. *Identities in North America: The Search for Community*. Stanford, CA: Stanford University Press.

Ehrenreich, Ben. 2010. "A Lucrative War." *London Review of Books* 32, no. 20 (October 21): 18.

Elden, Stuart. 2013. *The Birth of Territory*. Chicago: University of Chicago Press.

Elliot, J. H. 2019. "Spain's America." *New York Times Review of Books*, May 9, 44–45.

Erickson., Winston P. 1994. *Sharing the Desert*. Tucson: University of Arizona Press.

Escobedo, Helen, and Paolo Gori, eds. 1989. *Mexican Monuments: Strange Encounters*. New York: Abbeville Press.

Evans, Tripp. 2004. *Romancing the Maya*. Austin: University of Texas Press.

Favata, Martin A., and José B. Fernández. 1993. *The Account: Alvar Núñez Cabeza de Vaca's Relación*. Houston: Arte Publico Press.

Feldman, Phil. 1968. "Phil Feldman Casts Mexican People as Heroes of the Wild Bunch." *Box Office*, March 18, K-3.

Fields, Virginia M., John M. D. Pohl, and Victoria I. Lyall. 2012. *Children of the Plumed Serpent: The Legacy of Quetzalcóatl in Ancient Mexico*. Los Angeles: Los Angeles County Museum of Art in association with Scala Publishers.

Finnegan, William. 2010. "In the Name of the Law." *New Yorker*, October 18, 65.

Fojas, Camilla. 2019. "Border Securities, Drone Cultures, and Alex Rivera's Sleep Dealer." In *Latinx Ciné in the Twenty-First Century*, edited by Frederick Luis Aldama, 237. Tucson: University of Arizona Press.

Fox, Claire F. 1999. *The Fence and the River: Culture and Politics at the US-Mexico Border*. Minneapolis: University of Minnesota Press.

Freeman, Judith. 2007. *The Long Embrace: Raymond Chandler and the Woman He Loved*. New York: Pantheon Books.

Fregoso, Rosa Linda. 2003. *Mexicana Encounters: The Making of Social Identity on the Borderlands*. Berkeley: University of California Press.

Frodon, Jean-Michel. "Amos G., an Outline for a Portrait." *Culturesfrance*, 21–23.

Gandy, Matthew. 2021. "Film as Method in the Geohumanities." *GeoHumanities* 7, no. 2: 605–24. https://doi.org/10.1080/2373566X.2021.1898287.

García Canclini, Néstor. 2003. "Rewriting Cultural Studies in the Borderlands." In *Postborder City: Cultural Spaces of Bajalta California*, edited by Michael Dear and Gustavo Leclerc, 277–86. New York: Routledge.

———. (1990) 1995. *Hybrid Cultures Strategies for Entering and Leaving Modernity*. Minneapolis: University of Minnesota Press. (Original in Spanish.)

García Riera, Emilio. 1963. *El Cine Mexicano*. Mexico City: Ediciones Era.

Gardner, Erle S. 1962. *The Hidden Heart of Baja*. New York: William Morrow.

Gates, Henry Louis, Jr. 2019. *Stony the Road*. New York: Penguin Books.

Gertz, Nurith, and Gal Hermoni. 2008. "History's Broken Wings: 'Narrative Paralysis' as Resistance to History in Amos Gitai's Film 'Kedma.'" *Framework: The Journal of Cinema and Media* 49, no. 1: 134–43.

Gitai, Amos. 2019. *La Caméra est une Sorte de Fétiche: Filmer au Moyen-Orient*. Paris: Fayard et College de France.

Glaude, Eddie S., Jr. 2020. *Begin Again: James Baldwin's America and Its Urgent Lessons for Our Own*. New York: Crown.

Glendinning, Jim. 2000. *Mexico: Unofficial Border Crossings*. Alpine, TX: Alpine Company Press.

Gómez-Peña, Guillermo. 1996. *The New World Border: Prophecies, Poems and Loqueras for the End of the Century*. San Francisco: City Lights Books.

González, Jennifer A., et al., eds. 2019. *Chicano and Chicana Art*. Durham, NC: Duke University Press.

González Rodríguez, Sergio. 2012. *The Femicide Machine*. Los Angeles: Semiotexte; Cambridge, MA: Distributed by MIT Press.

Grillo, Ioan. 2021. *Blood Gun Money: How America Arms Gangs and Cartels*. New York: Bloomsbury Press.

———. 2012. *El Narco: Inside Mexico's Criminal Insurgency*. New York: Bloomsbury Press.

Griswold del Castillo, Richard. 1990. *The Treaty of Guadalupe Hidalgo: A Legacy of Conflict*. Norman: University of Oklahoma Press.

Grossman, Edith, trans. 2014. *Sor Juana Inés de la Cruz: Selected Works*. New York: Norton.

Guillermoprieto, Alma. 2010. "The Murders of Mexico." *New York Review*, October 28, 46–48.

———. 2003. "A Hundred Women Letter from Mexico." *New Yorker*, September 29, 83.

Gutiérrez, Ramón A., and Richard J. Orsi, eds. 1998. *Contested Eden: California before the Gold Rush*. Berkeley: University of California Press.

Haas, Lisbeth. 1995. *Conquests and Historical Identities in California, 1769–1936*. Berkeley: University of California Press.

Hackel, Steven W., ed. 2010. *Alta California: Peoples in Motion, Identities in Formation, 1769–1850*. Berkeley: University of California Press.

Hagerman, María Eladia, ed. 2006. *Babel: A Film by Alejandro González Iñárritu*. Culver City: Taschen.

Hahn, Steven. 2016. *A Nation without Borders: The United States and Its World in an Age of Civil Wars, 1830–1910*. New York: Viking.

Hämäläinen, Pekka. 2008. *The Comanche Empire*. New Haven, CT: Yale University Press.

Haygood, Wil. 2021. *Colorization: One Hundred Years of Black Films in a White World*. New York: Knopf.

Heinle, Kimberly, Octavio Rodríguez Ferreira, and David A. Shirk. 2014. *Drug Violence in Mexico: Data and Analysis through 2013*. San Diego: Justice in Mexico Project, Department of Political Science and International Relations, University of San Diego, April.

Hernández, Anabel, et al. 2013. *Narcoland: The Mexican Drug Lords and Their Godfathers*. London: Verso Books.

Hernández, Kelly L. 2010. *Migra! A History of the U.S. Border Patrol*. Berkeley: University of California Press.

Hershfield, Joanne. 1996. *Mexican Cinema, Mexican Woman, 1940–1950*. Tucson: University of Arizona Press.

Hershfield, Joanne, and David R. Maciel, eds. 1999. *Mexico's Cinema: A Century of Film and Filmmakers*. Wilmington, NC: Scholarly Resources Books.

Herzog, Lawrence A. 2003. "Global Tijuana." In *Postborder City: Cultural Spaces of Bajalta California*, edited by Michael Dear and Gustavo Leclerc, 119–142. New York: Routledge.

———. 1990. *Where North Meets South*. San Diego: Center for US-Mexico Studies, University of California San Diego.

Hing, Bill Ong. 2019. *American Presidents, Deportations, and Human Rights Violations: From Carter to Trump*. Cambridge: Cambridge University Press.

Hoberman, J. 2019. *Make My Day: Movie Culture in the Age of Reagan*. New York: New Press.

——. 2017. "Julio Bracho." *Artforum*, February. www.artforum.com/print /201702/julio-bracho-66051.

——. 2012. *Film after Film: Or, What Became of 21st-Century Cinema?* Brooklyn, NY: Verso.

Hondagneu-Sotelo, Pierrette. 2001. *Domestica: Immigrant Workers Cleaning and Caring in the Shadows of Affluence*. Berkeley: University of California Press.

Hurtado, Albert L. 1988. *Indian Survival on the California Frontier*. New Haven, CT: Yale University Press.

Hyland, Justin R. 2006. "The Central Sierras." In *The Prehistory of Baja California*, edited by Don Laylander and Jerry D. Moore, 117–34. Gainesville: University Press of Florida.

Iglesias [Prieto], Norma. 2015. "Transcendiendo Límites: La Frontera México–Estados Unidos en el Cine." In *Key Tropes in Inter-American Studies*, edited by Wilfried Raussert, Brian Rozema, Yolanda Campos, and Marius Littschwager, 179–210. Tempe, AZ: Bilingual Press/Editorial Bilingüe.

——. 2013. "Tijuana Provocadora. Tranfronteridad y Procesos Creativos." *Concurso*, no. 16 (December 10). www.arquine.com/tijuana-provocadora -tranfronteridad-y-procesos-creativos/.

——. 2008. *Emergencias, las artes visuales en Tijuana*. Tijuana: Centro Cultural Tijuana.

——. 2006. "Tijuana: Between Reality and Fiction." In *Strange New World*, 74–76. San Diego: Museum of Contemporary Art.

——. 1999. "Reconstructing the Border: Mexican Border Cinema and Its Relationship to Its Audience." In *Mexico's Cinema: A Century of Film and Filmmakers*, edited by Joanne Hershfield and David R. Maciel, 232–48. Wilmington, NC: Scholarly Resources Books.

——. (1985) 1997. *Beautiful Flowers of the Maquiladora: Life Histories of Women Workers in Tijuana*. Austin: University of Texas Press (Original in Spanish.)

——. 1991. *Entre Hierba, Polvo y Plomo: Lo Fronterizo Visto por el Cine Mexicano*. 2 vols. Tijuana: El Colegio de la Frontera Norte.

Ikeda, Marcelo. 2020. "The Ambiguities of Bacurau." *Film Quarterly* 74: 81–83.

Irwin, Robert McKee, and Maricruz Castro Ricalde. 2013. *Global Mexican Cinema: Its Golden Age*. London: British Film Institute/Palgrave Macmillan.

Jackson, Robert H. 1994. *Indian Population Decline: The Missions of Northwestern New Spain, 1687–1840*. Albuquerque: University of New Mexico Press.

Jackson, Robert H., and Edward Castillo. 1996. *Indians, Franciscans, and Spanish Colonization: The Impact of the Mission System on California Indians*. Albuquerque: University of New Mexico Press.

Jacobson, Brian R., ed. 2020. *In the Studio: Visual Creation and Its Material Environments.* Oakland: University of California Press.

——. 2015. *Studios before the System.* New York: Columbia University Press.

Jacoby, Karl. 2008. *Shadows at Dawn: A Borderlands Massacre and the Violence of History.* New York: Penguin Press.

James, David. 2016. *Rock 'n' Film: Cinema's Dance with Popular Music.* New York: Oxford University Press.

——. 2005. *The Most Typical Avant-Garde: History and Geography of Minor Cinemas in Los Angeles.* Berkeley: University of California Press.

James, Nick. 2008. "Who Needs Critics?" *Sight and Sound* 18, no. 10: 16–18.

Jones, Reece. 2021. *White Borders: The History of Race and Immigration in the United States.* Boston: Beacon Press.

——. 2016. *Violent Borders: Refugees and the Right to Move.* London: Verso.

——. 2012. *Border Walls: Security and the War on Terror in the United States, India and Israel.* London: Zed Books.

Juhasz, Alexandra, and Jesse Lerner, eds. 2006. *F Is for Phony: Fake Documentary and Truth's Undoing.* Minneapolis: University of Minnesota Press.

Kapchan, Deborah A., and Pauline T. Strong. 1999. "Theorizing the Hybrid." *Journal of American Folklore* 112, no. 445: 239–53.

Katzew, Ilona. 2004. *Casta Painting: Images of Race in Eighteenth Century Mexico.* New Haven, CT: Yale University Press.

Katzew, Ilona, and Susan Deans-Smith, eds. 2009. *Race and Classification: The Case of Mexican America.* Stanford, CA: Stanford University Press.

Kessell, John L. 2002. *Spain in the Southwest: A Narrative History of Colonial New Mexico, Arizona, Texas, and California.* Norman: University of Oklahoma Press.

King, John. 2000. *Magic Reels: A History of Cinema in Latin America.* 2nd ed. New York: Verso.

Klawans, Stuart. 1999. *Film Follies: The Cinema Out of Order.* London: Cassell.

Knight, Alan. 2016. *The Mexican Revolution: A Very Short Introduction.* Oxford: Oxford University Press.

——. 2002a. *Mexico: From the Beginning to the Spanish Conquest.* Cambridge: Cambridge University Press.

——. 2002b. *Mexico: The Colonial Era.* Cambridge: Cambridge University Press.

Konrad, Victor. 2015. "Toward a Theory of Borders in Motion." *Journal of Borderlands Studies* 30, no. 1: 1–17. https://doi.org/10.1080/08865655.2015.1008387.

Kracauer, Siegfried. 2006. "Introduction to *From Caligari to Hitler* (1947)." In *American Movie Critics: An Anthology from the Silents until Now*, edited by Pillip Lopate, 166–74. New York: Library of America.

——. 1994. "The Task of the Film Critic" (1932). In *The Weimar Republic Sourcebook*, edited by Anton Kaes, Martin Jay, and Edward Dimendberg, 634–35. Berkeley: University of California Press.

Kuhn, Annette, and Guy Westwell. 2012. *Oxford Dictionary of Film Studies*. Oxford: Oxford University Press.

Kun, Josh. 2010. "Minstrels in the Court of the Kingpin." *New York Times*, March 7, AR22.

Kun, Josh, and Fiamma Montezemolo, eds. 2012. *Tijuana Dreaming: Life and Art at the Global Border*. Durham, NC: Duke University Press.

Lacey, Marc. 2011. "In Echo of Pancho Villa: Modern Raid Shakes Town on the Verge of Extinction." *New York Times*, June 19, A16.

Lakhani, Nina, et al. 2020. "Murder in Mexico: Journalists Caught in the Crosshairs." *Guardian*, December 6. www.theguardian.com/world/2020/dec/06/murder-in-mexico-journalists-caught-in-the-crosshairs-regina-martinez-cartel-project.

Lamar, Howard Roberts. 1998. *The New Encyclopedia of the American West*. New Haven, CT: Yale University Press.

Landemore, Helene. 2020. *Open Democracy: Reinventing Popular Rule for the Twenty-First Century*. Princeton, NJ: Princeton University Press.

Lane, Anthony. 2020. "Mid-century Murk." *New Yorker*, June 8 and 15, 80.

———. 2002. *Nobody's Perfect: Writings from the New Yorker*. New York: Alfred A. Knopf.

Laylander, Don, and Jerry D. Moore, eds. 2006. *The Prehistory of Baja California: Advances in the Archeology of the Forgotten Peninsula*. Gainesville: University Press of Florida.

Le Clézio, J. M. G. (1988) 1993. *The Mexican Dream: Or, The Interrupted Thought of Amerindian Civilizations*. Translated by Teresa Lavender Fagan. Chicago: University of Chicago Press. (Original in French.)

Leclerc, Gustavo, Michael Dear, and Raul Villa, eds. 1999. *Urban Latino Cultures: La Vida Latina en LA*. Thousand Oaks, CA: Sage Publications.

Lehmbeck, Leah, Britt Salveson, and Vanessa Schwartz, eds. 2022. *City of Cinema: Paris 1850–1907*. Los Angeles: Los Angeles County Museum of Art and DelMonico Books.

Leonard, Elmore. 2018. "Valdez Is Coming." In *Elmore Leonard: Westerns*. New York: Library of America.

Lerner, Jesse. 2011. *The Maya of Modernism: Art, Architecture and Film*. Albuquerque: University of New Mexico Press.

Lerner, Jesse, and Rita González. 1998. *Cine Mexperimental: 60 Años de Medios de Vanguardia en México/60 Years of Avant-Garde Media Arts from Mexico*. Ciudad de México: Impresos Ocampo.

Lerner, Jesse, and Luciano Piazza. 2017. *Ism, Ism, Ism: Experimental Cinema in Latin America*. Berkeley: University of California Press and Los Angeles Film Forum.

Lockhart, James, ed. and trans. (1993) 2004. *We People Here: Nahuatl Accounts of the Conquest of Mexico*. Vol. 1. Berkeley: University of California Press. Reprint, Eugene, OR: Wipf & Stock.

Lopate, Phillip, ed. 2006. *American Movie Critics: An Anthology from the Silents until Now*. New York: Library of America.

López, Ana M. 1993. "Tears and Desire: Women and Melodrama in the 'Old' Mexico Cinema." In *Mediating Two Worlds: Cinematic Encounters in the Americas*, edited by John King, Ana M. López, and Manuel Alvarado, 158. London: British Film Institute.

Lozano, Jennifer M. 2019. "Digital Rasquachismo: Alex Rivera's Multimedia Storytelling, Humor, and Transborder Latinx Futurity." In *Latinx Ciné in the Twenty-First Century*, edited by Frederick Luis Aldama, ch. 14. Tucson: University of Arizona Press.

Lucero Velasco, Héctor M. 2003. "Peopling Baja California." In *Postborder City: Cultural Spaces of Bajalta California*, edited by Michael Dear and Gustavo Leclerc, 83–150. New York: Routledge.

———. 2002. *Mexicali Cien Años*. México, DF: Grupo Patria.

Maciel, David. 1995. "Chicano Cinema: A Panoramic View." *Voices of Mexico*, April–June, 19–24.

Maciel, David R. 1992. "The Cinematic Renaissance of Contemporary Mexico, 1985–1992." *Spectator* 13, no. 1: 70–85.

———. 1990. *El Norte: The US-Mexican Border in Contemporary Cinema*. San Diego: Institute for Regional Studies of the Californias, San Diego State University.

Magaña, Lisa. 2003. *Straddling the Border: Immigration Policy and the INS*. Austin: University of Texas Press.

Malkin, Elisabeth, and Ginger Thompson. 2010. "In Mexico, Official Promises Do Little to Ease a Stricken City's Pain." *New York Times*, March 17, A6.

Malone, Michael S. 2020. *El Tercer País: San Diego & Tijuana*. Saratoga, CA: Silicon Valley Press.

Marez, Curtis. 2004. "Subaltern Soundtracks: Mexican Immigrants and the Making of Hollywood Cinema." *Aztlan, a Journal of Chicano Studies* 29, no. 1: 57–82.

Martínez, María Elena. 2008. *Genealogical Fictions: Limpieza de Sangre, Religion, and Gender in Colonial Mexico*. Stanford, CA: Stanford University Press.

Martínez, Oscar. 1994. *Border People: Life and Society in the U.S.-Mexico Borderlands*. Tucson: University of Arizona Press.

Martínez-Cabrera, Alejandro. 2011a. "Calderón Highlights Successes in Juárez." *El Paso Times*, May 21, 1A.

———. 2011b. "Juárez to Add 'Heroic' to Name." *El Paso Times*, May 19, 1A.

Massey, Douglas S., Jorge Durand, and Nolan J. Malone. 2003. *Beyond Smoke and Mirrors: Immigration in an Era of Economic Integration*. New York: Russell Sage Foundation Publications.

Mathews, Joe. 2021. "Let Local Residents Govern the California-Baja Border." *City Watch*, November 4. www.citywatchla.com/index.php/375-voices/22957-let-local-residents-govern-the-california-baja-border.

McAtackney, Laura, and Randall H. McGuire. eds. 2020. *Walling In and Walling Out: Why Are We Building New Barriers to Divide Us?* Albuquerque: University of New Mexico Press.

McCarthy, Cormac. 1992. *All the Pretty Horses*. New York: Vintage Books.

McWilliams, Carey. 1990. *North from Mexico: A Spanish-Speaking People of the United States*. New York: Praeger.

Meeks, Eric V. 2007. *Border Citizens: The Making of Indians, Mexicans, and Anglos in Arizona*. Austin: University of Texas Press.

Meighan, Clement W. 1966. "Prehistoric Rock Paintings in Baja California." *American Antiquity* 3, no. 3.1: 372–92.

Meissner, Doris. 2020. *Rethinking the U.S.-Mexico Border Immigration Enforcement System: A Policy Road Map*. Washington, DC: Migration Policy Institute.

Mendoza, Mary E. 2021. "Nature Knows No Bounds: Mapping Challenges at the US-Mexico Border." In *Mapping Nature across the Americas*, edited by Kathleen Brosnam and James Ackerman, 202–22. Chicago: University of Chicago Press.

Mesa-Bains, Amalia. 2001. "Spiritual Geographies." In *The Road to Aztlan: Art from a Mythic Homeland*, edited by Virginia M. Fields and Victor Zamudio-Taylor, 332–41. Los Angeles: LACMA.

Miller, Todd. 2021a. "A Lucrative Border-Industrial Complex Keeps the US Border in Constant Crisis." *Guardian*, April 19. www.theguardian.com /commentisfree/2021/apr/19/a-lucrative-border-industrial-complex-keeps -the-us-border-in-constant-crisis?

———. 2021b. *Build Bridges, Not Walls: A Journey to a World without Borders*. San Francisco: City Lights Book.

———. 2019. *Empire of Borders: The Expansion of the US Border around the World*. London: Verso.

Miranda, J. V. 2019. "Techno/memo: The Politics of Cultural Memory in Alex Rivera's Sleep Dealer." In *Latinx Ciné in the Twenty-First Century*, edited by Frederick Luis Aldama, ch. 13. Tucson: University of Arizona Press.

Miroff, Nick. 2022. "Where Trump's Border Wall Left Deep Scars and Open Gaps, Biden Plans Repair Job." *Washington Post*, February 19.

Mora, Carl J. 2005. *Mexican Cinema: Reflections of a Society, 1896–2004*. 3rd ed. Jefferson, NC: McFarland.

Morris, Stephen D. 2005. *Gringolandia: Mexican Identity and Perceptions of the United States*. Lanham, MD: Rowman & Littlefield.

Morrison, Toni, ed. 1998a. *James Baldwin: Collected Essays*. New York: Library of America.

———, ed. 1998b. *James Baldwin: Early Novels and Essays*. New York: Library of America.

Morseberger, Robert E., ed. (1975) 2009. *Viva Zapata! The Original Screenplay by John Steinbeck*. New York: Penguin Books.

Mundy, Barbara E. 2015. *The Death of Aztec Tenotchtitlan, the Life of Mexico City*. Austin: University of Texas Press.

———. 2011. "Hybrid Space." In *Mapping Latin America: A Cartographic Reader*, edited by Jordanna Dym and Karl Offen, 51. Chicago: University of Chicago Press.

Munk, Yael. 2019. "The Borders We Cross in Search of a Better World: On Border Crossing in Three of Amos Gitai's Feature Films." In *Border Cinema: Reimagining Identity through Aesthetics*, edited by Monica Hanna and Rebecca Sheehan, 179–94. New Brunswick, NJ: Rutgers University Press.

Neumann, Dietrich, ed. 1996. *Film Architecture: Set Designs from Metropolis to Blade Runner*. New York: Prestel.

Nevins, Joseph. 2002. *Operation Gatekeeper: The Rise of the "Illegal Alien" and the Making of the U.S.-Mexico Boundary*. New York: Routledge.

———. 2000. "The Remaking of the California-Mexico Boundary in the Age of NAFTA." In *The Wall around the West*, edited by Peter Andreas and Timothy Snyder, 99–114. Lanham, MD: Rowman & Littlefield.

Nicholas, John H. 1980. *Tom Mix: Riding up to Glory*. Oklahoma City: Persimmon Hill Publications.

Nicholson, H. B. 2000. *Topiltzin Quetzalcóatl: The Once and Future Lord of the Toltecs*. Boulder: University of Colorado Press.

Nielsen, Henrik Dorf. 2020. "Perception of Danger in the Southern Arizona Borderlands." *Fennia* 198, nos. 1–2: 74–90. https://doi.org/10.11143/fennia.87338.

Noble, Andrea. 2011. "El Llanto de Pancho Villa." *Archivos de la Filmoteca* 68 (October): 38–59.

———. 2005. *Mexican National Cinema*. New York: Routledge.

Noriega, Chon. 2000. *Shot in America: Television, the State, and the Rise of Chicano Cinema*. Minneapolis: University of Minnesota Press.

Noriega, Chon A. 1996. "Imagined Borders: Locating Chicano Cinema in America/América." In *The Ethnic Eye: Latino Media Arts*, edited by Chon A. Noriega and Ana M. López, 3. Minneapolis: University of Minnesota Press.

Nuwer, Rachel. 2020. "'Tiger King' May Be Dangerous for Big Cats." *New York Times*, April 14.

Osio, Antonio M. 1996. *The History of Alta California: A Memoir of Mexican California*. Madison: University of Wisconsin Press.

Owen, Evans. 2011. "'The Many Ways of Looking at Cinema': *Sight and Sound* and the Value of Film." In *Valuing Films: Shifting Perceptions of Worth*, edited by Laura Hubner, 167–82. Houndmills, UK: Palgrave Macmillan.

Parker, T. Jefferson. 2010. *The Iron River*. New York: Dutton.

Paskin, Willa. 2018. "'True Detective' Director Cary Fukunaga Is Bringing His Obsessions to Netflix." *New York Times Magazine*, September 11, 27.

Pastor, Robert A. 2011. *The North American Idea: A Vision of a Continental Future*. Oxford: Oxford University Press.

Pastor, Robert A., and Jorge G. Castañeda. 1988. *Limits to Friendship: The United States and Mexico*. New York: Vintage Books.

Payan, Tony. 2016. *The Three US-Mexico Border Wars: Drugs, Immigration, and Homeland Security*. 2nd ed. Santa Barbara, CA: Praeger.

———. 2014. "Ciudad Juárez: A Perfect Storm on the US-Mexico Border." *Journal of Borderlands Studies* 29, no. 4: 435–47. https://doi.org/10.1080/08865655.2014.982468.

Paz, Octavio. 1988. *Sor Juana, o, Las Trampas de la Fe (The Traps of Faith)*. Translated by Margaret Sayers Peden. Cambridge, MA: Harvard University Press.

Peña, Elaine A. 2020. *¡Viva George! Celebrating Washington's Birthday at the US-Mexico Border*. Austin: University of Texas Press.

Peterson, Jeanette Favrot, and Kevin Terraciano, eds. 2019. *The Florentine Codex: An Encyclopedia of the Nahua World in Sixteenth-Century Mexico*. Austin: University of Texas Press.

Pierce, Sarah, and Jessica Bolter. 2020. *Dismantling and Reconstructing the U.S. Immigration System: A Catalog of Changes under the Trump Presidency*. Migration Policy Institute, July.

Pitt, Leonard. 1998. *The Decline of the Californios: A Social History of the Spanish-Speaking Californians, 1846–1890*. Berkeley: University of California Press.

Pohl, John M. D., and Clair L. Lyons. 2010. *The Aztec Pantheon and the Art of Empire*. Los Angeles: J. Paul Getty Museum.

Pratt, Geraldine. 2012. *Families Apart: Migrant Mothers and the Conflicts of Labor and Love*. Minneapolis: University of Minnesota Press.

Radke, Bill. 2009. "Mexican Dream Tied to American Dream." *Marketplace*, May 15. www.marketplace.org/2009/05/15/mexican-dream-tied-american-dream/.

Rebert, Paula. 2001. *La Gran Línea: Mapping the United States-Mexico Boundary, 1849–1857*. Austin: University of Texas Press.

Recinos, Adrián. 1950. *Popul Vuh: The Sacred Book of the Ancient Quiché Maya*. Translated by Delia Goetz and Sylvanus Morley. Norman: University of Oklahoma Press.

Reed, John. (1914) 1983. *Insurgent Mexico*. Harmondsworth, UK: Penguin Books.

Reséndez, Andrés. 2016. *The Other Slavery: The Uncovered Story of Indian Enslavement in America*. Boston: Houghton Mifflin Harcourt.

———. 2007. *A Land So Strange: The Epic Journey of Cabeza de Vaca*. New York: Basic Books.

Richards, H. 2003. "Memory Reclamation of Cinema-going in Bridgend." *Historical Journal of Film, Radio and Television* 23: 341–55.

Ripley, Marc. 2017. *A Search for Belonging: The Mexican Cinema of Luis Buñuel*. New York: Wallflower Press.

Rivera Garza, Cristina. 2020. *Grieving: Dispatches from a Wounded Country*. Translated by Sarah Booker. New York City: Feminist Press.

Robinson, Cedric J., and Luz Maria Cabral. 2003. "The Mulatta on Film: From Hollywood to the Mexican Revolution." *Race and Class* 45, no. 2: 1–20.

Rocha, Gregorio C. 2006. "La Venganza de Pancho Villa: A Lost and Found Border Film." In *F Is for Phony: Fake Documentary and Truth's Undoing*, edited by Alexandra Juhasz and Jesse Lerner, 50–58. Minneapolis: University of Minnesota Press.

Rodríguez, Teresa, and Diana Montané with Lisa Pulitzer. 2007. *The Daughters of Juárez*. New York: Atria Books.

Romero, Simon. 2020. "New Mexico Removes Statue of Conquistador Known for Atrocities." *New York Times*, June 16, A18.

———. 2017. "Statue's Stolen Foot Reflects Divisions Over Symbols of Conquest." *New York Times*, September 30, A1.

Romero, Simon, and Zolan Kanno-Youngs. 2020. "A Rush to Expand the Border Wall That Many Feel Is Here to Stay." *New York Times*, November 30, A1.

Rouse, Roger. 1996. "Mexican Migration and the Space of Postmodernism." In *Between Two Worlds: Mexican Immigrants in the United States*, edited by David G. Gutiérrez, 247–63. Wilmington, NC: Jaguar Books.

Ruiz-Alfaro, Sofía. 2020. "Domestic Matters: Hollywood and the Politics of Representing *la domestica* in *Babel* and *Cake*." In *Domestic Labor in the Twenty-First Century Latin American Cinema*, edited by Elizabeth Osborne and Sofía Ruiz-Alfaro, 209–30. Cham, Switzerland: Palgrave Macmillan.

Sahagún, Bernardino de. 1932. *A History of Ancient Mexico: Anthropological, Mythological, and Social*. Translated by Fanny R. Bandelier. Nashville, TN: Fisk University Press.

Sammon, Paul M. 2007. *Future Noir: The Making of Blade Runner*. 2nd ed. London: Gollancz.

Sanselme, Marie-José, ed. 2016. *Amos Gitai*. Paris: Galerie Enrique Navarra.

Sariñara-Lampson, Stephen. 2011. "Silent Images of Latinos in Early Hollywood." Interview with Stephen Sariñara-Lampson. June 10. https://cinesilentemexicano.wordpress.com/2011/06/10/silent-images-of-latinos-in-early-hollywood/.

Saunders, Robert A. 2019. "Geopolitical Television at the (b)order: Liminality, Global Politics, and World-Building in *The Bridge*." *Social and Cultural Geography* 20: 981–1003. https://doi.org/10.1080/14649365.2017.1404122.

Schladen, Marty. 2011. "Mayor Lauds Development." *El Paso Times*, May 19, 1B.

Schroeder Rodríguez, Paul A. 2016. *Latin American Cinema: A Comparative History*. Berkeley: University of California Press.

Scott, Allen J. 2005. *On Hollywood: The Place, the Industry*. Princeton, NJ: Princeton University Press.

Serna, Laura Isabel. 2020. "Estudios Churubusco: A Transnational Studio for a National Industry." In *In the Studio: Visual Creation and Its Material Environments*, edited by Brian R. Jacobson, 85–102. Oakland: University of California Press.

———. 2014. *Making Cinelandia: American Films and Mexican Film Culture before the Golden Age*. Durham, NC: Duke University Press.

Sheridan, Mary Beth. 2020. "Violent Criminal Groups Are Eroding Mexico's Authority and Claiming More Territory." *Washington Post*, October 29. www.washingtonpost.com/graphics/2020/world/mexico-losing-control/mexico-violence-drug-cartels-zacatecas/.

Shiel, Mark. 2010. "A Regional Geography of Film Noir." In *Noir Urbanisms*, edited by Gyan Prakash, 75–103. Princeton, NJ: Princeton University Press.

Shirk, David A. 2014. "A Tale of Two Mexican Border Cities: The Rise and Decline of Drug Violence in Juárez and Tijuana." *Journal of Borderlands Studies* 29, no. 4: 481–502. https://doi.org/10.1080/08865655.2014.982470.

Silver, Alain, and James Ursini. 1998. *Film Noir: A Reader*. 4th ed. New York: Limelight Editions.

Simmons, Marc. 1991. *The Last Conquistador: Juan de Oñate and the Settling of the Far Southwest*. Norman: University of Oklahoma Press.

Smith, Robert E. 1998. "Mann in the Dark." In *Film Noir: A Reader*, 4th ed., edited by Alain Silver and James Ursini, 197. New York: Limelight Editions.

Spagat, Elliot. 2017. "Stopped at U.S. Border, Haitians Find 'Mexican Dream' Instead." *Denver Post*, September 20. www.denverpost.com/2017/09/20/haitians-find-mexican-dream/.

Sohn, Christophe. 2022. "The Border as a Semiotic Resource for Place Branding: The Case of the Cali Baja Bi-National Mega-Region." *Geoforum*, 135: 82–92.

St. John, Rachel. 2011. *Line in the Sand: A History of the Western US-Mexico Border*. Princeton, NJ: Princeton University Press.

Staudt, Kathleen. 2014. "The Border, Performed in Films: Produced in Both Mexico and the US to 'Bring Out the Worst in a Country.'" *Journal of Borderlands Studies* 29, no. 4 (October 2): 465–79.

Stavans, Ilan. 2018. *Sor Juana: Or, The Persistence of Pop*. Tucson: University of Arizona Press.

———. 2011. "Juan de Oñate, 1550–1626." In *The Norton Anthology of Latino Literature*, 77–78. New York: W. W. Norton.

Stoddard, Ellwyn. 1990. "Frontiers, Borders and Border Segmentation: Toward a Conceptual Clarification." *Journal of Borderlands Studies* 6, no. 1 (Spring): 1–22.

Stratton, W. K. 2019. *The Wild Bunch: Sam Peckinpah, a Revolution in Hollywood, and the Making of a Legendary Film*. New York: Bloomsbury Publishing.

Tedlock, Dennis, trans. 1985. *Popol Vuh: The Mayan Book of the Dawn of Life*. New York: Simon & Schuster.

Terraciano, Kevin. 2019. "Reading between the Lines of Book 12 [of the Florentine Codex]." In *The Florentine Codex: An Encyclopedia of the Nahua World in Sixteenth-Century Mexico*, edited by Jeanette Favrot Peterson and Kevin Terraciano, 45–62. Austin: University of Texas Press.

Thomson, David. 2017. *How to Watch a Movie*. New York: Vintage Books.

———. 2012. *The Big Screen: The Story of the Movies*. New York: Farrar Straus and Giroux.

———. 2005. *The Whole Equation: A History of Hollywood*. New York: Alfred A. Knopf.

Tolson, Melvin B. 2006. "Gone with the Wind Is More Dangerous Than Birth of a Nation." In *American Movie Critics: An Anthology from the Silents until Now*, edited by Phillip Lopate, 140–44. New York: Library of America.

Tomadjoglou, Kimberly. 2017. "Introduction: The Culture of Mexican Silent Cinema." *Film History* (spring), v–xiii.

Torres, Elias L. (1931) 1973. *Twenty Episodes in the Life of Pancho Villa*. Austin, TX: Encino Press.

Toubiana, Serge. 2005. *The Cinema of Amos Gitai*. New York: Film Society of Lincoln Center.

UN Habitat. 2011. *Housing Finance Mechanisms in Mexico*. Nairobi: UN Human Settlements Programme.

United States Court of Appeals for the Ninth Circuit. 2016. Rodríguez v. Swartz, "Brief for Scholars of U.S.-Mexico Border Issues as *Amici Curiae* in Support of Plaintiff-Appellee Araceli Rodríguez and Affirmance," May 6.

Uribe, Ana B. 2009. *Mi México Imaginada: Telenovelas, Televisión y Migrantes*. Mexico: El Colegio de la Frontera Norte, Universidad de Colima, Miguel Angel Porrua.

Vasey, Ruth. 1997. *The World According to Hollywood, 1918–1939*. Madison: University of Wisconsin Press.

Vega Alfaro, Eduardo de la. 1999. "The Decline of the Golden Age and the Making of the Crisis." In *Mexico's Cinema: A Century of Film and Filmmakers*, edited by Joanne Hershfield and David R. Maciel, 165–91. Wilmington, NC: Scholarly Resources Books.

Velasco Ortiz, Laura. 2005. *Mixtec Transnational Identity*. Tucson: University of Arizona Press.

———. 2004. "Migraciones y fronteras. Ser indígena más allá de la nación." *Aztlán: A Journal of Chicano Studies* 29, no. 1: 135–43.

Vila, Pablo. 2000. *Crossing Borders, Reinforcing Borders: Social Categories, Metaphors, and Narrative Identities on the U.S.-Mexico Frontier*. Austin: University of Texas Press.

Villavicencio, Karla Cornejo. 2021. "Bad Dream." *New Yorker*, January 25, 31.

von Tunzelmann, Alex. 2015. *Reel History: The World According to the Movies*. London: Atlantic Books.

Vulliamy, Ed. 2010a. "As Juárez Falls." *Nation*, December 27, 39, 42.

———. 2010b. *Amexica: War along the Borderline*. New York: Farrar, Straus and Giroux.

Walsh, Raoul. 1974. *Each Man in His Time*. New York: Farrar, Straus and Giroux.

Wasson, Sam. 2020. *The Big Goodbye: Chinatown and the Last Years of Hollywood*. New York: Flatiron Books.

Weber, David J. 2005. *Bárbaros: Spaniards and Their Savages in the Age of Enlightenment*. New Haven, CT: Yale University Press.

———, ed. 2003. *Foreigners in Their Native Land: Historical Roots of the Mexican Americans*. Albuquerque: University of New Mexico Press.

———. 1992. *The Spanish Frontier in North America*. New Haven, CT: Yale University Press.

Weber, Martin. 2018. *Mapa de suenos latinoamericanos/Map of Latin American Dreams*. Buenos Aires: Ediciones Lariviere SA.

Weisman, Alan, and Jay Dusard. 1986. *La Frontera: The United States Border with Mexico*. New York: Harcourt Brace Jovanovich.

Wheatley, Thomas. 2022. "Ditching ICE Made Communities Safer, Georgia Sheriffs and Activists Say." *AXIOS*, February 22. www.axios.com/ditching -ice-ae81dd84-7724-405e-845e-fd14b517ea47.html.

Whitaker, Gordon. 2021. *Deciphering Aztec Hieroglyphics: A Guide to Nahuatl Writing*. Oakland: University of California Press.

Wood, Jason. 2006. *The Faber Book of Mexican Cinema*. London: Faber and Faber.

———. 2021. *The Faber Book of Mexican Cinema*. Updated ed. London: Faber and Faber.

Wulf, Andrea. 2015. *The Invention of Nature: Alexander von Humboldt's New World*. New York: Knopf.

Ybarra-Frausto, Tomas, in conversation with Michael Dear. 1999. "*El movimiento*: The Chicano Cultural Project since the 1960s." In *Urban Latino Cultures: La Vida Latina en LA*, edited by Gustavo Leclerc, Michael Dear, and Raúl Villa, 23–34. Thousand Oaks, CA: Sage.

Zúñiga, Víctor, and Rubén Hernández-León, eds. 2006. *New Destinations: Mexican Immigration in the United States*. New York: Russell Sage Foundation.

# Index

Academy Awards: for Mexican directors, 62–63; for others, 147
accuracy of film narratives, 60–62, 246; authenticity in representations of Pancho Villa, 81–85
Akwesasne Mohawk Nation, 236–37
*¡Alambrista!* (Robert M. Young), 58, 168–70, 171
*All the Pretty Horses* (Billy Bob Thornton), 179–81, 189
Ambos Nogales. *See* Nogales, Arizona; Nogales, Sonora
American Dream: defined, 203–4, 279n6; in film, 99, 109, 145, 168, 203–4, 209, 230. *See also* Mexican Dream
*And Starring Pancho Villa as Himself* (Bruce Beresford), 77–81, 219
Anzaldúa, Gloria, 235
Ariel Awards, for film in Mexico, 164; Arizona, 157, 172; as police state, 30, 31
*Aventurera* (Alberto Gout), 107–9; place of border in, 109

*Babel* (Alejandro González Iñárritu), 171–72, 174
Babitz, Eve, 49–50, 269n9

*Bacurau* (Kleber Mendonca Fihlo/Juliano Dornelles), 220, 226
*Bajo California* (Carlos Bolado Muñoz), 57, 210–12, 214, 219, 279n8
Baldwin, James, 8, 67, 246, 251
*Ballad of Gregorio Cortes, The* (Roberto Young), 170–71
*Band's Visit, The* (Eran Kolirin), 225–26
Big Bend, Texas, 26, 27*fig.*, 184
*Birth of a Nation, The* (D. W. Griffith), 42–43, 50, 270n11
bisected bodies, 34–38, 157, 200
*Boatman, The* (Greg Morgan), 222
Bonfil Batalla, Guillermo, 126–27
*Border* (Ali Abbasi), 226
*Border, The* (Tony Richardson), 186–87, 190
border crossings, 17, 41; as adventure, 180; as pilgrimage, 185–6, 210–12; as rebirth, 210–12; as redemption, 184, 211–12; as transformational, 138–39; as transition, 102; as trap, 103; as trial 211–12
border fences: in film, 191–96; in history 16–17, 87
border film after 2000, 147, 171–75; definition of, 3–5, 6–8, 38–39, 268n3; genre, 217–31; golden age of, 145, 217–31; in history,

303

Founded in 1893,
UNIVERSITY OF CALIFORNIA PRESS
publishes bold, progressive books and journals
on topics in the arts, humanities, social sciences,
and natural sciences—with a focus on social
justice issues—that inspire thought and action
among readers worldwide.

The UC PRESS FOUNDATION
raises funds to uphold the press's vital role
as an independent, nonprofit publisher, and
receives philanthropic support from a wide
range of individuals and institutions—and from
committed readers like you. To learn more, visit
ucpress.edu/supportus.